The Illustrated Lives of the Great Composers.

Gilbert & Sullivan

Dr. Alan James
Opera synopses by *Andrew Codd*

W9-ARM-334

Omnibus Press
London/New York/Sydney/Cologne

Cover design and art direction by Pearce Marchbank Studio.
Cover photography by Julian Hawkins.

Printed in Great Britain by Dotesios Ltd, Trowbridge, Wiltshire

© Alan James 1989.
This edition published in 1989 by Omnibus Press, a division of Book Sales Limited.

Hardback
Order No. OP44924
ISBN 0.7119.1627.6

Softback
Order No. OP45251
ISBN 0.7119.1753.1

Exclusive Distributors:
Book Sales Limited,
8/9 Frith Street,
London W1V 5TZ,
England.
Music Sales Pty Limited,
120 Rothschild Avenue,
Rosebery,
Sydney,
NSW 2018,
Australia.
Music Sales Corporation,
225 Park Avenue South,
New York,
N.Y. 10003,
U.S.A.
To The Music Trade Only:
Music Sales Limited,
8/9 Frith Street,
London W1V 5TZ,
England.

A catalogue record for this title is available from The British Library.

Contents

1 Gilbert's Early Life and Works

William Schwenck Gilbert (his middle name, which he disliked but which his family tended to use when addressing him, was the same as that of his great-aunt and godmother) was born on 18 November 1836 at 17 Southampton Street, off the Strand, in London. Southampton Street was prophetically only a stone's throw from the place where the famous Savoy Theatre was to be built. His father was a naval surgeon and his mother, from Scotland, was the daughter of a medical doctor. The boy had three younger sisters – Jane, Maud and Florence. The family had servants, lived an affluent life in Hammersmith at 4 Portland Place, and often travelled in Europe. Indeed, when W. S. Gilbert was two years old he was kidnapped in Naples while in the care of a maid and then held for ransom until £25 had been paid to secure his release. Gilbert, much later, made use of this experience when devising the plots of *H.M.S. Pinafore*, *The Gondoliers* and *The Pirates of Penzance*; in each of which a child was lost, exchanged or kidnapped while being cared for by a nurse. His parents did not get along together and parted when Gilbert was nineteen. There had always been a coldness and an aloofness in their personal relationship. It was an unhappy home where there was frequent discord, and it is more than likely that this unfortunate family life left indelible prints on the personality of their playwright son.

He first attended school in Boulogne at the age of seven and remained proficient in French – sometimes, in later years, writing his diary in French, probably in a successful attempt to confuse his servants! Next he attended Great Ealing School at the age of thirteen, following in the footsteps of such distinguished writers as Huxley, Marriot, Newman and Thackeray. At first he was lazy

W. S. Gilbert, aged 31.

5

but then knuckled down to work and won prizes. He produced plays for his fellow pupils and wrote verses. Gilbert's serious interest in matters theatrical began whilst still at school. He played Guy Fawkes in a school play. At the age of fifteen he went to the theatre where Charles Kean was appearing and asked him for a job, but Kean knew Gilbert's father and packed him back off to school where he belonged. By the age of sixteen he had become Head Boy and was able to translate Latin and Greek verse with facility. Following typhoid fever, he convalesced in Paris and watched the Emperor Napoleon III and the Empress Eugénie travel along the street. He later wrote a verse in which he noted that the royal pair had observed the thin youth with the shaven head:

> When the horses, white with foam,
> Drew the Empress to her home
> From the place whence she did roam,
> The Empress she did see
> The Gilbert Familee.
> To the Emperor she said:
> 'How beautiful the head
> Of that youth of gallant mien,
> Cropped so neat and close and clean –
> Though I own he's rather lean.'
> Said the Emperor: 'It is!
> And I never saw a phiz
> More wonderful than 'is.'

Gilbert was to become a great literary figure and his interest in literature and in comic verse began at an early age. Edward Lear published his *Book of Nonsense* when Gilbert was a child of ten. Dickens was a favourite author all his life and he read his novels regularly, usually packing one with his luggage when going off on a journey.

After school he went to King's College, London to study law in 1853 but part of the way through his course he decided to work for a commission in the Royal Artillery. He developed a keen interest in uniforms – hence the uniforms found in abundance in the Gilbert and Sullivan operas. He evinced great interest in the Crimean War (even in later life wanting to write a book on the subject) and intended to become a regular soldier:

When I was nineteen years old, the Crimean War was at its height, and commissions in the Royal Artillery were thrown open to competitive examination. So I . . . read for the examination for direct commissions, which was to be held at Christmas, 1856. The limit of age was twenty, and as at the date of examination I should have been six weeks over that age, I applied for and obtained from Lord Panmure, the then Secretary of State for War, a dispensation for this excess, and worked away with a will. But the war came to a rather abrupt and unexpected end, and no more officers being required, the examination was indefinitely postponed. Among the blessings of peace may be reckoned certain comedies, operas, farces, and extravaganzas which, if the war had lasted another six weeks, would in all probability never have been written.

In October 1855 he registered as a student at Inner Temple and also recommenced the study of law. Astonishingly, he succeeded in turning the Scientific Society at King's College into a Dramatic Society although it reverted to its original title on his departure! He wrote amusing verse caricaturing both friends and lecturers during this period and in 1857 gained a BA degree in the Department of General Literature and Science. Gilbert next sat a competitive examination and later in 1857 entered the Civil Service as an assistant clerk in the Education Department of the Privy Council at a salary of £120 a year. He considered that the office was ill-organised and ill-governed, and found the laborious business of writing out legibly numerous dull figures and the bureaucratic organisation indescribably irksome; but to ease the boredom he drew sketches illustrating the absurdity of officialdom. He remained in this post for four difficult years and stated: 'I was one of the worst bargains any government ever made.' As a form of relief from the tedious office life he became a volunteer, part-time officer – being gazetted Ensign in the 5th West Yorkshire Militia. In 1865 he transferred to the Royal Aberdeenshire Militia, became captain and wore a kilt on dress occasions.

Perhaps the writing he had done as a student was responsible for his being asked to make a translation for the Promenade Concert programmes of 'The Laughing Song' from Auber's *Manon Lescaut*. This was his first work to appear in print and he went along to the concert given by Madame Euphrosyne Parepa, not to hear her singing, but for the thrill of observing people reading his words:

I remember that I went night after night to those concerts to enjoy the intense gratification of standing at the elbow of any promenader who might be reading my translation, and wondering to myself what that promenader would say if he knew that the gifted creature who had written the very words he was reading was at that moment standing within a yard of him? The secret satisfaction of knowing that I possessed the power to thrill him with this information was enough and I preserved my incognito.

This first success whetted his appetite for more and he became eager to publish again. By the time he was twenty-four he had written fifteen works for the stage – but each was rejected. However, in 1860 he inherited £300 from an aunt. Eagerly, he left his office job – 'on the happiest day of my life I sent in my resignation.' Within three years he was called to the Bar and set up as a barrister:

With £100 I paid my call to the bar . . . with another £100 I obtained access to a conveyancer's chambers, and with the third £100 I furnished a set of chambers of my own, and began life afresh as a barrister-at-law.

At first he worked in the London courts and then joined the Northern Circuit where he made his first appearance as prosecuting counsel at Liverpool. He was not particularly successful in this calling, averaging about five clients a year for a period of about four years and even in court he filled notebooks with amusing sketches. On one occasion he defended an old woman accused of pick-pocketing. But when she was sentenced to eighteen months of hard labour, despite Gilbert's pleading, she is believed to have thrown a boot at him across the courtroom. Whether or not this incident actually occurred in court, Gilbert used the scenario to develop a short story of the episode published in the *Cornhill Magazine*. Perhaps he made less than £100 in his career as a barrister. He spent three years living at a boarding-house in Pimlico, but he seldom wasted ideas or experiences and the four years in which he worked in the law bore fruit in the very frequent references to law and legal matters in his later plays and in the Gilbert and Sullivan operas.

It was when he was twenty-five that the artistic and literary aspects of his creativeness were brought together effectively and lastingly. Gilbert had long amused himself by writing articles, poems and comic verse and then sent them to magazines and papers in the hope of making money. *Punch* had seen the light of day in 1841 and popular journalism was a fruitful field for a successful writer because of the very multiplicity of such magazines. It was in one of these, *Fun*, that Gilbert began his career in publishing as he himself later reminisced:

In 1861 *Fun* was started, under the editorship of Mr H. J. Byron. With much labour I turned out an article three-quarters of a column long, and sent it to the editor, together with a half-page drawing on wood. A day or two later the printer of the paper called upon me, with Mr Byron's compliments, and staggered me with a request to contribute a column of 'copy' and a half-page drawing every week for the term of my natural life. I hardly knew how to treat that offer, for it seemed to me that into that short article I had poured all I knew. I was empty. I had exhausted myself: I didn't know any more. However, the printer encouraged me (with Mr Byron's compliments), and I said I would try. I did try, and I found to my surprise that there *was* a little left, and enough indeed to enable me to contribute some hundreds of columns to the periodical throughout his editorship, and that of his successor, poor Tom Hood. And here I may mention, for the information and encouragement of disheartened beginners, that I never remember having completed any drama, comedy, or operatic libretto, without feeling that into that drama, comedy or operatic libretto I had poured all that I had, and that there was nothing left. This is a bogey which invariably haunts me, and probably others of my kind, on the completion of every work involving sustained effort. At first it used to scare me; but I have long learnt to recognise it as a mere bogey, and to treat it with the contempt it deserves.

What actually seems to have happened was that Gilbert, weary of receiving rejections for plays as well as poems and articles, decided to by-pass the editor on this occasion and so he sent the article and sketch to the owner of the penny magazine entitled *Fun*. This proprietor, Maclean, liked the work so much that he instructed H. J. Byron, the magazine's editor, to print it forthwith.

Since Gilbert had considerable artistic skill, he illustrated his poems with appropriate sketches. These illustrated poems remain some of the most amusing verses that have come down to us from nineteenth-century English writings. He wrote verses for a variety of magazines, including a few for *Punch*, but principally for *Fun*. He called his poems the 'Bab' ballads – imitating in doing so other illustrators of the time who used a suitably eye-catching name with which to sign their cartoons – people such as 'Spy' (Leslie Ward), 'Ape' (Carlo Pellegrini) and 'Phiz' (Hablot Knight Browne). Gilbert chose the name 'Bab' with which to sign his work because this was the name his family had used for him as a young child – 'Bab' being derived from baby or babby.

A collection of his poems (mostly illustrated) was published in 1869 as the *Bab Ballads* and this was followed in 1873 by a further collection of thirty-five ballads (all illustrated) entitled *More Bab Ballads*. In 1877 he published *Fifty Bab Ballads*, selecting ballads from the earlier books but by then he omitted some well-liked poems and, since readers were critical of this, these were reinstated in 1882. No book published in Gilbert's own lifetime had more than eighty of these poems represented. Altogether there are 139 poems – published together for the first time in 1970. The stark and often ferociously funny illustrations are part of the innate cruelty and crudity of these poems; and yet, surprisingly, much later, in 1898, a more sedate and older Gilbert prepared a further edition and re-drew many of the illustrations, replacing them with a set of friendlier and kindlier characters. Various minor changes in the ballads, for instance to improve rhythm, were also made at that time.

9

Gilbert became a regular contributor to *Fun* and was engaged as a permanent member of staff. His work appeared in *Fun* (often referred to as 'the penny *Punch*') alongside that of many notables including H. J. Byron (who wrote the farce *Our Boys*); Clement Scott (dramatic critic of the *Daily Telegraph*); Tom Robertson (the producer); Artemus Ward (the American humorist); and F. C. Burnand (who later became editor of *Punch* and wrote the libretto for *Cox and Box*). But Gilbert felt the need to belong rather more securely to the literary world of journalism and theatre; so in the early 1860s he founded a group calling it 'The Serious Family' and this was composed of personalities from the world of journalism and theatre. It was Gilbert's role to feed this group at their regular Saturday evening meetings at his chambers in Gray's Inn. The group included Tom Robertson, Tom Hood (by then editor of *Fun*), Clement Scott and others. Each member paid a subscription of two guineas except for Gilbert:

in consideration of my undertaking to supply a rump-steak, cold boiled beef, a Stilton cheese, whisky and soda and bottled ale, every Saturday night for the term of my natural life. Although, financially speaking, this was one of the worst bargains I ever made, I have never regretted it.

Gilbert earned rather less than £3 for a ballad of average length. Each contributor to *Fun* – whether writing prose or poem – received the same payment, £1 per column, the length of contributions being measured by the cashier with a piece of string! The first of his poems to be published with an illustration signed as 'Bab' appeared in *Punch* in October 1865 and was entitled 'To My Absent Husband'. But the editor of *Punch* refused to publish Gilbert's poem 'The Yarn of the *Nancy Bell*' because he thought it too cannibalistic for his readers' tastes:

> For a month we'd neither wittles nor drink,
> Till a-hungry we did feel,
> So we drawed a lot, and accordin' shot
> The captain for our meal.

But 'The Story of Gentle Archibald' is often regarded as the first of the series of *Bab Ballads* since this was the earliest to appear in *Fun* with a 'Bab' illustration and it was in *Fun* that these poems made their mark:

> The change had really turned his brain;
> He boiled his little sister Jane;
> He painted blue his aged mother;
> Sat down upon his little brother;
> Tripped up his cousins with a hoop;

Put pussy in his father's soup;
Placed beetles in his uncle's shoe;
Cut a policeman right in two.

The ballads (written between 1861 and 1879) had a narrative form and dealt with everyday incidents and characters but often with a violent twist that illustrated the selfish aspect of an individual's nature. This was something with which any reader was able to identify. Gilbert tried to show that however important a person became he remained in many respects a child who refused to grow up wholly. The truth is that Gilbert was often critical and contemptuous of people and their deeds and so he delighted in illustrating human foibles and weakness. He is supposed not to have thought very highly of the *Bab Ballads* but it is known that he had his favourite verses. He said that the ballads were:

composed hastily, and under the discomforting necessity of having to turn out a quantity of lively verse on a certain day in each week.

Even when he published them collectively he excused them by saying that he had:

ventured to publish the little pictures with them, because while they are certainly quite as bad as the ballads, I suppose they are not much worse.

The *Bab Ballads* have had both critics and advocates. The *Athenaeum* reviewer of 1869 described them as the dreariest, dullest fun, and others described Gilbert as essentially cruel and delighting in cruelty. G. K. Chesterton and Max Beerbohm were ecstatic in their praise; and Chesterton wrote:

This is the pure and holy spirit of Nonsense; that divine lunacy that God has given to men as a holiday of the intellect . . . and rather especially to Englishmen.

A line that Gilbert was later to put into the mouth of Jack Point, the jester in *The Yeomen of the Guard*, may be taken as typical of his personal and professional creed:

For, look you, there is humour in all things, and the truest philosophy is that which teaches us to find it and to make the most of it.

Gilbert also illustrated works written by his father including his father's first novel, *Shirley Hall Asylum* (1863) and *The Magic Mirror* – a collection of stories for children. In this topsyturvey world of Gilbert's imagination it seemed perfectly natural that William Gilbert senior should follow in the footsteps of his son and commence a career in writing!

W. S. Gilbert's interest in ballad-writing developed into a mania. Even whilst setting out on the train to Folkestone, on the first leg of his honeymoon in France after his marriage to Lucy Agnes Turner in 1867, he is believed to have composed one of the 'Babs'. He was then thirty-one years old. She was seventeen when they married, the daughter of an army officer in India. She remained with him throughout his life and was his strength and helpmate and someone for whom he, in turn, felt lasting warmth and affection. She built him a home in which peace and tranquility reigned – a stark contrast with the life he led outside it. The couple lived in Kensington.

But within a year or so, and certainly by mid-1869, the number of new poems dwindled and he turned instead to drama. He had produced various new plays (including the burlesque *Dulcamara* in 1866) and in 1870 one of these, *The Palace of Truth*, was a success. Later that year *Pygmalion and Galatea* appeared at the Haymarket and this was his most successful play and one which, with revivals, was to earn him about £40,000. The nervous tension involved in meeting deadlines for magazine journalism had become less appealing than the thrill of writing for the stage and Gilbert soon found that the latter was financially more rewarding. But, in addition to the money to be made from drama, he had found in writing for the stage a creative medium in which he excelled.

Perhaps a facet of Gilbert's own character may be gleaned in the ballad 'The Half-Crown Day':

> No, I'm not in the least democratic,
> I object to a mob and a crush,
> *My* tastes are too aristocratic,
> *My* way through a crowd to push.

In another ballad, 'The Three Bohemian Ones', there are three portraits of Gilbert himself – as an actor, a magazine writer and a comic artist. Gilbert believed in an economy of ideas and where possible he re-used and re-worked an older story-line. Some of the *Bab Ballads* were important sources of inspiration when he searched for ideas for a libretto for his operas written in collaboration with Sullivan. It was natural enough that he should look again at his many poems and raid some of his earlier works as a valuable source of ideas. 'Trial by Jury' was a ballad from *Fun* that became an opera of the same name. 'The Rival Curates' was used as a story-line for *Patience*. 'General John', 'Joe Golightly', 'The Bumboat Woman's Story' and 'Captain Reece' were transformed into *H.M.S. Pinafore*. 'A Bad Night of It' and 'The Fairy Curate' (in which a child was born to a fairy and a mortal)

Selection of Gilbert's cartoons from the *Bab Ballads*.

were sources of inspiration for *Iolanthe*. Similarly, 'Haunted' was used in *The Pirates of Penzance*; 'King Borria Bungalee Boo' in *The Mikado*; 'Annie Protheroe' and 'Jester James' in *The Yeomen of the Guard*; 'The Two Majors' in *Utopia Limited*; 'The Ladies of the Lea' and 'The Cunning Woman' in *The Sorcerer*; 'The Modest Couple' in *Ruddigore*; 'A and B' in *The Gondoliers*; and it seems at least possible that 'The Railway Guard's Song' provided the germ of an idea towards a song in the first Gilbert and Sullivan opera, *Thespis*, in which there was a song about a democratic railway company called the Diddlesex Junction and a railway director who undermined his influence by association with inferiors.

Some ballads provided a vague lead and others a very clear inspiration for the later operas and the following lines from 'Captain Reece', for instance, illustrate some similarity to events in *H.M.S. Pinafore*:

My daughter, that enchanting gurl,
Has just been promised to an earl,
And all my other familee,
To peers of various degree.

But what are dukes and viscounts to
The happiness of all my crew?
The word I give you I'll fulfil;
It is my duty, and I will.

Only two Gilbert and Sullivan operas do not appear to have derived any direct inspiration from the ballads – *The Grand Duke* and *Princess Ida*. For the latter of these Gilbert reworked an earlier play he had written, *The Princess*, following a poem by Tennyson.

The volume Gilbert published in 1898 was entitled *The Bab Ballads with which are included Songs of a Savoyard*. The book is a curious mixture of eighty ballads interspersed with rather more than that number of lyrics from the Gilbert and Sullivan operas. Gilbert had originally intended to entitle this work 'The Savoy Ballads' in order to emphasise the close relationship of the ballads with the Savoy operas and the debt the latter owed to the former.

Gilbert used Donizetti's theme of *L'Elisir d'Amore* and had written the play entitled *Dulcamara: or the Little Duck and the Great Quack*, and this was produced at St James's Theatre in 1866 by Tom Robertson – who was to become an important model for Gilbert himself as a practical and pioneering stage producer. Gilbert could not have been more fortunate in learning the techniques of theatrical management from such an innovator as Robertson who moved actors about the stage with precision and to achieve the best effect. Prior to Robertson's influence principal actors had been eccentric free-agents who had done precisely as they pleased. Robertson wrote plays (and then produced them) in which characters appeared to become real people – involving such commonplace actions as eating a meal on stage in his so-called 'cup and saucer comedies'. Gilbert was slowly mastering a skilled craft. Much of what he produced was doggerel and some of the *Bab Ballads* had been forced and tedious, but the experience of producing a number of frankly indifferent plays stood him in good stead. His material gradually rose in significance and the technique of improved play-production evolved in his mind. Gilbert's skill in drawing was also to be of great value in later years, enabling him to make sketches both of costumes and scenes for the Gilbert and Sullivan operas. Much later Gilbert stated that the art of a playwright:

does not call for the highest order of intellect – it demands shrewdness of observation, a nimble brain, a faculty for expressing oneself concisely, a

14

sense of balance both in the construction of plots and in the construction of sentences.

He was a man of many passions and one of his personal interests was croquet – and he admitted that he once played the game in the dark using candles. In the *Broadwood Annual* of 1868 he wrote an article on the game:

It is an outdoor game, and differs from leap frog in being one of the very few in which both sexes can join with propriety. It is allied to many pleasant associations – a fine day, a smooth lawn, pretty boots, bewildering petticoats, and agreeable interludes.

Gilbert was a man of his time – punctilious, proper and courteous with the opposite sex and yet someone who was clearly fond of younger women and enjoyed their company. His wife, considerably younger than himself, always remained his 'kitten' and during the forty-three years in which they were together she had the sense to make more than adequate allowance for his foibles and wider interests. They had no children. In many senses his wife was his child, his pretty young thing; but he also enjoyed giving parties for children – upwards of a hundred at a time – at his home. Gilbert was tall, good-looking, with blue eyes and fair hair. He was imposing and had a military presence. Gentleman though he was, his fiery impatience caused him endless problems, and frequently at law, since he spoke first and then, sometimes, thought about whether he should have done so or not, but only much later when the hackles of others were raised and the damage was done.

The year in which he married – 1867 – was, with hindsight, to become a momentous year for yet another reason. In that year he reviewed in *Fun* a work by the composer Arthur Sullivan. This work was Sullivan's first comic opera, *Cox and Box*, produced at the Adelphi Theatre. Gilbert the reviewer believed that Sullivan's music was ill-matched for the play because the music was too good for the latter:

Mr Sullivan's music is, in many places, of too high a class for the grotesquely absurd plot to which it is wedded. It is funny here and there, and grand or graceful where it is not funny; but the grand and the graceful have, we think, too large a share of the honours to themselves.

Gilbert thought that Sullivan, by attracting too much attention to the music, had failed to understand the kind of music that was needed for this libretto – a strangely early form of a grievance that, again and again, in their later partnership was to cause friction between the two of them. They did not meet at this stage but at least they had become conscious of the existence of one another.

15

The house in Bolwell Street,
Lambeth, where Arthur
Sullivan was born in May 1842.

2 Sullivan's Early Life and Works

Arthur Seymour Sullivan was born at 8 Bolwell Street, Lambeth, in south London on 13 May 1842. His father, Thomas, was an Irish musician who played the clarinet in a theatre. The family lived in a working-class district of cockney London and money was always a problem necessitating Thomas Sullivan to supplement his income by teaching and copying out music. Arthur had an older brother, Frederic, and both of them were encouraged to take an interest in music. Arthur Sullivan played the piano in the front parlour. His father became bandmaster at the Royal Military College at Sandhurst and this position, with an enhanced salary, eased the family's financial worries, but only to an extent. Sullivan's mother, Maria Coughlan, is thought by some to have been partly Jewish by descent.

By the age of eight Sullivan was able to handle and play the various instruments in his father's band – including the clarinet, horn, cornet, trombone and flute. He played at rehearsals of the band; and at that early age composed an anthem to 'By the waters of Babylon' – the 137th Psalm. His mother became a governess, living away from home for a while, in order to earn more money to help further the family's slender financial resources. At the age of eight he began four years at a boarding school in London. Effectively, then, he left home at this age – since he never returned there for any length of time – and so it is the more remarkable that he always remained devoted to and involved with his family during his entire life. When he was ten he wrote home to his mother from school:

One of our boys, Higham, has taken a great fancy to my knife. He has a little gold pencil-case which I have taken a great fancy to. He asked me whether, if he gives me the pencil and a two-bladed knife, I will give him mine. I have submitted this to your discretion. Mr Plees has a lodger, Miss Matthews, who has a nice piano, and I often go up to her room and play.

Sullivan had a very good voice and in 1854 his singing ability afforded him a place in the prestigious choir of the Chapel Royal, St James's Palace, when he was twelve. The years he spent there provided him with a first-rate choral training. Just over a year after entering the Chapel Royal, Novello published his song 'O Israel' in 1855. He was thirteen and a composer who had appeared in print. His letters to his parents now showed a growing awareness and appreciation of music:

The cake is all gone, and *I shall soon be in want of another*. I like Mr Goss's anthem very much; it is very fine. It opens with a fine chorus, 'Praise the Lord, O My Soul'. *Very fine*.

In his heavy scarlet and gold coat he looked a perfect picture and sounded angelic. The Duke of Wellington gave him half a sovereign after a service; the Prince Consort praised his singing, which had pleased the Queen, and gave him ten shillings; and a bishop had presented him with half a sovereign on finding that Sullivan had been singing one of his own songs – the first recorded occasion on which the thirteen-year-old Sullivan received 'payment' for one of his compositions!

In 1857 Thomas Sullivan was appointed as professor of the clarinet at the Royal Military School of Music at Kneller Hall in Twickenham. The family went to live that autumn at 3 Ponsonby Street in Pimlico.

The Mendelssohn Scholarship – established in memory of the composer – was a formidable test of present knowledge and potential ability. Each of the competitors who reached the final stage was older than Sullivan who was then only just fourteen. His success in 1856 in being awarded the first Mendelssohn Scholarship for a year filled him with ambition:

I have chosen music, and I shall go on, because nothing in the world would ever interest me so much. I may not make a lot of money, but I shall have music, and that will make up if I don't.

Still a chorister, Sullivan, in addition, was now able to attend the Royal Academy of Music, under Sterndale Bennett, on a regular basis for lessons on the piano and harmony. The scholarship was renewed for a second year when he took the examination again. He became the pupil who showed the greatest

The Chapel Royal in the late 1850s at the time when Sullivan sang there in the choir.

Sullivan aged eighteen as a student in Leipzig.

progress and potential. He continued to show an interest in composition, and it was decided that he should be sent to Leipzig to continue his musical education. He was offered free German lessons twice a week in preparation for this stay abroad; and hence he was re-elected a Mendelssohn Scholar for a third year to allow him to study at Leipzig. He arrived there, at the Conservatoire that Mendelssohn had founded, in September 1858. Contemporaries of his at Leipzig were Carl Rosa and Grieg. The Conservatoire had an enormous reputation due to the drive of its leading-light, Ignez Moscheles; and in this environment the sixteen-year-old Sullivan thrived. He became friendly in Leipzig with an English family with children at the Conservatoire. One of these students, Clara Barnett, remarked on Sullivan's appealing manners:

It was part of Sullivan's very nature to ingratiate himself with everyone that crossed his path. He always wanted to make an impression, and what is more, he always succeeded in doing it. Whenever some distinguished person came . . . to visit the Conservatorium, Sullivan always contrived to be on hand to render some little service which brought him to their notice and formed an entering wedge to their acquaintance. In this way he got into personal touch with most of the celebrities . . . He was a natural courtier; which did not prevent him, however, from being a very lovable person.

Sullivan had been attracted both to Clara and her sister Rosamund. Clara recalled that when an established pianist arrived at the Conservatoire he:

flirted with her so violently as he was wont to do with every newcomer of note. I had long since concluded, however, that these flirtations were only fires of straw which quickly burnt out.

Whilst in Leipzig he had received acclaim for the incidental music he had written for *The Tempest*. He met Robert Schumann and Franz Liszt. He was thrifty in expenditure because his parents had to finance his living expenses although the Mendelssohn Committee again renewed his Scholarship to enable him to study for a second year at Leipzig. But eventually his days there were drawing to a close in 1860 and a dilemma ensued; it had been suggested to him by his teachers that he would derive enormous benefit if he stayed on at Leipzig until the following spring. The Sullivan family somehow managed to raise the money to keep him there. Sullivan's father obtained an extra income from working at Broadwoods, the piano-makers, where he gave lessons four nights a week. The young Sullivan was full of gratitude:

How can I thank you sufficiently, my dearest Father, for the opportunity you have given me of continuing my studies here. I am indeed very grateful and will work very hard in order that you may soon see that all your sacrifices (which I know you make) have not been to no purpose, and I will try to make the end of your days happy and comfortable. I had given up all idea of staying longer, and indeed was making preparations for my journey home, therefore the surprise was greater for me.

The financial situation for Tom Sullivan was eased slightly when the director of the Conservatoire released Sullivan from payment of tuition fees for this additional period. When he returned to London from Leipzig in the summer of 1861 he had extensive knowledge and sound training in the areas of orchestration as well as of counterpoint and fugue. He remained enthusiastic about the music of Schumann, at that time unknown in Britain. He soon met George Grove who accepted *The Tempest* for a performance at the Crystal Palace in April 1862; and nineteen-year-old Sullivan suddenly became well-known. His compositions showed a Mendelssohn influence and this made his music acceptable to the appreciative Queen Victoria and Prince Albert. The Queen asked Sullivan to compose a *Te Deum* in honour of the marriage of the Prince of Wales and Princess Alexandra. He became Master of the Queen's Music.

He taught part of the normal curriculum for a period to boys at the Chapel Royal; and was also appointed Professor of Pianoforte and Ballad Singing at the Crystal Palace School of Art. But his compositions and the few lessons in music he was able to give did not provide much of an income; so in order to help make a living he became organist at St Michael's Church in Chester Square at a salary of £80 a year. He improved the church choir considerably and solved the problem of a deficit of tenors and basses by recruiting policemen from the local police station as new choir members. He later wrote:

I used to think of them sometimes when I was composing *The Pirates of Penzance*.

The 1860s were the years of expansion and experiment for Sullivan. He stopped selling songs outright and instead demanded a royalty for each copy sold and this improved his finances. George Grove remonstrated with him that he was receiving next to nothing for his songs – just as in the same way a friendly theatrical manager once pointed out to Gilbert that he should never sell so good a play as *Dulcamara* as cheaply as £30 again.

At the end of 1862 Sullivan went to Paris with Charles Dickens, the Lehmanns and Chorley who was then writing the libretto of *The Sapphire Necklace* to be set by Sullivan. In Paris they met Rossini and Sullivan played duets from *The Tempest* with him.

In 1864 he wrote a ballet entitled *L'Ile Enchantée* for Covent Garden, and he became organist at the theatre, attended rehearsals and took part in performances. His own first opera, *The Sapphire Necklace*, did not get performed. He composed a cantata, *Kenilworth*, for the Birmingham Festival. He had collaborated with the librettist Henry F. Chorley on *Kenilworth* and also on the opera *The Sapphire Necklace*; and so the seeds of his interest both in serious and in lighter music were shown in these collaborations with this one individual!

In October 1867 he visited Vienna as an assistant of George

Grove and to their joy they discovered two lost symphonies by Schubert and the music for *Rosamunde*. This was the same George Grove who was later to write the *Dictionary of Music and Musicians*.

Crossing the Channel they met on board Johann Strauss (the younger). After conducting singers in Paris, they met Clara Schumann at Baden-Baden. Sullivan wrote to his mother from the continent about their visit to Salzburg:

We went and saw the house Mozart was born and lived in . . . when we wrote our names in the Visitors' Book the librarian asked me if I was the composer of whom he had often read in the *Signale* and the other musical papers. I modestly owned that I did now and then write a little music and we bowed and complimented each other.

In Vienna they met Eduard Schneider, a nephew of Schubert, and even an elderly clerk named Döppler in the firm that had published Schubert's music – the clerk claiming that he was present at Schubert's christening, as well as being a pupil of Schubert's father. He also remembered Beethoven's visits to the music shop where he had sold him sheet music. They were able to discover a number of lost pieces: the Overture in D (Die Freunde von Salamanca) and two symphonies – C minor (no. 4, D.417) and C major (no. 6, D.589). Yet, as Grove related:

I had failed in one chief object of my journey. The *Rosamunde* music was almost dearer to me than the symphonies . . . we still required the accompaniments to the Romance and the two Choruses, as well as the total number of pieces and their sequence in the drama . . . It was Thursday afternoon and we proposed to leave on Saturday for Prague. We made a final call on Dr Schneider, to take leave and repeat our thanks, and also, as I now firmly believe, guided by a special instinct . . . I again turned the conversation to the *Rosamunde* music – he believed that he had at one time possessed a copy of a sketch of it all. Might I go into the cupboard and look for myself? Certainly, if I had no objection to being smothered with dust. In I went, and after some search, during which my companion kept the doctor engaged in conversation, I found, at the bottom of the cupboard and in the farthest corner, a bundle of music books two feet high, carefully tied round and black with the undisturbed dust of nearly half a century . . . There were the part books of the whole of the music in *Rosamunde*, tied up after the second performance, in December 1823, and probably never disturbed since . . . it was now late in the day, but we summoned our kind and faithful friend Pohl to our aid, and by dint of dividing our work into three, and writing our hardest, we contrived before two in the morning to get all the missing accompaniments copied, as well as every note and stage direction that could throw light on the connection between the drama and the music.

George Grove and Sullivan then concluded their labour of love by celebrating with a game of leap-frog – and weeks later, in November 1867, the first complete *Rosamunde* was presented at the Crystal Palace. Later in the same continental trip Sullivan made his way back to the Leipzig he had left five years before. He conducted his overture *In Memoriam* at the Gewandhaus Concert and then wrote to his mother:

You will like to know about the Overture. It was a great success. I went to the Orchestra undaunted by the frigid audience, made my bow and began. It went splendidly – with great delicacy and great fire. I expected applause but I got more – a hearty recall after I left the Orchestra. Everyone of note came and congratulated me, and I think it has laid a firm foundation to a good reputation in Germany. Next Monday the Symphony is to be tried, and then I leave for Paris. Grove arrived yesterday and is happy, the separation was telling on his health!* He sends his love; so do I.
Yours. A.
*Bosh! Yours affectionately, G. Grove.

Between 1867-72 Sullivan became organist at the more fashionable church of St Peter's, Cranley Gardens. In 1866 he wrote his symphony and a cello concerto. In 1869 he produced the oratorio, *The Prodigal Son*, for the Worcester Festival; and in 1870 wrote the *Overture di Ballo* for the Birmingham Festival. He also became guest conductor at a number of important musical festivals. At the age of twenty-four he was appointed professor of composition at the Royal Academy of Music, although teaching did not excite him. By the late 1860s Sullivan was living at Claverton Street in Pimlico. W. S. Gilbert was also, strangely, residing in Pimlico.

Sullivan drew on various styles of music and was able to produce parodies of Bellini, Purcell, Handel, Schubert, Bizet, Verdi, Donizetti, Mendelssohn and Arne. English folk songs and English ballad operas also influenced him, as did the works of Mozart and Offenbach. But, in addition, he had his own innate melody, rhythm, sense of musical fun and a flair for orchestration – and all these gifts were able to complement his librettist so well when the comic operas came to be written.

Sullivan always remained the respectable church organist and aspects of this role percolated into his writings for the operas. His hymn tunes were mainly composed in the years 1867-74 and most were published in *The Hymnary* and *Church Hymns*. Sullivan was musical editor of the latter publication. His most famous hymn tune was 'Onward Christian Soldiers'; and another favourite was the carol 'It came upon the midnight clear'.

Sullivan's love for his mother remained an abiding passion:

The Crystal Palace at Sydenham where Sullivan's *The Tempest* established his fame. Sullivan taught for a time in the School of Art nearby.

Dearest Mum,
I am coming home. I want quiet – and you. I want to work. The *Overture* last night was a great success; I was recalled, flowers etc. But I am coming home to work. Better still, I am coming home for your birthday.

He was perhaps a bit carefully prissy in dress and also apparently in speech as the brief recording of his voice made in 1888 appears to testify. Thomas Edison wanted recordings of the voices of famous people and Sullivan's message was almost belligerent:

For myself I can only say that I am astonished and somewhat terrified at the result of this evening's experiment. Astonished at the wonderful form you have developed, and terrified at the thought that so much hideous and bad music will be put on record forever.
But all the same I think it is the most wonderful thing that I have ever experienced and I congratulate you with all my heart on this wonderful discovery.
Arthur Sullivan.

Sullivan was short, prim and a bit stout. He wore an eye-glass. He had thick dark, curly hair, a moustache and a dark complexion – probably inherited from his mother who had Italian origins. His manner was gentle and his bright eyes were kindly. He became a person able to suffer distress and setbacks stoically.

In the years following his return from Leipzig in the summer of 1861, Sullivan had become a frequent visitor at the homes of a number of musical families living at Sydenham. This was where the concerts organised by George Grove at the Crystal Palace were held on Saturday afternoons and trains took audiences to

25

George Grove helped further Sullivan's early musical career.

Sydenham for the day. Sullivan was especially friendly with the Groves, the Scott Russells and the Glehns. John Scott Russell was an engineer who worked with Isambard Kingdom Brunel on the *Great Eastern*, the largest ship of the period. He had three daughters, Louise, Rachel and Alice. Each was intelligent, attractive and interested in music. Sullivan, an incorrigible, self-centred flirt, became friendly with each of them, and had sexual relationships with Rachel and then with her sister Louise. For many years these love affairs, beginning in 1864 and lasting until

1870, remained secret. Sullivan kept the letters he received from the girls until his death. There are more than two hundred of these letters and they became available only fairly recently. Sullivan's relationship with the Scott Russell sisters is of great interest since it presents fascinating asides on his character and lifestyle.

It was Rachel, the middle daughter in the family, with whom he had the most intense relationship. She was determined that he should succeed as a musician and, undoubtedly, Sullivan found her influence exciting and stimulating and he produced almost all the symphonic music he ever composed during the years of their friendship:

Oh, strain every nerve for my sake – women love to be proud of their friends – and I don't think you know *how* ambitious I am. I want you to write something for which all the world *must* acknowledge your talent.

Rachel desperately wanted to marry Sullivan and they became secretly engaged. Her parents would have disapproved since Sullivan did not have the income to support their daughter adequately. Nonetheless, Rachel continued her support:

I have so often said you could and will be the first musician of the time . . . I wish I had you here that I could talk to you. There is nothing you cannot do if you will only *will* it – No man ever had such a chance as you, never – you have a name already and scarcely any rivals.

In 1866 and the following year Sullivan wrote a symphony, a concerto and two overtures. But the truth was that Sullivan was lazy in composition. He needed to be pushed and he found life much easier when he had the words of a piece available as a source of ideas and inspiration. Rachel also encouraged him in this direction:

I want you to write an opera – such an opera – and I feel it must be done this winter – a grand and vigorous great work.

But Rachel did not admire aspects of the lifestyle Sullivan enjoyed in London and she was hardly reticent about letting him know her views:

I cannot think how you can go on living the life you do – going to miserable sickly London parties, smoking half the night through – and then getting up seedy and limp and unfit for any good honest work.

In October 1866 Sullivan's father had died suddenly. It had been due to his father's sacrifices that Sullivan had achieved his training and current success. Sullivan now knew that he could never repay his father in old age. He wrote to a close friend, Nina Lehmann:

My dear, dear Father, whom I loved so passionately and who returned my love a hundredfold if that were possible! Oh, it is so hard, it is so terribly hard to think that I shall never see his dear face again, or hear his cheery voice saying, 'God bless you, my boy!'

The death of Thomas Sullivan provided the inspiration Sullivan needed to write the oratorio, *In Memoriam*, for the Norwich Festival in October 1866. This oratorio was very well received and Sullivan was acclaimed even by doubting critics. At this time Rachel's father found himself in a state of financial crisis and there were suggestions that he might need to go abroad to find work; and, of course, his family would go with him. These events tended to push Sullivan and Rachel, momentarily, rather closer emotionally. But, following his father's death, his mother went to live with him at Claverton Street; and the continual presence of his mother in his home – as housekeeper – probably did not help to advance his relationship with Rachel. Sullivan had a lifestyle beyond his financial means. Marriage to Rachel was out of the question in the foreseeable future.

In 1866 Sullivan dedicated a song, 'If Doughty Deeds My Lady Please', to Rachel's mother, but this was before Rachel's parents found out his true feelings towards their daughter. When they did discover his intentions, in the summer of 1867, there was a storm of protest from Mrs Scott Russell about her daughter's proposal to marry a penniless musician and Sullivan was banned from the family home. But the lovers continued to meet and correspond in secret. Louise posted Rachel's letters to Sullivan. Sullivan's friend, Fred Clay, who was an intimate friend of Rachel's sister, Alice, carried Sullivan's letters to Rachel.

At the beginning of May 1867 Rachel had spent an evening with Sullivan in London and they had returned by train to Sydenham where they made love for the first time. Rachel later in 1868 remonstrated with him:

When I think of those days when cooing and purring was enough for us – till we tried the utmost – and that is why I fancy *marriage* spoils love. When you can drink *brandy* water tastes sickly afterwards . . . that is the reason why marriage gets so commonplace that people see and have so much of each other morally and physically that they get satiated and the freshness of the charm and attraction wears off. Darling, why are you not coming today? Because you had enough of me yesterday, and are quietly contented to wait till another opportunity occurs? When will you come again – Don't you want to see me darling . . . I feel as if my heart would break if your love grew cold.

28

Maria Sullivan, Sullivan's beloved mother.

Rachel enjoyed the love affair with Sullivan at different levels of consciousness. One of these was love by correspondence, in which she became cloying and choking in her demands:

Keep up your courage my own one – and write to me daily a long long letter that I may have it to help me tomorrow. Oh! my love, tell me all I want to hear . . . Oh Arthur, I put my arms round you and kiss you darling as I *never* kissed you before. God bless and keep you my own one – and some day Arthur I will stand before you waiting till you hold out your arms and clasp me in them for *ever*.
Your own one I am
true until death.

Arthur Sullivan – the young and presentable socialite.

But Rachel was not the only sister to receive letters from Sullivan. He actually wrote to all three sisters and they tended to share one another's missives when these arrived from him! In the latter part of 1867 Sullivan was cooling in his ardour towards Rachel. He did not bother to send her a Christmas card or a greeting at New Year. Yet things had improved between them within weeks and Rachel told her parents that they had kept their relationship alive and intended to marry that spring. Her father – who knew how seriously she felt, having spent the previous autumn with her in Switzerland – wanted them to marry at once but Rachel knew that Sullivan still had little money. By the spring he was cooling again. His letters became hostile and hers

30

desperate. Fred Clay told Rachel that he did not really think that Sullivan was a man given to matrimony; and George Grove advised her that Sullivan did not understand what devotion was all about. Perhaps Rachel already realised that she would never possess him totally, but she would not yet admit this; her fantasies were becoming more comforting than reality. Sullivan had dedicated the song, 'O Fair Dove! O Fond Dove!' to Rachel – a song which he set to music at her suggestion. This was a public statement of his regard for her and it became her reality. She was his dove. He addressed her as Fond Dove and she addressed him as Birdie. The name she aptly used to describe herself was Passion Flower.

Rachel again went to Switzerland with her father in the summer of 1868, and her mother later joined them. Alice, the youngest sister, whose romance with Fred Clay was now ended, was preoccupied with parties. Louise, the eldest, began seeing Sullivan in the autumn. She had already written to him on various occasions and it is clear that their relationship and her feelings for him ran deep:

I can offer not the slightest reward for good behaviour because you have taken as your right the only thing I have to give, but I can try to be even more tender and loving.

Louise was doting on her sister's lover:

Suppose we arrange not to meet at all till it becomes an absolute necessity, and then suppose we say there is to be no petting. Would you like that? We could talk and be near one another and enjoy each other's society; would it be nice? Or is there really only one thing that makes one thoroughly comfy and warm? Oh how sad and that that one thing should be wicked, though I can't find any passage in the Bible where it is forbidden or even alluded to, so perhaps if *they* take no notice of it, *we* need not!

Sullivan really does seem to have been spoilt for choice. Rachel wrote to him from Switzerland:

My little bed is turned back all ready for use and oh! how I wish a little curly black head were lying on it and that I might lay mine down beside it.

Rachel was shortly to return to England, and hence the dilemma. But Sullivan was able to extricate himself from Louise emotionally by admitting to her that he was continuing to see other women. This was too much for her to take. Next, Sullivan decided that he must end his relationship with Rachel. He went to

Switzerland and talked to her in Zurich. Shortly after, she wrote to him:

What I write to say now is 'Goodbye' . . . You have others to work for and your beautiful genius to live for, and I – nor any other woman on God's earth is worth wasting one's life for.

And yet she continued to write to him – one letter still bears the tear stains – and she did so even after her return home. But, eventually, in the autumn of 1869, she decided to join her brother, Norman, who was working in Russia. She wrote to Sullivan to arrange to see him in order to burn all the letters she had ever sent him; although in the end she allowed him to keep them. Louise still wrote occasionally to Sullivan:

If I shrink from seeing you it is because you say you are hard and I cannot go through that pain again. It is like clinging to a marble pillar trying to get warm. It would at least be some gratification if the pillar would only say, 'Do try and warm me,' but no – it rejoices in its iciness.

By the autumn of 1872 Rachel had decided to burn all the letters that Sullivan had ever sent her – hence the one-sided nature of the correspondence that can be presented now. She married and moved to India where she had two daughters and forgot Sullivan, but maintained some interest in music – translating into English the autobiography of Hector Berlioz. This appeared in 1884 two years after her death in India in 1882 at the early age of thirty-six. But Sullivan always kept her letters and the others from her family. She and Sullivan had met again at a party in 1881 but by then more than a decade had gone by and they were different people. Louise, who never married, had died in 1878 of consumption.

Perhaps these tangled relationships and the emotional energy Sullivan needed to expend in attempting to unravel himself from them had served as a permanent warning to him, for there was never again any suggestion that he would give so much of himself to another. The private life of even a well-known national personality of the nineteenth century must in some degree remain shrouded in intimacy and mystery and each of the principal characters in this biography enjoyed privacy and anonymity in at least part of his lifestyle. It might be argued that Sullivan's personal and sexual preferences have nothing to do with us now, and that a century and more since no-one cares very much anyway. And yet a number of writers have chosen to comment on such matters in recent years – indicating very different opinions. Caryl Brahms (1975) made a number of references to Sullivan's supposed homosexuality; Arthur Jacobs (1984) clearly believed

Alfred, Duke of Edinburgh, shown here in an 'Ape' cartoon from 1874, was a friend of Sullivan and a musical patron.

32

that Sullivan was heterosexual. Faced with such divergent opinions, some further comment seems to be desirable.

It may be the case that, especially in his earlier life, Sullivan overtly enjoyed the company of like-minded, musical young men and he was merely sixteen and susceptible when he first went to study at Leipzig. But it seems to be going a bit far to categorize him as having homosexual inclinations, even in these early years, on such flimsy evidence as has been adduced by some writers. Indeed, once he had a few years of maturity the evidence shows his preference in his love affairs with two of the Scott Russell sisters. Although cartoonists were later to have a field day sketching Gilbert and Sullivan together (on occasions portraying Sullivan wearing a dress – sometimes, but not always, more a reflection of his opera *H.M.S. Pinafore* than of anything else) this probably means little. It is possible, of course, that there was an element of bi-sexuality in Sullivan's nature. His relationships with women went so far but no further – fires of straw, as they have been called. His friendships with men, on the other hand, appear to run deep and were long-lasting; and his intimate relationship with the Duke of Edinburgh was parodied by cartoonists in the press.

It appears from his diary that in later life he evolved an elaborate code of noting his not infrequent visits to brothels. His friendship

Mary Frances Ronalds was Sullivan's closest female friend.

33

with Mrs Ronalds lasted for many years and in his diary he used a variety of symbols to denote engagements with and visits from that lady. He even confided to his diary the degree of sexual satisfaction and also the precise nature of the sexual act on a particular day by using a numerically graded system. He was a complex character. Mrs Ronalds was his friend, his confidante, his companion, his hostess – even when he entertained Royalty – and it seems, from the evidence of his lifestyle and his diary, that she was his regular lover as well. Sullivan never married and, as far as is known, had no children. It could be said that his music was his life, his wife and his child; although he later chose to adopt one of his nephews, Herbert, who lived in his home as his son and who eventually became his heir.

Sullivan's friend, Fred Clay (the son of a peer), introduced him to the men's clubs in London in which people of means and aspirations met others in society, ate, drank and gambled. Sullivan quickly became interested in these gatherings. He also liked to sit at a piano and entertain, informally, an audience of artistic people and there were many such opportunities at parties where recitals and private theatrical performances were presented.

Sullivan's ballads were becoming so popular that he was paid an annual retainer of £400 to write ballads for the music publishers, Boosey. He became the foremost composer in England. Rachel had been right about that! Frequent requests were made for him to write oratorios for the major music festivals including Birmingham, Leeds, Manchester, Norwich and Edinburgh. He led a hectic existence – composing during the day, then travelling on a train through the night to conduct in the provinces the following day. His notebook was his constant companion and he often sketched out music for songs during his travels.

John Goss, one of his old teachers at the Royal Academy, in writing to Sullivan after the performance of *The Prodigal Son* in 1869 (a very commendable first attempt at oratorio), had this advice to offer the aspiring musician:

All you have done is most masterly. Your orchestration superb, and your efforts, many of them, original and first-rate. Some day you will I hope try at another oratorio, putting out all your strength – not the strength of a few weeks or months. Show yourself *the best man in Europe*! Don't do anything so pretentious as an oratorio or even a Symphony without *all your power*, which seldom comes in one fit. Handel's two or three weeks for the 'Messiah' may be a fact, but *he* was not always successful, and was not so young as you.

In 1869 Sullivan was still only twenty-seven. Queen Victoria wrote to him in that year requesting a complete set of his works –

F. C. Burnand with whom
Sullivan wrote *Cox and Box*.

an unequalled honour. She later sent him music composed by the
Prince Consort on Sunday mornings, asking if Sullivan would
correct its technique.

In the early 1870s Sullivan produced such major works as music
to *The Merry Wives of Windsor*, the Festival *Te Deum* as well as
numerous hymns, songs and choruses. But the oratorio *The Light
of the World*, declared by Gounod to be a masterpiece and by
Queen Victoria as destined to uplift British music, gave Sullivan
an enviable and unshakeable position of musical authority.

His first performed opera was *Cox and Box* with lyrics by
Francis Burnand – later editor of *Punch*. In 1866 Burnand had met
Sullivan on the street and suggested that they work together. The
title of J. Maddison Morton's play *Box and Cox* was reversed by
Burnand and became *Cox and Box*. Sullivan wrote the music
without charging a fee as it was to be performed by friends in an
amateur theatrical company. A member of the Glehn family
recalled an early private performance of this opera:

At my own home we used to indulge a good deal in private theatricals . . . and on a few occasions Sullivan would act with us – but the memorable occasion was the first (or nearly the first) performance of *Cox and Box* at our house, in which Sullivan played Box; Fred Clay, Cox and Norman Scott Russell, Bouncer; while Franklin Taylor officiated as orchestra. Both Sullivan and Clay had voices of great beauty, and this delightful little operetta went with a charm and go which I don't think has been equalled by any other performers since.

Sullivan's agreement to compose the music for this comic opera in collaboration with Burnand might almost be viewed as a diversion from his main areas of musical interest. It was first produced at Burnand's home at the end of 1866 and, when in 1867 it was presented to the public at the Adelphi Theatre as a benefit performance, it met with such success that Sullivan was astounded. It was given performances in a number of venues. The success of *Cox and Box* encouraged Sullivan to try again with Burnand and in December 1867 they produced *The Contrabandista* about a band of brigands in Spain. This was not reviewed too kindly and, as with *Cox and Box*, it was felt that his music was an advance on the libretto, so causing an imbalance in the total effect.

The stage was now almost set for the fateful meeting. Possibly late in 1869 or more probably in the summer of 1870, Sullivan went to see a rehearsal of a play written by his friend Fred Clay, with words by W. S. Gilbert. Gilbert and Sullivan thus met; and fairly shortly afterwards they began their notable collaboration – Sullivan with his carefully framed melodies and Gilbert with his humorous and even ludicrous words provided the perfect partnership of minds. The difference between Sullivan and the other composers in the field was that he worked with the care of a professional and brought to the task the wealth of his training in Leipzig. The training, it is true, was never intended to produce comic operas but it often appears that it is the gods and not men who write the final scripts of destinies and so it was to be in this case.

3 Collaboration and the First Opera: 1871

In the 1850s French operettas and burlesques were being played in most of the London theatres – the former re-written in English and the latter with light music by French composers. An English style had yet to develop and early champions of this style were the German Reeds. Priscilla Reed was an actress with a fine voice and Thomas German Reed an entertainer, composer and conductor. They began to produce stage performances in 1854 at St Martin's Hall but wisely advertised their offerings as 'Illustrative Gatherings' in an attempt to obviate Victorian reticence and social fear of attending theatres. Later, they moved to a larger building, the Royal Gallery of Illustration in Regent Street, Waterloo Place. Their productions were tasteful and anyone could visit them without feelings of embarrassment. The production was usually very simple – a small cast, little scenery and a piano or harmonium accompaniment. By the mid-1860s their theatre could be referred to by one newspaper as incomparably the best entertainment house in London. In 1867 they also leased the even larger St George's Hall in Langham Place and this time employed a chorus and an orchestra of forty musicians. The first entertainment presented in this building was *La Contrabandista*, a comic opera with words by F. C. Burnand and music by Arthur Sullivan. The opera lasted only a few weeks.

In March 1869 the German Reeds tried again and presented a revival of another opera by the same pair, at their smaller Royal Gallery of Illustration, and this one – *Cox and Box* – ran for three hundred performances! Sullivan's sense of humour saw the possibilities of the piece – in which an unscrupulous landlord let the same room to two people, a printer by day and a hatter by night

COX AND BOX QUADRILLE

ON SULLIVAN'S BY OPERETTA

CHARLES COOTE

LONDON.
BOOSEY and Co., 28 HOLLES St. W.

Pp 4/−

Illustrated music cover of dance arrangement of *Cox and Box.*

Gilbert's *Ages Ago* was performed at the Royal Gallery of Illustration in 1869. Pictures came to life and the idea re-emerged years later in *Ruddigore.*

– and the *Daily Telegraph* enthused about his ability to link exquisite melodies with idiotic words.

Playing on the same programme as *Cox and Box* was a piece written by W. S. Gilbert called *No Cards*, and with music by German Reed, although this operetta had a limited run. So on this occasion Gilbert and Sullivan, each working separately with other collaborators, had written a work presented by German Reed. Their names appeared on the same programme, but with responsibility for separate pieces!

In November 1869 another of Gilbert's stories was produced by the German Reeds at the Gallery of Illustration. This was called *Ages Ago*, and the music was written by Fred Clay, perhaps Arthur Sullivan's closest friend. Indeed the work was dedicated to Sullivan. We know that Clay asked Sullivan to call in at the theatre to watch a rehearsal and hence, Gilbert, who happened to be present, was introduced to Sullivan. This meeting was ultimately to have historic consequences. The setting of the meeting – a theatre during a rehearsal of an operetta – was in itself prophetic.

But we do not know with any certainty the date of this meeting. Gilbert, true to form, instantly set Sullivan up with a ludicrous question:

You will be able to decide a question for me, Mr Sullivan. I maintain that a composer can express a musical theme perfectly upon the simple tetrachord of Mercury, in which there are no diatonic intervals at all, as upon the much more complicated diapason . . . which embraces in its perfect consonance all the single, double and inverted chords.

Although Sullivan asked Gilbert to repeat his question, and then offered to think about it further, Gilbert never did get a reply. The words Gilbert used had come from a musical encyclopaedia article on harmony which he needed for his play, *The Palace of Truth*. Gilbert's *Ages Ago* ended its run in June 1870 but was quickly revived in a revised version in the following month from Monday, 11 July. As we know that Gilbert and Sullivan met at a rehearsal of *Ages Ago*, it seems likely that they were introduced to one another around the time of the re-opening – very possibly on the afternoon of Monday 11 July 1870, at a final rehearsal prior to the first performance of the re-opening that evening. It is much more likely that Gilbert would have been working on material for his play *The Palace of Truth* in July 1870 than in November 1869 – since this play was not first produced until November 1870. But the important point was that the two artists had at last met. Subsequently, their paths crossed again on a number of occasions when, occasionally, they each happened to be present at a gathering of mutual friends, but the two men had entirely different characters and temperaments. They were not the sort to become friends – and, indeed, they never did become so, but enjoyed a professional alliance only.

Fred Clay (1838-89) was a close friend of Arthur Sullivan.

Gilbert continued to produce successful pieces for the Gallery – including *Our Island Home*, *A Sensation Novel* and *Happy Arcadia*. Of the six of Gilbert's comedies that were produced in London in 1871, *Pygmalion and Galatea* at the Haymarket was most successful and ran for more than two hundred performances. Gilbert later used ideas from these plays for his opera plots written with Sullivan. *Patience* shows similarity with *No Cards*; *The Pirates of Penzance* and *H.M.S Pinafore* relied on *Our Island Home*; and *Ruddigore* was built on ideas from *Ages Ago*. Hence, Gilbert's joke that the operas later written with Sullivan were indeed cradled by the Reeds.

Gilbert was an adept at writing short stories for magazine publication. Such titles as 'The Poisoned Postage Stamp', 'Foggerty's Fairy', 'Creatures of Impulse', 'The Wicked World', 'The Burglar's Story' and 'The Finger of Fate' suggest the range of his interest and the story content indicates something of the intriguing and many stranded mind of the author – disclosing the fairyland of his unique and vivid imagination.

For his part, Sullivan continued to compose ballads; but their first joint production was soon to occur. The venue for this collaboration was at another London theatre, the old Gaiety Theatre, which was situated at the east end of the Strand near the church of St Mary-le-Strand. The theatre, opened by John Hollingshead as recently as 1868, provided a variety of entertainment from opera to burlesque. The offerings on the opening night of the theatre had included Gilbert's play *Robert the Devil: or The Nun, the Dun and the Son of a Gun;* and Sullivan was a member of the first-night audience. Little did either know that their first production together would take place in that very theatre.

Late in 1871 Hollingshead contacted Gilbert about the possibility of working for him again. Hollingshead wanted Gilbert to write a comic opera for the Christmas season, and he asked Gilbert whether Arthur Sullivan would be a suitable composer to write the score. The German Reeds had previously tried to get Sullivan to work with Gilbert on a joint production in 1870:

Gilbert is doing a comic one-act entertainment for me – soprano, contralto, tenor, baritone and bass. Would you like to compose the music? If so – on what terms? Reply at once, as I want to get the piece going without loss of time.

John Hollingshead (1827-1904) opened the old Gaiety Theatre in the Strand in 1868.

But Sullivan had rejected this invitation to work with Gilbert, probably owing to the pressure of choral and orchestral demands. Yet, on this occasion, Sullivan agreed to do the work and *Thespis: or The Gods Grown Old* became the first Gilbert and Sullivan opera. The work went ahead quickly. The libretto was written in record time by Gilbert, and Sullivan completed the music in December. Gilbert read the opera to the company in the middle of the month; less than two weeks remained for rehearsals and the piece was first performed on Boxing Day 1871. It followed on the programme H. J. Byron's *Dearer Than Life*, and was produced by Gilbert himself.

Thespis was a two-act opera with an amusing story-line that entailed switching the roles of mortals and the ancient gods of Mount Olympus, together with all the expected chaos that resulted. Nellie Farren played the young god, Mercury, and the part of Thespis, the stage manager of the theatrical troupe of mortals who stumbled on the lair of the gods, was played by the comedian, J. L. Toole. Sullivan's brother, Frederic, played Apollo. Sullivan moaned that:

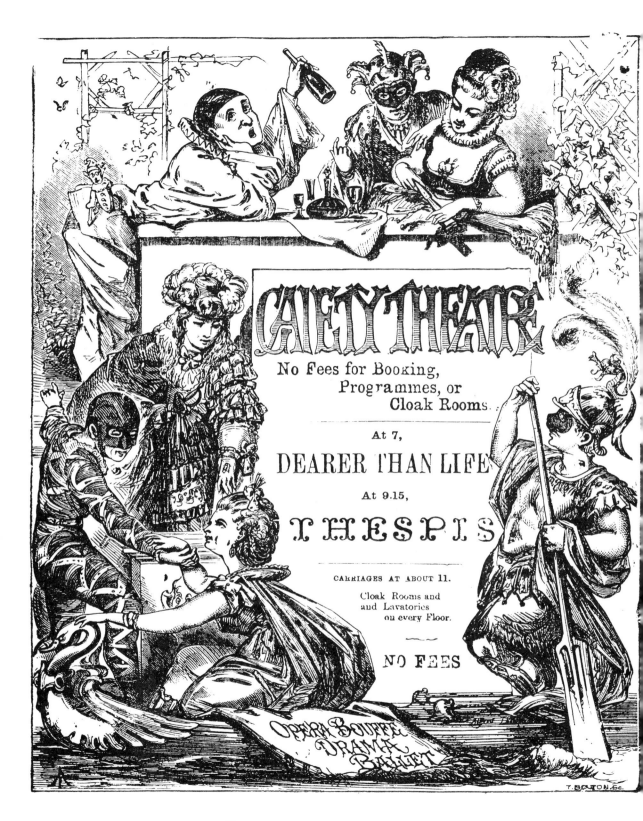

Few actors in the cast could sing, and of those who pretended to hardly any could be said to compass more than six notes.

Ideally, the opera should have had more proficient singers than were assembled on stage and it needed more than a week or so of rehearsal to even begin to do it justice. Gilbert was learning a great deal from this production and insisted that the chorus had to be an integral part of the story, and so he involved them in effective movement. The Gaiety was crowded on the opening night but, unfortunately, the opera was not well-received. Members of the pit and the gallery booed the performance, there were boring hold-ups and the performance did not end until late, as *Punch* recorded:

It was past midnight when the curtain descended and the audience was in a fidgety state to get away.

Much of the audience was quite unused to hearing about such esoteric characters as the ancient gods and so the characters of Apollo, Jupiter and Mars were unknown to them. Certainly Sullivan felt restricted in having to write music for people without good singing voices. But the opera had some initial enthusiastic reviews. Clement Scott, the *Daily Telegraph* critic, wrote:

The story, written by Mr W. S. Gilbert in his liveliest manner, is so original, and the music contributed by Mr Arthur Sullivan so pretty and fascinating that we are . . . disappointed when we find the applause fitful, the laughter scarcely spontaneous, and the curtain falling not without sound of disapprobation . . . The verdict of last night cannot be taken as final. . . . *Thespis* is too good to be put on one side and cold-shouldered in this fashion.

Similarly, the *Standard* commented:

Mr Gilbert has happily provided the composer with everything he could desire. . . . The composer in return has wedded Mr Gilbert's verses to some exquisite music, has pleasingly coloured his scenes, and given character to some of his mythological personages. . . . Mr Sullivan has been very happy in infusing a certain amount of sentiment into several of the characters.

These were surprisingly accurate forecasts considering the lengthy and continuing success of the joint partnership. It was Gilbert who once remarked:

Sullivan and I have the same sense of humour. When I tell him a joke he understands it immediately. I never have to tell it twice, which is fatal.

Programme for *Thespis*, the first Gilbert and Sullivan opera, produced at the Gaiety Theatre from Boxing Day, 1871.

Thespis ran for sixty-four performances. This was a very

43

D.H.FRISTON GAIETY

A drawing from *The Illustrated London News*, January 1872, of a scene from *Thespis* in which Fred Sullivan played Apollo.

respectable run for a piece produced as an entertainment for Christmas. Days after the first performance, Sullivan wrote to his mother:

I have rarely seen anything so beautifully put upon the stage. The first night I had a great reception, but the music went badly, and the singer sang half a tone sharp, so that the enthusiasm of the audience did not sustain itself towards me. Last night I cut out the song, the music went very well, and consequently I had a hearty call before the curtain at the end of Act 2.

Expense had not been stinted in staging the work and the audience was treated to a transformation in Act 1 when the fog lifted revealing the ivy-covered classical columns of the set for Mount Olympus. Jupiter was able to demonstrate his powers effectively by means of flash-paper in his fingers which ignited when he sent a thunderbolt – such a device clearly delighting the audience.

The Green Room at the Gaiety Theatre. Standing is J. L. Toole who played Thespis.

Sadly, Gilbert in later years found *Thespis* to be an embarrassment he would rather forget all about. The music for *Thespis* long ago disappeared, although Gilbert's libretto still survives. Possibly Sullivan, ultimately dissatisfied with the music,

44

destroyed all the copies. It is known that he went to the bother of obtaining the full score and the band parts from Hollingshead a number of years after the production of *Thespis*.

Later, Sullivan used the music of one chorus from this opera in *The Pirates of Penzance*: 'Climbing Over Rocky Mountain'. Again, one song has survived as it became popular and was published in music form – 'Little Maid of Arcadee'. It is very likely that Sullivan did use other music from *Thespis* in some of his later works – as, indeed, he claimed to have done when people asked him what had become of this opera – but we do not know this with any certainty. It is a tragedy that the music of the first Gilbert and Sullivan opera should have disappeared – the more so when it is rumoured that a copy of the vocal score was held secretly in London by Chappell, a firm of music publishers, but was accidentally destroyed by fire in 1964. Other material by Sullivan was believed to have been destroyed at the same time, including a copy of his unpublished cello concerto which had been given a broadcast performance in 1953. It is, of course, conceivable that one day a stray copy of the music from *Thespis* will come to light again. Many enthusiasts have attempted to unearth such a copy but so far the search has been fruitless.

After the run of *Thespis* came to an end Gilbert and Sullivan went their own ways. It was to be three years before they worked together on their second joint opera.

4 Richard D'Oyly Carte and Trial by Jury: 1875

Richard D'Oyly Carte was born in London on 3 May 1844 in Soho. His father, Richard Carte, played the flute (and even invented a variant on existing flutes) and was also partner in Rudall, Rose and Carte, a firm in Charing Cross that made musical instruments. The Belgian, Adolphe Sax, who greatly influenced the form of many instrument designs, gave the sole agency for the sale of his instruments in Britain to this company in 1853, including saxhorns and saxophones to which he gave his name.

The boy grew up in a cultured environment. His mother was a clergyman's daughter and she had made visits to Europe. Musicians and other artists were frequent visitors to the well-appointed family home where French was spoken on several days of the week. Richard D'Oyly Carte entered this family business after leaving University College, London but his heart was never in the work. The 'D'Oyly' in his name was actually a second Christian name which was often used when addressing him, rather than Richard, within the family. So really he should be referred to as 'Mr Carte' but as he is universally known as 'D'Oyly Carte' this convention is maintained here, even though the name was not double-barrelled.

He was a composer of songs (including 'Come Back to Me' and 'The Setting Sun') and wrote the music of several operettas produced by the German Reeds at St George's Hall; and also at the Opéra Comique. One of these operettas was called *Happy Hampstead*. He soon left the family firm and opened a concert and operatic agency, operating from an office in Craig's Court, Charing Cross from 1870. He arranged the programmes of lecturers and singers and even managed a number of London

Richard D'Oyly Carte: 1844-1901.

47

theatres. He was especially interested in the development of light opera and worked hard to promote the growth of an English operatic tradition. D'Oyly Carte had the sense to recognise that his own musical accomplishments were not sufficient to make him a regular living. But, as a manager of the accomplishments of others, he excelled. He was often given the nickname 'Oily Carte' due to his shrewdness and businesslike demeanour.

D'Oyly Carte had a beard, dark hair and was of medium height. He watched, listened and weighed up people; and spoke but little. He was, however, popular throughout the theatrical world amongst actors, producers and fellow managers. Helen Black (1852-1913) was his secretary for a lengthy period. She had appeared on the stage under the surname of Lenoir and shared with him the task of building up the position and status of a theatrical agent as a respectable middle-man. In 1888 she married him, becoming his second wife, and continued to be his valued business partner. She was practical and sensible and complemented D'Oyly Carte by ensuring that at least someone in the office always had both feet firmly on the ground whilst perhaps searching towards further goals. D'Oyly Carte became so well-respected in his field of managing performers that celebrities were numbered amongst his clients. These included Adelina Patti (the noted operatic singer), Charles Gounod (who composed *Faust*), the poet Matthew Arnold and the esoteric writer Oscar Wilde.

D'Oyly Carte had seen *Thespis* when it had its Christmas run in 1871-72. Perhaps he then had the vision to understand, more than many, that this first offering by Gilbert and Sullivan was a seminal statement which indicated that there was much more to come. After *Thespis* Sullivan reverted to his more serious music, and Gilbert to his plays, and they probably thought little of each other, apart from collaborating on two songs – 'Sweethearts' and 'The Distant Shore'. A prospective financial backer offered to find £1,000 to fund a second Gilbert and Sullivan opera but the money did not materialise. In all events, when the opportunity arose to bring the pair back in harness together, D'Oyly Carte jumped at the chance – and this occurred in 1875. D'Oyly Carte was two years younger than Sullivan and seven years younger than Gilbert. He was still thirty years old early in 1875, when his partnership with Gilbert and Sullivan began.

At the beginning of that year D'Oyly Carte was Selina Dolaro's business manager. She was presenting Offenbach's *La Périchole* at the Royalty Theatre, Dean Street. This was a small theatre in Soho which she had leased. D'Oyly Carte had dreams of developing comic operas and, once these became established and successful, to concentrate more on English operas.

The fashion in theatres at the time was for a lengthy period of

Vanity Fair cartoon of Sullivan from 1874, by 'Ape'.

evening entertainment. An audience, whatever else it wanted, insisted on good value for money – and this often meant a long programme in return for the price of an admission ticket. Offenbach's opera required accompanying pieces to make the evening a suitably lengthy one. The first piece of the evening had the amazing title *Cryptoconchoidsyphonostomata* (or While It's To Be Had) by R. H. Edgar and Charles Collette, but a third piece was still needed as an end-of-evening filler. Several pieces were considered and rejected. It was then that D'Oyly Carte had the inspiration to get Gilbert and Sullivan together for their second united effort. A number of factors worked in his favour. He knew each of them and, indeed, he could be considered to have a friendship with Sullivan of some standing. By 1869 D'Oyly Carte had had pipe-dreams:

The starting of English comic opera in a theatre devoted to that alone was the scheme of my life.

A Faustin caricature of Richard D'Oyly Carte.

In the following year he had mentioned this idea to Sullivan and then to Gilbert and Sullivan in 1874 but shortage of money stopped him from going ahead at that stage. In 1875 Gilbert showed D'Oyly Carte a libretto he had written and for which he had drawn heavily from one of the *Bab Ballads* for inspiration. It had been planned that this libretto of *Trial by Jury* was to have been set to music by Carl Rosa, who that year had founded the Carl Rosa Opera Company. Carl Rosa's wife, Euphrosyne Parepa-Rosa, was to sing the soprano lead but, on her sudden death in 1874, arrangements became fluid and Gilbert had had his script returned to him. D'Oyly Carte told Gilbert that he wanted the opera but on condition that Sullivan and not Carl Rosa set the music.

D'Oyly Carte wanted Sullivan to hear the script as soon as possible and thought that Gilbert himself should read it to the composer. So Gilbert went round to Sullivan's house and the two of them sat by the fire while Gilbert read the libretto aloud to him – but was fearful that Sullivan would think little of it. Sullivan, however, later recalled:

He read it through, as it seemed to me, in a perturbed sort of way, with a gradual crescendo of indignation, in the manner of a man considerably disappointed with what he had written. As soon as he had come to the last word he closed up the manuscript violently, apparently unconscious of the fact that he had achieved his purpose so far as I was concerned, in as much as I was screaming with laughter the whole time.

Sullivan was enchanted with the story-line and its humour and set to work at once. In only three weeks the opera was written and rehearsed. D'Oyly Carte probably recalled that Gilbert had pulled out all the stops and had produced the libretto for *Thespis* very quickly when it was required by Hollingshead in 1871. Now he was impressed and gratified to find that Sullivan, similarly, could work under pressure and produce the music for *Trial by Jury* in just a few weeks. D'Oyly Carte shrewdly realised that he was working with a special kind of talent.

Trial by Jury was first produced at 10.15pm on 25 March 1875 at the Royalty Theatre and was billed as a dramatic cantata. Fred Sullivan, Arthur Sullivan's older brother, played the role of the Learned Judge. Fred Sullivan was a great success on the stage. He had been an architect before abandoning the drawing-board for

A scene from *Trial by Jury* in a drawing that appeared in the *Illustrated Sporting and Dramatic News*.

the stage and commented dryly that even as an actor he was still drawing big houses! Both he and his brother Arthur had long been interested in dramatics and had been members of the Pimlico Dramatic Society as early as 1857; Fred as an actor and Arthur conducting. Fred Sullivan was part of Selina Dolaro's company and was appearing in *La Périchole* before *Trial by Jury* was envisaged as an after-piece. *Trial by Jury*, although merely at first regarded as a fill-in to the main event of the evening, continued to run and draw audiences when *La Périchole* had to be replaced by other works.

Sullivan's fame at this stage meant that, initially, he received an undue proportion of the praise for *Trial by Jury*. Even posters described the work as a dramatic cantata by Arthur Sullivan. The poor librettist appeared to receive short shrift. This was common practice in advertising operas and D'Oyly Carte was aware that Sullivan – the favourite composer of Queen Victoria – would draw greater crowds than Gilbert the playwright, even though at that time he was the most noted dramatist in the country.

The *Times* said it all in praising this opera performed straight after an opera by Offenbach:

To judge by the unceasing and almost boisterous hilarity which formed a sort of running commentary on the part of the audience, *Trial by Jury* suffered nothing whatever from so dangerous a juxtaposition. On the contrary, it may fairly be said to have borne away the palm.

It seems, as in the great Wagnerian operas, as though poem and music had proceeded simultaneously from one and the same brain.

The *Daily Telegraph* praised Gilbert's libretto and Sullivan's music:

Here in fact is the happiest idea caught to perfection by Mr Arthur Sullivan's music and faultlessly executed by the company. The true enjoyment of laughter has not yet been discovered by those who have not yet seen *Trial by Jury*.

The opera is a sparkling example of Gilbert and Sullivan at work. Some would regard it as one of their finest works; a blending of superb music and witty dialogue in this hilarious breach of promise of marriage farce. Sullivan wrote tunes that people sang, hummed and whistled and Gilbert made them laugh at national institutions and standard caricatures. The Lord Chief Justice went to see *Trial by Jury* – but only once – and decided not to go again in case people thought he was encouraging the performance. He feared that the subject matter of the opera might make people begin to ridicule the Bench but it was also the case that Fred Sullivan was made-up to look like the then Lord Chief Justice, Sir Alexander Cockburn!

Trial by Jury is the only opera Gilbert and Sullivan wrote in one act. It is also their only opera without spoken dialogue between the songs and choruses. It is the shortest (about forty minutes) of the fourteen operas they wrote together. Gilbert enjoyed himself in producing *Trial by Jury*. He had two months to prepare the performance (unlike the twelve days for *Thespis*). He designed the set himself – basing the courtroom scene on the Clerkenwell Sessions. The costumes were attractive, up-to-date and tasteful.

A lithograph showing Fred Sullivan on the sheet music cover of the 'Judge's Song' from *Trial by Jury*.

He was precise in his instructions both to chorus and soloists. There was no doubt in anyone's mind that Gilbert was in charge of the production; even if on the programmes of the first night his name was listed as W. C. Gilbert. The imbalance was soon rectified, however, and the pair worked together as master with master. Indeed, later, Gilbert was not only the first librettist to enjoy equal billing with the composer but had the satisfaction of seeing his name appear first!

Gentle satire was prominent in this opera. Angelina, the jilted bride, appeared in court wearing her wedding-dress and accompanied by her bridesmaids similarly attired – an ingenious way to get a female chorus into a courtroom. The Learned Judge in the end married her himself; and at this point Gilbert allowed himself the extravagance of having plaster cupids wearing legal wigs descending to the set.

Sullivan, too, enjoyed working on *Trial by Jury*. The music contains the parodies of other operas – with echoes of a phrase or even a single bar which are developed by him into something new and unique. Sullivan burlesqued Handel as well as Italian and French operas but the parody was more one of stylistic pattern, and not so much of actual musical notation. Sullivan ruefully reminded those who questioned the originality of his music that all composers have only the same seven notes with which to work.

The early death of Fred Sullivan whilst still in his thirties occurred at the beginning of 1877. His brother's sad illness resulted in Sullivan writing the song 'The Lost Chord'. Fred Sullivan, as creator of the part of the Judge, had met with widespread acclaim. The *Daily Telegraph* reported:

The greatest hit was made by Mr F. Sullivan, whose blending of official dignity, condescension and, at the right moment, extravagant humour, made the character of the Judge stand out with all requisite prominence, and added much to the interest of the piece.

Following the success of *Trial by Jury*, D'Oyly Carte knew that he had backed a winning team. He reinforced his relationship with Gilbert and Sullivan by exacting a promise of further operas in the future. D'Oyly Carte wanted a revival of *Thespis* with an improved story and revised music. The collaborators agreed to do this but tried to pin D'Oyly Carte to a guaranteed run of one hundred performances with two guineas for each of them a night, but with fifty nights paid in advance. Within a few weeks of these discussions Sullivan received a letter from Gilbert:

I have heard no more about *Thespis*. It's astonishing how quickly these capitalists dry up under the magic influence of the words 'cash down'.

D'Oyly Carte needed financial assistance from others to bring his dream of promoting English opera to the fore. Financial backers, however, were not falling over themselves to invest in productions of English operetta at a time when Offenbach was overwhelmingly popular. But he managed to interest a number of backers and in 1876 a company was formed called the Comedy Opera Company. A lease was secured on the Opéra Comique – not a particularly popular or fashionable theatre situated between Wych Street and the Strand. *Trial by Jury* played for 131 performances at the Royalty from March until December 1875. It then transferred to the Opéra Comique from January to May 1876 and subsequently to the Royal Strand from March to May 1877. It had three hundred performances in total in this interrupted run.

By 1877 Gilbert and Sullivan had time to prepare their third joint opera, when they produced *The Sorcerer*. In 1878 *Trial by Jury* was to appear again alongside *The Sorcerer*. Two years and more elapsed between *Trial by Jury* and the appearance of *The Sorcerer*. In the meantime, Sullivan showed his continuing interest in producing comic operas by writing the music to *The Zoo* (set in London Zoo) with words by Bolton Rowe (actually B. C. Stephenson). This was presented at the St James's Theatre.

When George Bernard Shaw commented on the importance and influence of Gilbert and Sullivan operas on the English theatre he stressed the pivotal significance of Richard D'Oyly Carte in the joint venture. Without D'Oyly Carte's leadership and drive it is more than likely that the Gilbert and Sullivan partnership would not have endured or become anything like as successful as it became under his pervading and paternal oversight. Writer and composer were both, indeed, most fortunate to work with a man of sound business knowledge and who also had the musical experience, taste, ambition, vision and driving force that willed him to succeed with English works.

The triumvirate of Gilbert, Sullivan and D'Oyly Carte was to work well together, despite temperamental flare-ups on occasions. Each partner in this trio was a skilled practitioner with a vision. Sullivan was already a musician with an increasing reputation nationally; Gilbert was already a successful writer of plays who was gaining in repute; D'Oyly Carte was already well-known and respected in the field of theatrical management and was dreaming the dream of further success. He wanted to become a noted impresario and would strive to any lengths to achieve this ambition.

5 *Evolving a Pattern –* The Sorcerer: *1877*

Flushed with the initial success of *Trial by Jury*, in 1875 Sullivan went to Lake Como for the summer with friends. Then he wrote songs, including 'Let Me Dream Again' which was so popular that it sold thousands of copies in a few months. In 1876 he accepted the position of Principal of the newly-formed National Training School of Music – which later became the Royal College of Music – and held the post until 1881. Sullivan composed feverishly and then travelled the country by train to conduct concerts. He wrote to his mother:

I am dead tired today. Next week I shall be knocked up I fear.

From 1872 he appeared to have suffered agonies from a stone in his kidney or possibly from a bladder infection. This affected his life and work cruelly and the complaint persisted for the remainder of his life. In 1876 he was awarded the honorary degree of Doctor of Music from Cambridge and Oxford awarded him similar honours in 1879. He remained extremely busy. Again he wrote to his mother:

There are so many things I want to do for music if God will only give me two days for every one in which to do them.

On the death of his brother Fred, Sullivan's mother went to Fulham to live with his widow and children, but Sullivan wrote to her constantly:

My Princess Louise [daughter of Queen Victoria] is coming tomorrow,

Sullivan in 1876.

so I had better do all I can to make her happy! Bring a lot of roses – never mind what it costs – I don't get her here every day. I want nothing but roses about the rooms, masses of them and one in every single thing I've got. Hooray! Blow the expense. I hope neither you nor Charlotte will be late as there is a good deal to do. God Bless You.

He also added 'Don't forget the tea-spoons,' and enclosed a guest list of distinguished visitors. The list included a close friend of his, Mary Frances Ronalds, a wealthy and attractive American who was separated from her husband and was living at Cadogan Place. He wrote to her frequently, often daily, when away from London. She was a talented singer and held Sunday evening musical sessions at her home. Her rendering of 'The Lost Chord' was one of the first phonograph recordings made in England. Her interest in music and talent in singing appealed to him. She also moved in circles which interested Sullivan – as she was a friend of the Prince of Wales and Princess Alexandra. She was Sullivan's hostess when he gave dinner parties at his home and they went together to the theatre, the opera and even to race meetings – to which Sullivan was addicted. It seems to be almost indisputable

56

that Fanny Ronalds, as she was known to friends, was Sullivan's mistress. He made constant references to her in his diary (L.W. standing for Little Woman, for instance) and the timing of many of their meetings at her home and the secretive symbols that he used in his diary seem to provide virtually conclusive evidence. His diary was kept locked and as closely protected as many of the secrets it contained, even for many years after his death. Perhaps because Fanny Ronalds was a decade older than Sullivan, he took her advice in professional as well as personal areas. She sat in a box in the theatre when auditions were taking place, and on her verdict might depend whether an aspirant became a principal singer in the Gilbert and Sullivan operas – and this undoubtedly irritated those being auditioned.

Gilbert, too, was by no means idle. He considered a collaboration with Carl Rosa; and wrote several pieces including *Princess Toto* with Fred Clay. His plays *Broken Hearts*, *Charity*, *Sweethearts* and *Engaged* were all produced in London. But the next, and third, Gilbert and Sullivan opera was soon to be written.

Richard D'Oyly Carte now fulfilled his dream of becoming an independent presenter of operas. In 1876 he had formed the Comedy Opera Company Ltd. There were four directors as financial backers, each of whom contributed £500. George Metzler was a music publisher, Frank Chappell was an associate of Metzler, Collard Augustus Drake was from a firm of piano-makers and Edward Hodgson Bayley – or 'water-cart Bayley' – owned a business which sprinkled water on the dust of London's streets. D'Oyly Carte was General Manager of the Company. The Comedy Opera Company came into being:

for the purpose of establishing permanently in London a theatre which shall have for its staple entertainment light opera of a legitimate kind, by English authors and composers.

Various English writers were invited to submit works – F.C. Burnand, James Albery, Frederic Clay and Alfred Cellier but D'Oyly Carte's real aim was to attract Gilbert and Sullivan together again. He now had the financial resources at his disposal to make a full-length, two-act work by Gilbert and Sullivan a viable proposition. In July 1877 D'Oyly Carte signed an agreement with Gilbert and Sullivan which promised them an advance of two hundred guineas each on *The Sorcerer* when they delivered to him the words and music.

So in 1877 Gilbert, as was to happen so often in the future, returned to an earlier idea for this next collaboration with Sullivan. His short story 'An Elixir of Love' had appeared in the *Graphic*. That story told of a love potion which was obtained from a firm of magicians in London by a curate in the country in order to hand it out to his parishioners. Gilbert worked on this idea to form the next opera, *The Sorcerer*, in which unlikely couples fell in love after drinking the potion in a cup of tea; although the potion only had an effect on unmarried imbibers!

Love potions and their potential effects were to be an abiding interest of Gilbert's. He used the idea in a *Bab Ballad*, 'The Cunning Woman'. He also developed a similar idea in his early play, *Dulcamara*, which burlesqued Donizetti's opera, *L'Elisir d'Amore*. Later in life he even wrote another opera using the same theme, *The Mountebanks*, with music by Alfred Cellier. It was a magic potion theme which years later he wanted Sullivan to accept yet again – his infamous 'Lozenge Plot' – but which Sullivan consistently rejected. Perhaps Sullivan felt that stories about the effect of love potions already figured prominently enough in the operatic catalogue without adding further to the listing. These offerings included Wagner's *Tristan und Isolde*, Auber's *Le Philtre*, Donizetti's *L'Elisir d'Amore* and others such as the magic bullets in Weber's *Der Freischütz*.

Gilbert completed the libretto for *The Sorcerer* by the spring but Sullivan did not set to work on the music for months, and it was not ready until the middle of November, a day or so before the first night. Indeed, such last minute panic was to become a regular feature of Sullivan's personal composing and scoring programme. By the beginning of November 1877 Sullivan wrote:

I am just putting the finishing touches to my opera, and tomorrow begin the scoring. I have been slaving at this work and I hope it will be a success. Everything at present promises very well. The book is brilliant and the music, I think very pretty and good. All the company are good and like it very much.

Gilbert was given freedom to choose the cast for this first opera to be performed by the new company. He by-passed established professional singers and engaged actors who could also sing and whom he believed he would be able to train successfully to play his personal ideas of the character roles. He engaged George Grossmith (despite opposition from the directors) to play the part of the sorcerer. Grossmith had been a press reporter at Bow Street Police Court and was also an entertainer on the piano. In astonishment at being offered the comic lead as an opera singer, he suggested to Gilbert that perhaps a fine man with a fine voice would fill the bill more precisely; but Gilbert assured him that that was just what he didn't want!

Mrs Howard Paul was chosen to play the part of Lady Sangazure ('blue blood'). She was an actress who ran her own touring company and was important at this early stage of recruiting for *The Sorcerer* since she encouraged Grossmith to join the cast despite his doubts that, once he had appeared on the stage, the YMCA halls, where he sang sentimental songs, might never engage him again. Mrs Paul pushed Grossmith into playing the sorcerer, John Wellington Wells, and considering his long-standing success with the company she clearly saw a sparkling future for him on the stage:

It is a splendid part – better than you think, I fancy – and the 'patter' song is great in its way. I think, if you will arrange, it will be a new and *magnificent introduction* for you, and be of great service afterwards.

In fact, both Gilbert and Sullivan had previously seen George Grossmith act. He had been a juror in a benefit performance of *Trial by Jury* at the Haymarket Theatre towards the end of 1875 attended by Sullivan. Sullivan had also heard him sing in a private house entertainment after a dinner party. The idea of using him in this opera was suggested to Sullivan by the playwright, Arthur Cecil. Grossmith related how he met Sullivan:

Afterwards I met him in Society, and on one occasion went round to his rooms after a dinner party. The following year I received a note from him asking, 'Are you inclined to go on the stage for a time? There is a part in the new piece I am doing with Gilbert which I think you could play admirably. I can't find a good man for it.'

Subsequently, Grossmith had played the part of the Learned Judge in a production of *Trial by Jury* at Bayswater that was not only seen but also rehearsed by Gilbert.

Mrs Paul was also instrumental in ensuring that a young member of her own touring group joined the new company and so Rutland Barrington (an actor who had little singing experience) joined the team. He was to create and play almost all the important bass-baritone parts in later Gilbert and Sullivan operas, just as George Grossmith was to play the comic baritone roles. Gilbert described Barrington thus: 'He's a staid, stolid swine and that's what I want.'

But whilst Gilbert purposely declined to select established theatrical stars, the actors and actresses who played these leading roles in the Gilbert and Sullivan operas were to become stars in their own right and some held this position for very lengthy periods. Many of them were amateurs, others merely students and others still performers on the concert platform, the musical stage or provincial professionals who had not already reached the dizzy heights of appearing in London itself. Only a few came from the established operatic tradition. Much of the chorus came from the

Entrance to the Opéra
Comique.

Royal Academy of Music, and Alfred Cellier was hard at work
testing voices and engaging singers. He, together with his younger
brother François, had been a chorister at the Chapel Royal. Apart
from composing the music for his own operas, he was conductor of
the Gilbert and Sullivan operas, as was his brother at a later date
and for a much longer period.

D'Oyly Carte had negotiated for the lease of the Opéra
Comique, a theatre off the Strand, to house the new opera
company. This theatre was small, literally underground, and the
main entrance was reached by a long tunnel under the Strand; but
it was the best that he was able to manage. Front of house was
adequate enough but the facilities backstage were primitive with a
few minute dressing-rooms below the stage and others in nearby
houses. The wall at the back of the stage was a party wall with the
Globe Theatre next door – so performers in one theatre could
actually hear their counterparts performing in the other theatre!

The Sorcerer opened at the Opéra Comique on 17 November 1877, and ran for 178 performances. It opened with *Dora's Dream* (with words by Arthur Cecil and music by Alfred Cellier) as a curtain-raiser. This curtain-raiser was replaced by *The Spectre Knight* by James Albery and music again by Alfred Cellier in February 1878.

Rutland Barrington played the part of Dr Daly, the village rector, in *The Sorcerer*. This was the only clergyman for whom Gilbert dared to write a part in any of the operas. Barrington played the part commendably but George Bentham, who played the leading tenor, Alexis, did not have an easy opening night. His face was swollen because of a heavy cold and D'Oyly Carte had to apologise to the audience in advance for Bentham's appearance! The latter had to change his stage name from the Italian pseudonym of Signor Benthamo to the more ordinary Mr Bentham for D'Oyly Carte did not want a tenor – or anyone else for that matter – to appear to be Italian in his English production. Richard Temple was another fortunate find. He played Sir Marmaduke Pointdextre and on the opening night his minuet with Lady Sangazure was encored.

The story-line of this opera was a bit thin and sketchy – relying too heavily on the love theme alone – and this was a failing that Gilbert was to improve upon vastly in subsequent libretti. Yet the critics were mostly enthusiastic, although the *Figaro* of London noted that Sullivan had not written an overture (he just hadn't had time!) but had used part of his incidental music from Henry VIII instead. Later, for the revival of 1884, an overture was probably written by Alfred Cellier using themes from the opera.

The *Times* said:

Messrs W. S. Gilbert and Arthur Sullivan have once again combined their efforts with the happiest result.

The *Examiner* commented that with *The Sorcerer* had at last appeared:

a work of entirely English growth, which bids fair to hold its own by the side of numberless foreign importations.

The *Musical Times* noted that George Grossmith sang:

as well as he could, considering that nature has not gifted him with a voice.

But this was just what Gilbert had wanted from the comic lead – an actor who could articulate his words with such precision and clarity that the audience could follow every line, even when the songs proceeded extremely quickly.

A few days after the opening night Sullivan wrote:

They are doing tremendous business at the Op. Comique, I am glad to say. I was on the stage last night and heard *three* encores before I left. If it is a great success it is another nail in the coffin of Opéra Bouffe from the French.

Sullivan always conducted the first-night performance of a new opera himself and also special performances. But the usual day-to-day performances were conducted by one of the Cellier brothers. *The Sorcerer* was the only two-act opera written jointly by Gilbert and Sullivan that did not have a sub-title. The eleven joint operas that followed it each had sub-titles, as had *Thespis*, the first opera, but

George Grossmith played John Wellington Wells in *The Sorcerer*. He remained with the Company from 1877 to 1889.

not *Trial by Jury*, the second opera, that was only a one-act piece. Continental operettas were usually written in one act and operas had three or more acts. Gilbert and Sullivan broke fresh ground in planning their operas in two acts.

The group of actors and actresses whom Gilbert and Sullivan recruited for *The Sorcerer* were to make theatrical history. They were to form the nucleus of the D'Oyly Carte Company. But Richard D'Oyly Carte experienced continual friction with the directors who blew hot and cold over *The Sorcerer*, wanting to close it down one day by giving a fortnight's notice when sales of tickets slumped, but deciding to keep the show going by the following day whenever sales showed an increase. D'Oyly Carte quickly realized that he would do better without the hindrance of such fair-weather directors, and doubtless looked forward to the time when he could dispense with their involvement and financial support.

Gilbert became patterned in the writing of his libretti from *The Sorcerer* onwards. The roles found in the story-line of this opera can be traced through every opera that followed. George Grossmith, having played John Wellington Wells, then went on to play the roles of Sir Joseph Porter, Major-General Stanley, Reginald Bunthorne, the Lord Chancellor, King Gama, Ko-Ko, Robin Oakapple and Jack Point. Rutland Barrington, having played Dr Daly, then played Captain Corcoran, the Sergeant of Police, Archibald Grosvenor, the Earl of Mountararat, King Hildebrand, Pooh-Bah, Sir Despard Murgatroyd, Giuseppe, King Paramount and Ludwig. Indeed, this typecasting of an established group might even be said to have begun earlier still. Frederic Sullivan had played Apollo in *Thespis*, the Learned Judge in *Trial by Jury*, and the part of John Wellington Wells in *The Sorcerer* had been written with him in mind – before his early demise.

Each of these operas had a world of its own. Each was unique with its particular character and mood, and yet each opera, different though it was from all the others, was written for much the same company of artists, whether of principals or chorus. The principals who became well-known celebrities in the theatrical world included George Grossmith, Rutland Barrington, Richard Temple and Jessie Bond – the latter of whom joined the Company for the production of *H.M.S. Pinafore*. There was always to be a tailor-made part for these and other leading lights in the Company, for each major role was virtually written for a specific artist. Gilbert knew precisely who would be playing the main parts in the next opera as he wrote the libretto, just as Dr Sullivan (as he had become in 1876) was equally aware of who would be singing the solo songs that he composed in his study.

Gilbert's plots often followed the pattern of a problem of personal interaction that appeared to be resolved at the close of act one, but then the problem was shown to be a continuing one early in act two, and further solutions needed to be devised by the characters by the conclusion of the opera. The six operas from *Trial by Jury* (1875) had their settings in Victorian England, but from *Princess Ida* onwards (1884) nearly all of the operas were set in more distant times and locations – Hildebrand's palace and a remote university for women, and then journeying to Japan, sixteenth-century London, Italy, a South Sea utopia and a German duchy. Gilbert included much topical social satire in the earlier operas set in contemporary England but, as the operas from *Princess Ida* onwards were set usually in distant locations, such satire could no longer be prominent or even relevant.

Each opera (excepting *The Yeomen of the Guard* which began with a solo from Phoebe) opened with an introductory scene-setting chorus. *The Sorcerer* and *The Grand Duke* opened with a joint male and female chorus, but in the remainder of the operas the opening chorus was of single sex and in about equal proportion. The other chorus entered mid-way through the first act. Despite often being at odds during the plot, the two choruses sometimes married by the end of the opera, as in *The Pirates of Penzance*, *Patience* and *Iolanthe* – though not in *The Mikado* with its disparate choruses of nobles and schoolgirls or in *H.M.S. Pinafore* with Sir Joseph Porter's tribe of relatives socially so very different from the common sailors. The social distinctions and stratas of society represented on stage were mirrored almost amusingly for the actors in the similar stratification of the audience they faced on the other side of the footlights – sitting as they were in segmented groups in boxes, front stalls, rear stalls, dress circle, upper circle and gallery.

Even at the early stage in the development of the Gilbert and Sullivan operas, Gilbert knew exactly what he wanted. He arrived at rehearsals knowing how he wished the chorus and minor principals to speak his words and how he wanted them to move about the stage; and in this way, tyrant though he might have seemed at times, he was able to mould the inexperienced group into a viable team. He had the sense to allow the principals considerable latitude in interpreting the major roles (in which they were often able to add to Gilbert's initial conception) but in cases of dispute Gilbert reserved the right of ultimate veto. Gilbert was emulating in the opera world what he had earlier seen Tom Robertson accomplish with theatrical plays. Each was an innovator in the realm of production technique.

In preparing a libretto Gilbert evolved a basic theme that was to serve as a guide for many other operas and, within this framework,

Quadrille music cover detail showing Sir Marmaduke Pointdextre's mansion and the assembled cast.

both Gilbert and Sullivan set to work in detail and devised somewhat limited variations on the standard pattern. Gilbert wrote magnificent finales to Act 1: *The Gondoliers, Iolanthe* and *The Mikado* are merely 'examples illustrative' which Sullivan orchestrated to perfection. Similarly, the entrances of the chorus, whether male or female, were given special attention by Sullivan when he prepared the music. The male chorus usually entered robustly to a military, jaunty or dignified strain; whilst for the female chorus Sullivan went to pains to ensure that they always had bright, welcoming and lively entrance numbers.

Many of Gilbert's heroines have slightly tainted sides to their characters in that they frequently appear to be on the lookout for the main chance, whatever the consequences. Aline, however, in *The Sorcerer*, is more straightforward and uncomplicated than many of Gilbert's later creations. With his male heroes, Gilbert seems to have gone to some lengths to make them characters who are self-centred and, at times, not particularly pleasant individuals. Alexis in *The Sorcerer*, Frederic in *The Pirates of Penzance* and Nanki-Poo in *The Mikado* are typical. Gilbert claimed that tenors had cursed each of his operas but, in fairness, it must be said that *he* wrote the parts for the tenors to play and so it was partly his own fault that they often appeared as unheroic characters; but, additionally, Gilbert found tenors to be so temperamental that they were prone to leave the theatre having a tantrum rather than staying behind to accept any advice:

They can never act and they are more trouble than all the other members of the company put together.

Gilbert quickly evolved a place in the operas for an older woman whom he tended to make rather a figure of fun. She was present (although not actually on stage) as early as *Trial by Jury* in the rich attorney's elderly ugly daughter; and earlier still as the ageing Diana in *Thespis*. Subsequently, Lady Sangazure in *The Sorcerer* gave way to Little Buttercup, and then came Ruth, Lady Jane, the Fairy Queen, Lady Blanche, Katisha, Mad Margaret, Dame Carruthers and Lady Sophy. In similar vein, the Learned Judge was followed by numerous other stereotyped comic leads, each of whom had a patter song in which he related his background. These roles included John Wellington Wells, Sir Joseph Porter, Major-General Stanley, the Lord Chancellor, Ko-Ko and the Duke of Plaza-Toro.

As early as *Thespis*, in the quartet 'You're Diana, I'm Apollo', the composer and librettist experimented with a musical form that was to become known as the ensemble of perplexity – in which several of the cast sang of the problems within the plot. The ensemble of perplexity in *Trial by Jury* was sung by the whole company in the number 'A nice dilemma'. Another was the quartet of Tessa, Gianetta, Marco and Giuseppi in *The Gondoliers* when they discovered that two husbands had managed to acquire three wives.

Gilbert appeared to be obsessed with the idea of role reversal. In *Thespis* the gods changed places with the mortals; in *The Sorcerer* people fell in love with the most unlikely villagers; in *H.M.S. Pinafore* Captain Corcoran changed stations with the common sailor Ralph Rackstraw; in *The Pirates of Penzance* the pirates at the end of the opera became respectable noblemen again – and Frederic sided one minute with the pirates, the next with the policemen, and then with the pirates again.

It was a characteristic that promising ideas such as Rose Maybud's book of correct behaviour in *Ruddigore* and the limited liability of a monarchy in *Utopia Limited* were not always developed very far. More usually, the plot ended with a twist of logic and this was not necessarily a particularly satisfactory way to conclude an opera. In four operas – *The Mikado, Ruddigore, Iolanthe* and *The Grand Duke* – there was a playing with words to find a 'legal' solution. In *Thespis, Trial by Jury, H.M.S. Pinafore, Patience, The Gondoliers, The Sorcerer, Princess Ida* and *The*

Yeomen of the Guard people changed places in one way or other to effect a solution. The endings of the second acts were often fairly stereotyped in consequence, and a weakness in the total scenario.

From the earliest days Gilbert included cynical social comment within the libretti of the operas. He had strident views on love and marriage and was able to paint satirical portraits of characters as they went about their courtship or married life, whether sad, happy, resigned or frustrated. He refuted the belief that love alone was enough; believing, rather, that differences in the ages of partners or their social position could result in such a union being doomed to failure. His general cynicism might have been regarded as coasting a bit near the mark at times bearing in mind Victorian standards of propriety; hence, the love potion administered to the villagers from the teapot in *The Sorcerer* only had an effect on unmarried people!

He parodied current ideas and national institutions – the stage and stage managers in *Thespis*; a Learned Judge whose law was fudge; a First Lord of the Admiralty who had never been to sea; fairies with far-reaching powers in Parliament; the social equality of roles, whether of king or footman, inside a royal palace; and a penniless duke reduced to lending his name to help the sale of products in order to raise himself some cash. A prevailing characteristic was that these operas, and especially the earlier ones, were absolutely British, whether examined from the viewpoint of words, subject matter, dress, humour or music. No national institution or group was to be safe from Gilbert's acute observation. Even *The Mikado*, set nominally in Japan, was brimful of English humour, though the characters shuffled and wore kimonos.

Rutland Barrington, writing in 1911, recalled that the quality of acting ability in these plots had been of prime importance:

One of the secrets, if not the all-important one, of the phenomenal success of these operas lies in the serious manner in which the delineation of each and every part should be sustained, a truism which has not invariably been recognized by the artists concerned. What a monument of fun and whimsicality is *Trial by Jury* when so attacked! And yet on many occasions I have seen it distorted almost out of recognition by artists who insisted on being funny.

The *Figaro* was disapproving of *The Sorcerer* when it appeared at the end of 1877 and voiced disappointment at the downward art course into which Sullivan appeared to be drifting; for although it was felt that he had the ability to become a great composer it was thought that he wilfully threw away his opportunities:

A giant may play at times but Mr Sullivan is always playing.

Nonetheless, *The Sorcerer* was to be an important milestone in the development of the partnership, since in this work Gilbert established a planning pattern regarding story-line and standard characters and Sullivan did not parody the works of other composers but began to create his own moods. This opera, at last, provided a work that was English by conception and growth.

6 The First Major Successes: 1878-81

H.M.S. Pinafore

Gilbert loved the sea and sailing and the subject matter of the next opera – *H.M.S. Pinafore* – was one which he tackled with tremendous enthusiasm and energy. He visited the *Victory*, Admiral Nelson's flagship, to make sketches of the details of deck and rigging, and a model of the deck was constructed on which he was able to experiment with placing the cast. Even when the opera had been written and composed, Gilbert went with Sullivan to inspect the real thing once more and the authenticity of the costumes was supervised by a tailor who supplied naval uniforms. Nothing was left to chance. When the curtain rose on the production the audience saw, in effect, a realistic ship on stage.

The opera opened on 25 May 1878 and ran until February 1880. On the first night Gilbert, as usual on these occasions, was attacked by agonies of fear at the possible reaction of the audience to the new piece. He rarely saw a first night but walked the streets of London instead. On this evening he was in and out of the theatre three or four times but, as usual, he need not have worried; there were enthusiastic calls at the end both for himself and for Sullivan.

H.M.S. Pinafore became a tremendous success – reaching 571 evening performances in the initial run – but there were problems in the early stages of this run. The temperature in the summer of 1878 became so high in London that audiences fell alarmingly; it was much too uncomfortable to sit for an evening in the heat of a theatre and by July the nightly takings were lower than £40. D'Oyly Carte's directors were constantly posting closing-down notices. Yet the cast agreed to a salary reduction of one-third until

A drawing of the principal characters from *H.M.S. Pinafore* given by the children's company at the Opéra Comique, 1879-80.

the situation improved, and it was Sullivan who had the inspiration to play selections of tunes from *H.M.S. Pinafore* at the Promenade Concerts held at the Covent Garden Theatre. The audiences there enjoyed the melodies and so bought tickets at the Opéra Comique to hear the complete opera. Phrases from the text were soon repeated everywhere and the tunes were sung and whistled in the streets. D'Oyly Carte quickly organised two touring companies to take the success of *H.M.S. Pinafore* into the provinces.

The comic lead in this opera, Sir Joseph Porter, KCB, the First Lord of the Admiralty, had never been to sea. At the same time, the First Lord of the Admiralty in Disraeli's Government was W. H. Smith, MP for Westminster, who founded the firm of booksellers and who, because his career had been landbound, quickly became dubbed as 'Pinafore Smith'.

The name 'Pinafore' in the title of the opera had no special significance. It was probably chosen simply because it rhymed with 'one cheer more' from the finale. The initial choice of title had been *Semaphore* but Sullivan suggested that *Pinafore* might be more suitable.

Neither playwright nor composer enjoyed good health during the preparations for this light and beautiful opera. Gilbert had headaches and gout and Sullivan suffered from his kidney complaint:

It is perhaps rather a strange fact that the music of *Pinafore*, which was thought to be so merry and spontaneous, was written while I was suffering agonies from a cruel illness. I would compose a few bars and then be almost insensible from pain. When the paroxysm was past, I would write a little more, until the pain overwhelmed me again.

In later operas this complaint of Sullivan's was to result in interrupted rehearsals. Gilbert began to write a diary at about the same time that Sullivan was engaged in composing *H.M.S. Pinafore*. A few such entries are noted here in order to illustrate his style:

Jan 27th (Sunday): bad headache. Walked out during church time – saw man trying to steal dogs – ordered him off. Short man, reddish whiskers. Met Mrs coming out of church. Headache lifted about four. Wrote letter to *Observer* but did not send it.

March 11th: Stopped ten minutes (at shop to buy a cigar case). Then home. Row with cabman – took six pence away from him. He is going to summons me.

May 25th: Went to Opéra Comique to superintend scene – remained there till 6.30 working at it . . . then went to Beefsteak to dine and dress. To theatre at 8 . . . Rowdy Gallery – singing songs etc. Piece went extremely well . . . enthusiastic call for self and Sullivan.

The cast, as usual, was expertly managed and trained. George Grossmith played Sir Joseph Porter, Rutland Barrington (with a heavy cold) was Captain Corcoran, Harriet Everard was Little Buttercup and Jessie Bond played the part of Hebe which was cut to a minor role in order that this newcomer would not have to contend with dialogue.

Many reviewers praised Gilbert's play and afforded Sullivan muted congratulation. The *Times* stated:

While recording this decided success of Mr Sullivan's new work we cannot suppress a word of regret that the composer on whom before all others the chance of a national school of music depends should confine himself, or be confined by circumstances, to a class of production which, however attractive, is hardly worthy of the efforts of an accomplished and serious artist.

The press and musical journals maintained a critical distance and did not describe *H.M.S. Pinafore* in glowing terms – despite the public ovation that the opera received after its somewhat shaky beginning. Its music was described as disappointing by the *Daily Telegraph*. The plot was thought to be thin and the comic material was not regarded as of a type to give a musician the opportunity to excel at his craft. The reserved comments in the press were probably another reason for the slow start to the popularity of this opera.

Yet *H.M.S. Pinafore* was an excellent book backed by splendid music and the public soon loved the way in which it tilted at British lifestyles, at the Senior Service and at class distinctions. By the autumn of 1878 the opera was making a small fortune. Sullivan seems to have been concerned that the directors were endeavouring to make economy cuts in the production in order to save cash. During the summer he wrote formally to D'Oyly Carte, probably in an attempt to give the latter some power to force the directors to rectify matters:

My dear Carte,
I regret to say that on my visit to the Theatre last Tuesday I found the Orchestra both in number and efficiency very different to what it was when I rehearsed the *Pinafore*.

There seemed two second violins short and the whole band is of very indifferent quality. I beg to give you notice that if the deficiencies are not supplied by Saturday and the efficiency of the orchestra increased by engaging better players both of the wind and the stringed instruments I shall withdraw my music from the theatre on Monday night.

You know perfectly well that what I say I mean. Kindly inform the Directors of this and oblige.
Yours very truly,
Arthur Sullivan

D'Oyly Carte's directors now changed their tune, deciding that the authors were receiving too much in returns. They argued that it had been their financial backing which had put on the show in the first place and that therefore the stage settings were their property. During the 374th performance on 31 July 1879 – and at a time when the lease of the Opéra Comique to the Comedy Opera Company had run its course – a group of heavies hired by the directors entered the theatre backstage and attempted to remove the scenery to another theatre where they intended to put on a rival production of *H.M.S. Pinafore*. It is possible only to guess at the amazement of the audience as heavies fought with stagehands and the curtain was eventually dropped. The directors had sent horse-drawn vans to the Opéra Comique in an unsuccessful attempt to transport away the scenery. D'Oyly Carte was in America at the

An 1879 programme of *H.M.S. Pinafore* at the Imperial Theatre – the rival company that set up in opposition to D'Oyly Carte's production.

time and Gilbert wrote to inform him of the events:

By the way, on Friday night they broke into the theatre with a mob of 50 roughs, during the performance, and tried to carry off the properties . . . Barker resisted their approach, and was knocked downstairs and seriously hurt. There was alarm among the audience who raised the cry of 'Fire!', appeased, however, by Grossmith who made them a speech

73

from the stage . . . I hear the performance at the Aquarium [the rival production] was wretched and that very few audience were present.

The rival company actually opened nearby at the Imperial Theatre adjoining the Royal Aquarium in Westminster. It then moved on to the Olympic – in the same street as the Opéra Comique and finally to the Standard in Shoreditch. It was a makeshift production which, however, managed to survive for ninety-one performances. Gilbert employed men with sandwich-boards to walk the streets of London to inform people that the authorised performances of *H.M.S. Pinafore* took place only at the Opéra Comique. The matter went to court and Gilbert, Sullivan and D'Oyly Carte won the action, but by then the offending company had gone bankrupt and the aggrieved trio not only got no damages but had to pay their own costs.

The directors were paid off by D'Oyly Carte who then set up a new company managed by Gilbert, Sullivan and himself on equal business terms. From 4 August 1879 the opera company was known as Mr D'Oyly Carte's Opera Company and a contract was drawn up by Gilbert, Sullivan and D'Oyly Carte. Each contributed £1,000 to the company. D'Oyly Carte was to receive a fee of £15 a week for management and both Gilbert and Sullivan were to receive four guineas for each performance.

Gilbert produced a children's version of *H.M.S. Pinafore* in London in December 1879 – from the Christmas holidays until March 1880. All the parts were played by children whose ages ranged from ten to thirteen. The music was rearranged for young voices and the performances were given as matinées – although Lewis Carroll was angered that young children were being encouraged to sing 'Damme!' on the stage!

H.M.S. Pinafore was also successful in America but the success angered Gilbert and Sullivan who made virtually nothing from such productions. Eight separate productions of *H.M.S. Pinafore* were playing at the same time in New York alone and six more in Philadelphia. Eventually, more than fifty makeshift companies were performing this opera across America. One American newspaper reported:

At present there are forty-two companies playing *Pinafore* about the country. Companies formed after six p.m. yesterday are not included.

Scribner's Magazine summed up the American response to *H.M.S. Pinafore*:

It was welcomed with an enthusiasm bordering on insanity.

George Grossmith as Sir Joseph Porter and Jessie Bond as Hebe in *H.M.S. Pinafore*.

The opera was actually described as the reigning sensation throughout all the world.

The copyright laws did not favour Gilbert and Sullivan and although it is customary to speak of 'pirate' performances the producers of these pieces were technically breaking no laws. Indeed, it was with the numerous performances of *H.M.S. Pinafore* that the widespread amateur productions of Gilbert and Sullivan operas began to develop into such a cult. In Britain *H.M.S. Pinafore* was first produced by amateurs – by the Harmonists' Choral Society at Kingston-upon-Thames Drill Hall – in April 1879.

The United States law allowed a work for the theatre to be used freely by anyone since it was argued that once it was published it became in effect public property. At that time there was not even an international convention on copyright. In one witty speech made in New York, Gilbert gibed:

Apart from the fact that we have no copyright, and we are not yet managers in the United States, we see no reason why we should be the only one not permitted to play the piece here!

D'Oyly Carte, in an attempt to combat these unauthorised productions, organised his own productions in America and he, together with Gilbert and Sullivan, went over towards the end of 1879 to supervise the proceedings as well as to add on-the-spot interest and personal appearances. The cast they took to America was chosen from that of the London company and the first authentic performance in America took place at the beginning of December at the Fifth Avenue Theatre in New York, the cast including Jessie Bond, Rosina Brandram and Alice Barnett. Gilbert himself appeared in the chorus as a sailor – heavily disguised with a beard – for the first night of the New York production. This was perhaps the only occasion in which he played in a first-night performance in one of his operas.

Americans went in droves to see this authorised performance and one newspaper commented:

Last evening *H.M.S. Pinafore* was under command of its builders. Mr Sullivan conducted, and the master-hand was clearly discernible . . . last night's performance was everywhere studded with new points . . . But the really noticeable difference in the interpretation was the orchestration. There was breadth, colour, tone, altogether with an harmonious blending with the vocalism which was utterly wanting in what may be called the home-made *Pinafores*.

An American journalist remarked with appreciation:

We've seen it as a comedy, we've seen it as a tragedy, but the play these Englishmen have brought over is quite a new play to us, and very good it is.

The Pirates of Penzance

Gilbert and Sullivan, both in New York staging their official version of *H.M.S. Pinafore*, began secret rehearsals in America of the next opera. They had taken to America the rough draft of *The Pirates of Penzance*. The plan was to present this opera in New York in order to get a copyright production in America in the hope of defeating pirate productions. Sullivan completed the score in a hotel in Manhattan. This proved to be an onerous task since his draft of Act 1 had been left in England in error and so the first act had to be re-written, virtually from memory. There was little time available and the music continued to be written over the period of the Christmas festivities. Sullivan worked non-stop on Christmas Day and the score was completed at seven o'clock in the morning on 28 December – only a day before the dress rehearsal and merely two days before the opening! The opera was rehearsed at the Fifth Avenue Theatre with security guards at each door to keep away unwelcome intruders.

It seems that Gilbert's original idea had been to have a plot about the activities of burglars interacting with policemen and it was initially titled *The Robbers*, with not a whiff of a pirate anywhere. The burglars were somehow changed to pirates whilst Gilbert was working in America – perhaps a reflection of his irritation at pirate performances of his works. The partners knew that there was only a slim chance of defeating American pirates but at least they could get copyright in England and, in order to secure this, they decided to hold a single nominal performance of *The Pirates of Penzance* in a quiet location where it would attract little attention. This token performance was to take place a day before the grand opening in New York.

The first performance of *The Pirates of Penzance* took place in England at the Royal Bijou Theatre at Paignton in Devon on 30 December 1879, and was given as a matinée production (with an audience of about fifty) by one of D'Oyly Carte's touring companies that was playing at nearby Torquay. There was only one full rehearsal on the stage at Torquay after the performance of *H.M.S. Pinafore*. There was then no overture ready. There were no proper costumes – only parts of the *H.M.S. Pinafore* costumes with added scarves for pirates, and the chorus of policemen wore sailors' dress. The cast held sheet music on the stage during the opera. This had only recently arrived from America and not all of it had turned up in time for this first performance. The Major-General, for instance, was unable to *sing* of his prowess and had to be content with introducing himself to the audience in verse only!

The opening in New York took place the following day, on New Year's Eve, with Sullivan, of course, conducting. The show boasted nine encores. Sullivan was most impressed by the designs for the New York production:

The dresses are something to be dreamed about. I never saw such a beautiful combination of colour and form on any stage. All the girls dressed in the old-fashioned English style, every dress designed separately by Faustin and some of the girls look as if they had stepped out of a Gainsborough picture.

But he admitted to his diary that he:

went into the orchestra more dead than alive, but got better when I took the stick in my hand. Fine reception. Piece went marvellously well. Grand success.

Gilbert directed the New York cast and preparations had gone fairly smoothly – although a matter of days before the first night the local orchestra struck for a higher rate of pay arguing that union regulations had varying scales for grand opera and mere operetta; and the musicians believed that *The Pirates of Penzance* fell into the former category because the opera contained so much music. Sullivan threatened to dismiss the orchestra and, bluffing further, said that he would ship the orchestra from Covent Garden to America in their stead; he even threatened to provide the music during the production until the alternative orchestra arrived from London – himself playing the piano and Alfred Cellier the harmonium! But things quietened down and the first night went well. The overture was completed by Sullivan and Cellier at about five o'clock in the morning on the day of the opening. After that, Sullivan needed to spend the morning rehearsing with the orchestra in the theatre.

In this opera Gilbert satirizes the *nouveau riche* as epitomized by Major-General Stanley and his daughters. He also pokes fun at a misplaced sense of duty. The alternative title for the opera finally became 'The Slave of Duty'. This had first been written as 'A Sense of Duty' in Gilbert's original manuscript and later as 'Love and Duty' as Sullivan revealed in a letter sent from America to his mother:

Our houses at the *Pinafore* have fallen off very much this week. All the theatres are doing badly, and we shall have no profits until the new piece comes out – so Gilbert and I are reducing our expenditure. We shall begin by not paying the postage of our letters home. We hope to have the new opera out on the 27th or 29th. It is called *The Pirates of Penzance*, or 'Love and Duty'. I can't help feeling sanguine of success although we ought never to be sanguine.

There are many memorable and tuneful songs, especially in

Programme cover of *The Pirates of Penzance* presented at the Opéra Comique in 1880, with the billing Sullivan and Gilbert.

78

OPERA COMIQUE

Licensed by the Lord Chamberlain to Mr. BARKER, 299, Strand.

Lessee and Manager - - MR. D'OYLY CARTE

EVERY EVENING,

The New and Original Melo-Dramatic
Opera, in Two Acts, entitled

THE

PIRATES OF PENZANCE

By Messrs. A. SULLIVAN and W. S. GILBERT.

Preceded at 8 by the New and Original Vaudeville,

IN THE SULKS.

By FRANK DESPREZ.   Music by ALFRED CELLIER.

No Booking Fees.

Box Office open daily
from 11 to 5.

BURNSIDE

Act 2, and the whole opera flows gracefully. Perhaps there is some lack of effective instrumentation caused probably by the speed of composition and the distractions of working in a foreign country. In *The Pirates of Penzance* Sullivan parodies once more Italian opera. He believed that the music of this opera was:

infinitely superior in every way to *Pinafore* – 'tunier' and more developed, of a higher class altogether.

Piracy persisted and Gilbert and Sullivan sent out four companies to tour America, and this helped to contain the problem to some extent. The opera was presented by the companies in Boston, Philadelphia, Newark (New Jersey), Buffalo, Chicago, Memphis, New Orleans, Louisville and in many other cities.

The music was only available in manuscript at this stage for, had it been printed and published, it would have become, in effect, public property. The manuscripts were collected and counted after each performance in America and locked in a safe until required the next evening. Pirate companies attempted to secure the music by sending musicians to the theatre as copyists to make extensive notes of the music as the opera was being played. Indeed, some judges in America interpreted the law to allow anyone able to memorize the music to produce it – since they held that a public presentation in a theatre was effectively a publication.

A week after the opening Sullivan wrote to his mother:

The Pirates of Penzance is still doing enormous business every night and likely to last, so that at last I really think I shall get a little money out of America. I ought to, for they have made a good deal out of me.

Perhaps the excitement of the American tour prompted Sullivan to begin a diary which he did shortly after his arrival and the habit, once fixed, persisted for the remainder of his life – for a further twenty-one years. His diary for 1879-80 is deposited at the Pierpont Morgan Library in New York which also houses his letters. His diaries for the years 1881-1900 are deposited at the Beinecke Library, Yale University. Some of the first entries relate to the days when he worked on *The Pirates of Penzance*:

10th December: Writing all day. Gilbert, Cellier, Rosavella, Clay called. Cellier stayed and finished 2nd Act. I wrote till 4.30am.

15th December: Rehearsal of music of 1st Act at the theatre. Wrote afterwards. Dined at the Manhattan Club with Gilbert. Went round to theatre. Then home to work.

17th December: Began scoring of Opera. Went to rehearsal 11-4. Came home tired. Couldn't work. Dined at Bett's. Then home. Wrote Trio (2nd Act) and Ruth's song (1st Act) and went to bed at 5am.

18th December: Rehearsal at my own rooms of Principals, 11.30 till 3.30. Very tired. Went to bed at 5.30 till 7. Then up, had a walk, dined with Gilbert. Came home; scored 2 numbers of 1st Act. Went to bed at 4.

25th Christmas Day: Worked all day. Dined at Grant's. Came home and worked till 5.30am.

26th December: Writing. First Act rehearsed with Band only.

Early in March 1880 Gilbert and Sullivan sailed home together from New York. Returning to England, they found that the score of *The Pirates of Penzance* was missing. To their great relief the package finally reappeared – having crossed the Atlantic several times before being discovered! The opera was to have a third 'first' night, this time in London on 3 April 1880 at the Opéra Comique. The London audience was appreciative, following the plot in their copies of the libretto that were popularly on sale and much used at that time during performance when the house lights were not turned out.

The well-known entry of chorus girls – 'Climbing Over Rocky Mountain' – had been taken almost word for word from *Thespis* – in a similar entry when the mortals climbed the slope of Mount Olympus!

Thespis	*The Pirates of Penzance*
Scaling rough and rugged passes,	Scaling rough and rugged passes,
Climb the hardy lads and lasses	Climb the hardy little lasses
Till the mountain top they gain.	Till the bright sea-shore they gain.

The critics were mostly fulsome in their praise, and the London production ran for a year – clocking the commendable number of 363 performances. The prior success of *H.M.S. Pinafore* made it a certainty that *The Pirates of Penzance* would be reviewed comprehensively in such journals as the *Musical World*, the *Musical Times* and the *Monthly Musical Record*. The critics commented that the composer had entered so thoroughly into the spirit of the dramatist that the result of their joint labours was as though it were the product of only one mind; that the masterly and discriminate skill in instrumentation accompanied the libretto hand-in-hand as a sister might go hand-in-hand with her brother. Clement Scott wrote in *Theatre* of Gilbert as a humorist:

It is a kind of comic daring and recklessness that makes fun of things . . . In a comical way he shows us all that is mean, and cruel, and crafty, and equivocal even in the world's heroes; and he makes us laugh at them because we are convinced such faults are lingering in the breasts of the best of us.

The *Monthly Musical Record* noted that various actors and actresses spoke perhaps too slowly – doubtless due to Gilbert's insistence on clear diction, but it is illuminating to find that his style was not everywhere welcomed:

There is a quaint eccentricity of ideas in several of the incidents which amuses sufficiently in most cases to justify the sublime anxiety not to speak too fast displayed by the ladies and gentlemen who have to interpret them. But those who ask for action and fun in dialogue will be disappointed.

The Pirates of Penzance was the first of the operas in which proceeds were divided into a three-way split amongst D'Oyly Carte, Gilbert and Sullivan as a result of their fresh contractual agreement. It seems that the way in which Sullivan in particular was lauded in America caused resentment in Gilbert. The public adulation of Sullivan must have rankled with Gilbert who saw much more of his partner in America than he ever saw when at home in England, and where the two partners usually worked together by correspondence rather than by personal meetings. Sullivan appears to have been sufficiently sensitive to note Gilbert's discomfort and perhaps that was why he asked Gilbert to re-work H. H. Milman's dramatic poem into suitable verse for his oratorio *The Martyr of Antioch*. This Gilbert did and the work was performed at the Leeds Festival.

Patience

The next opera, *Patience*, presented Gilbert with difficulties in the planning stages. His initial idea had been to write a play about aesthetics but he was concerned that such a chorus might not be able to act, dress and even make up effectively. So he then planned and wrote most of a play about two curates who attracted lady parishioners but he began to worry about the possibly adverse audience reaction to a comedy about clerics and about angering the Church. His hero in this farce was the Reverend Lawn Tennison! He also feared that a chorus composed of former cavalry officers who then became comic clerics might be regarded in poor taste. His plan to satirize the Anglo-Catholic movement within the Church of England, with its ritual and vestments, had seemed well enough at the planning stage, but he began to have cold feet once the opera appeared in a more detailed form. He then reverted to the story about aestheticism – a topical enough project since London at that time boasted many who were languid or

The soldier aesthetics from the original production of *Patience*, 1881.

affected in dress or demeanour. Gilbert re-wrote the story and this time had a chorus of love-sick maidens who were infatuated by Reginald Bunthorne, a poet. It may be that Gilbert had the writer Oscar Wilde, the painter James McNeill Whistler and the poet Charles Algernon Swinburne in mind as general models for Bunthorne and Archibald Grosvenor, the other aesthete in the opera. The fabric for the costumes was bought at Liberty's and Gilbert designed them.

Aestheticism as manifested in London in the last quarter of the nineteenth century contained praiseworthy aspects including an interest in beautiful things, a mania for blue and white china and for Japanese prints. It was the caricatures and excesses of the cult which Gilbert chose to parody. D'Oyly Carte wrote to the public in the programme of:

the outpourings of a clique of professors of ultra-refinement who preach the gospel of morbid languor and sickly sensuousness, which is half real and half affected by its high priests for the purpose of gaining social notoriety. The authors of *Patience* have not desired to cast ridicule on the true aesthetic spirit, but only to attack the unmanly oddities which masquerade in its likeness.

Once the story was prepared, Sullivan was tardy in writing the music. He spent much time in Nice and recorded:

My natural indolence, aided by the sunshine, prevents my doing any really serious work.

When he returned home, he engaged in the usual frenetic rush, working through the night, to get the music finished just before the opening. He orchestrated *Patience* in only ten days. The score was sent by him to the theatre piece by piece as soon as it was completed, arriving whilst rehearsals were well under way. The almost indecent rush to complete the work just before its public production was partly due to Sullivan's indolence, partly due to his busy and varied musical life, partly due to his many social engagements which often kept him away from his desk, partly due to his recurring illness and partly due to a desire not to waste time scoring material that might not be used in the final production. Gilbert frequently cut numbers during final rehearsals and so Sullivan found it advisable to wait almost until the last minute to see which pieces were likely to remain in the opera before bothering to score the final work.

The first performance took place at the Opéra Comique on 23 April 1881. There were eight encores that first night, including 'Prithee, pretty maiden', 'The magnet and the churn' and 'Silvered is the raven hair'. The press commented favourably. The *Daily News* reported:

The composer's settings of the lyrical portions of Mr Gilbert's witty satire are in nearly every case, bright and melodious. The sentiment and grace of most of Mr Sullivan's music gives the additional zest to the quaintness and humour of the other portions, and there is little doubt that these qualities and merits of Mr Gilbert's book will secure a success as great as any that hitherto resulted from the same co-operation.

Oscar Wilde went to see the opera. D'Oyly Carte, still an organiser of lectures through his agency, arranged for Wilde to go off on a tour of America. He appeared in the audience at a performance of *Patience* at the Standard Theatre in New York – providing useful publicity for the opera and the cult of aestheticism. D'Oyly Carte planned Oscar Wilde's lecture tour of the United States so that Wilde appeared in a particular city as *Patience* began to open there. He was, indeed, a sandwich-board man for the opera. When he spoke in Omaha a reporter observed in the press:

He wore the suit of black velvet with knee breeches which has been his usual dress in this country. His hair fell about his shoulders in heavy masses, his dreamy, poetic face grew animated, and his large dark eyes lighted up as he entered upon his subject.

D'Oyly Carte had major plans for a new theatre – the Savoy. It was designed by the theatre architect, C. J. Phipps, and was built in only a few months in red brick and Portland stone and was situated between the Embankment and the Strand. It had seats for 1,292 people, in the amphitheatre and gallery, balcony, circle, pit, stalls and private boxes. The theatre, an early example of a construction of the circle without pillars on the cantilever principle, had a spacious, uncluttered interior and afforded audiences splendid views of the stage – no matter how much or how little they had paid for their tickets. It also had electric lights. The Thames Embankment had been electrified in 1878, but in a handout D'Oyly Carte stressed that this was the first time that an attempt had been made to light a public building solely by using electricity:

The greatest drawbacks to the enjoyment of the theatrical performances are, undoubtedly, the foul air and heat which pervade all theatres. As everyone knows, each gas-burner consumes as much oxygen as many people, and causes great heat besides. The incandescent lamps consume *no* oxygen, and cause no perceptible heat.

Programme for *Patience* – produced at the Savoy Theatre in 1881 – showing electric lights in the border.

85

The Savoy Theatre was given its name as it stood on the site of a medieval palace of the Princes of Savoy. The theatre was built principally as a permanent home for performances of the joint works of Gilbert and Sullivan. D'Oyly Carte had tremendous faith in his composer and librettist; but he was a practical businessman, too, and 'Savoy operas', whilst nowadays denoting Gilbert and Sullivan, in the latter years of the nineteenth century meant, in addition, productions of works by other composers and librettists whom D'Oyly Carte engaged to play at the Savoy Theatre between the finish of one Gilbert and Sullivan opera and the appearance of the next one if, for some reason, the starting date of the next joint work was to be later than that which he required.

Patience was moved from the Opéra Comique to the Savoy and

The auditorium of the Savoy during a production of *Patience*. Engraving from the *Graphic*, 17 December 1881.

was first performed at the new theatre on 10 October 1881. To celebrate the occasion there was a larger chorus, and costumes and scenery were new. The Prince of Wales attended the opening of *Patience* at the Savoy and the theatre was crowded.

D'Oyly Carte announced that at the new theatre the attendants would all be paid fair wages. Tipping was to be abolished and programmes were to be free of charge. He also instituted orderly queues for unbooked seats prior to entry. The auditorium was decorated in white and gold. There were stage curtains of yellow satin instead of the usual painted drop-cloth. The seats were deep blue and the backs of the boxes were Venetian red. There were entrances on four sides. The theatre had a circular entrance vestibule paved with black and white marble. There was a refreshment saloon, a smoking-room and a lounge for ladies. There was even a stone staircase that was recommended for safety in the event of fire.

Initially, it was discovered that only the auditorium could be illuminated with electricity since the theatre contained 1,200 electric bulbs and it was found that the generator was too small and a second engine had to be installed to cope with the quantity of electricity required. So, at first, the stage was lit by gas – although within three months the stage (and also backstage) had electricity in use. The stage of the Savoy was illuminated with electricity for the first time at the matinée on 28 December 1881.

D'Oyly Carte enjoyed showmanship and put this to dramatic use on the first night for the audience, on entering, found the electric bulbs unlit. He ordered the gas light to be turned off and the *Daily Chronicle* reported:

As if by the wave of a fairy's wand the theatre immediately became filled with a soft, soothing light, clearer and far more graceful than gas.

D'Oyly Carte, ever the showman, appeared on stage holding an electric light. As the *Electrical Times* reported:

A hush fell upon the audience, who thought that electricity was always fatal. He then delighted with a sort of polytechnic lecture . . . respecting the safety of the electric light to a theatre. Finally, he placed a piece of muslin round the lamp and held it up . . . He then took a hammer and smashed the lamp which, naturally, went out. But when he held up the muslin unburnt the effect on the audience was electric, in both senses of the word. D'Oyly Carte bowed himself off amidst enthusiastic cheers, which were so prolonged that he had to go on and take two calls.

A theatrical 'Carte-oon' appeared with an illustration of D'Oyly Carte holding aloft an electric bulb together with a poem:

Although the world it will attract
To princely new Savoy;
And here the public gladly sits
With *Patience* every night,
While Mr Carte o'er every heart
Sheds his electric light.

Patience was popular with the public and had a run of 578 London performances. The opera contained more catchy tunes than any of its predecessors. Perhaps, too, the music was popular with theatre-goers because in this opera there were fewer solo arias – reminders of a 'grand opera' performance – and rather more duets, trios and ensembles than in previous Gilbert and Sullivan operas. Even Gilbert believed that the continued appeal of *Patience*, long after the cult of aestheticism had passed away, was mainly due to its delightful music.

Alice Barnett played Lady Jane; Leonora Braham played Patience; George Grossmith was Bunthorne; Rutland Barrington played Grosvenor; and Julia Gwynne was Saphir. The latter was a well-known giggler on stage. She was frequently fined for this misdemeanour by the stage manager, and eventually she told Gilbert that the Savoy Theatre had been built from the proceeds of her fines!

Several companies were sent on tour throughout the country. Apart from the American tours, a company also toured Australia. Pirate performances of *Patience* were presented in both these continents and lengthy legal action was brought by Gilbert, Sullivan and D'Oyly Carte but this was not always successful. Sullivan noted bitterly when speaking of American judges:

It seemed to be their opinion that a free and independent American citizen ought not to be robbed of his rights of robbing somebody else.

Both Gilbert and Sullivan each earned more than Gladstone, the Prime Minister. Gilbert built a large mansion in Harrington Gardens in South Kensington. His new home boasted central heating, a telephone and a bathroom on each floor. Sullivan could afford to move to Queen's Mansions in Victoria Street and he decorated his rooms lavishly. He remained there from 1881 for the rest of his life. His mother became ill in May 1882, rallied and then died. He wrote in his diary on 1 June:

Home feeling terribly lonely.

But within two days he was at work on the next opera, *Iolanthe*.

7 The First 'Savoy' Operas: 1881-85

Iolanthe

The first 'Savoy' opera was *Patience* when it was transferred to the newly-built Savoy Theatre on 10 October 1881. But *Iolanthe* has the distinction of being the first opera written for performance at the Savoy. In this opera Gilbert poked fun at the law, at parliament, at pretensions but especially at the institution of the House of Lords – and all within the context of peers interacting with a troupe of immortals from fairyland! The first performance of *Iolanthe* occurred at the Savoy on 25 November 1882. During the performance the audience was entranced to see stars glittering from the fairies' heads as battery-operated lamps were switched on to give a magical effect. The peers appeared to grow wings, prior to flying off to fairyland, by the device of pulling hidden cords concealed within their robes. Sullivan had earlier recorded:

The blinds were all down. I rushed upstairs and was alone in the room – alone, that is, with dear Mother's lifeless body – her soul had gone to God.

Just as his father's death in 1866 had inspired *In Memoriam* and his brother's death in 1877 had occasioned 'The Lost Chord', his mother's death in 1882 at the age of seventy-one gave him the strength and inspiration to tackle *Iolanthe*. The opera gave him the distraction he needed to side-step his grief and *Iolanthe* is perhaps the tenderest and most romantic of all the operas which he composed.

Gilbert's initial idea for this opera, following in outline his Bab Ballad 'The Fairy Curate', told of a marriage between a fairy and a

The façade of the Savoy Theatre facing, not the Strand but, the Embankment.

mortal – actually a commonplace solicitor. Then he decided that the chorus of fairies should wed barristers in the Northern Circuit and that the action of the opera should be set in a courtroom. But he later felt that a political jibe would have more thrust. His notes show that he intended the Fairy Queen to marry the Prime Minister (later the Foreign Secretary) with a setting in the House of Commons. Only later still did the setting change yet again to the environs of the House of Lords. Such alterations illustrate clearly the extent to which Gilbert studied and amended his plots before arriving at a satisfactory story. He wrote to Sullivan:

I am hard at work on Act 2 but have infinite difficulty with it.

Sullivan had written in his diary of 17 August 1882:

Wrote the first chorus of new opera and framed it.

The new opera was, of course, *Iolanthe*. Sullivan used the words 'write' or 'sketch' to refer to the planning of the form that the music would take. When he used the word 'frame' he referred to the writing of the score – but not yet to the detailed orchestration.

The overture was written a matter of days before the opening and Alfred Cellier had to put together an overture himself for the New York opening. Sullivan completed the overture at seven o'clock in the morning on 24 November. That evening there was a dress rehearsal from seven o'clock until one thirty the next morning – the actual day of the opening. That very day Sullivan received a letter from his financial adviser telling him of his own financial ruin and that Sullivan had lost his principal investment of £7,000 that he had entrusted to this stockbroker. The letter arrived just before he set out for the theatre. Sullivan was not totally destitute as he had shares held in the bank and also bank deposits, and his diary relates the events of that day (25 November 1882) with its usual abruptness:

Received letter from E. A. Hall saying that he was ruined and my money (about £7,000) lost, just before starting for the theatre. Dined with Smythe at home. 1st performance of *Iolanthe* at the Savoy Theatre. House crammed – awfully nervous, more so than usual on going into the orchestra. Tremendous reception. 1st act went splendidly – the 2nd dragged and I was afraid it must be compressed. However it finished well and Gilbert and myself were called and heartily cheered. Very low afterwards – came home.

Gilbert appears to have parodied Wagner's *Das Rheingold* when he makes Iolanthe surface from the bottom of a river. Sullivan,

Earl Tolloller and the Earl of Mountararat from *Iolanthe* played by Durward Lely and Rutland Barrington respectively.

Jessie Bond played the title role in *Iolanthe*.

too, satirizes Wagner in the music he wrote for *Iolanthe*. He made much use of musical themes. The Lord Chancellor, for instance, made his various entrances to fugal music and the word 'Iolanthe' as used by the fairies was also used in a thematic sense.

The secrecy surrounding previous new productions was maintained as *Iolanthe* was being rehearsed. Even the title of the opera was not known by the cast until the last rehearsal. Prior to this, where the word 'Iolanthe' would appear in the text the cast had to sing 'Come Perola'. When the name 'Iolanthe' was substituted for Perola at the final rehearsal some performers feared that they might forget the new name. Sullivan advised them to sing any name that occurred to them since no one would be any the wiser – no one, that is, except for Gilbert and, as usual, he would not be there but would be pounding the pavements of the Embankment.

Gilbert insisted that the peers must be a clean-shaven chorus. There were grumbles about losing moustaches, but all complied except for one who was dropped from the cast. The entry of the peers created a favourable stir amongst the audience, since Gilbert had researched insignia and fabrics for the peers' robes and insisted that they deport themselves as peers of the realm – wearing their coronets as though they were used to them!

Despite attempts to keep the subject matter of this new opera a secret, the story-line became fairly widely known. The music critic of the *World* published the story in some detail in advance of its production, and demand for tickets grew. D'Oyly Carte advised in the London newspapers on the morning of the première:

To accommodate to some extent the overflow of applications for boxes and stalls for tonight, the First Circle has been numbered and reserved. The remaining seats can be booked this morning at 4s each.

The audience enjoyed *Iolanthe* so much that the entire finale of Act 1 was encored – thus setting a tradition that was followed with this opera for many years, in London and also in the provinces. Captain Eyre Massey Shaw, a friend of Sullivan's and chief of the London Fire Brigade, was mentioned by name in *Iolanthe* when the Fairy Queen, played by Alice Barnett, sang from the footlights:

> O Captain Shaw!
> Type of true love kept under!
> Could thy brigade
> With cold cascade
> Quench my great love, I wonder?

Captain Shaw was sitting on that first night in the centre of the stalls. One can only hazard his reaction at being thus immortalised but it is believed that he took a bow!

Gilbert designed the fairies' dresses. These were made of blue, mauve, yellow, pink and apple-green chiffon but they were quickly replaced by a heavier silk from Liberty's. The wands carried by the fairies seemed to cause difficulties. Gilbert remonstrated with the chorus after the opening night:

You must not bang your fairy wands on the stage, ladies, the diamonds in the heads drop out. The stage was strewn with diamonds last night.

For the opening, copies of the libretto were available to the audience and, because the house lights could not be dimmed to any great extent, it was possible to follow the text. One enthusiast recorded:

Everyone was provided with a book and was so fascinated that they scarcely looked at the stage. When the time came for a 'turn-over' there was the rustling as of the leaves in a mighty forest. The audience followed the book as if it was the inspired oracles of Delphi and such roars of laughter were never heard before.

For the opening night the entry of the peers was heralded by part of the Band of the Grenadier Guards. The replicas of state robes worn by the peers were provided by the Queen's own robe-maker. Their coronets were an exaggerated Gilbertianism since peers did not wear such regalia, but the effect was magnificent.

The programmes for *Iolanthe* showed the electric bulbs at the theatre in a pattern around the cast list – a reminder that this was the first work specifically written for the new Savoy Theatre.

Captain Eyre Massey Shaw – Chief of the Metropolitan Fire Brigade – who is remembered in song by the Fairy Queen in *Iolanthe*.

94

George Grossmith made an admirable Lord Chancellor, Rutland Barrington and Durward Lely played the lords Mountararat and Tolloller and Jessie Bond was Iolanthe – the latter making her appearance on stage from a river of real water.

When *Iolanthe* opened on 25 November 1882 in London, it also opened on the same night at the Standard Theatre in New York. The performance in London ended an hour or so before the production in New York was to begin, and a cable was sent to New York from the Savoy Theatre relating the success of the London première and this was received in New York before the première there actually began!

Not all critics praised *Iolanthe*. *Punch*, a stern critic of Gilbert's work, thought that the opera was not within a mile of *Pinafore* nor a patch on *Patience*. The *Echo* was sharp:

Same set of puppets as Mr Gilbert has dressed over and over before.

The *Times* was subdued:

The public once more were indebted to their favourites for an evening of genuine, healthy, albeit not supremely intellectual enjoyment.

Vanity Fair thought:

the music decidedly superior to the libretto.

The *Era* noted that:

Mr George Grossmith as the Lord Chancellor brings all his comic talent and skill to bear upon one of the drollest impersonations imaginable.

The critic of *Theatre* enthused:

I do not hesitate to say that in fitting notes to words so exactly that the 'book' and the setting appear to be one and indivisible, our gifted composer is without a rival in England.

Some criticised Gilbert for the social conscience, regarded as out of place in a comic opera, which he showed in the song 'Fold your flapping wings' in which Richard Temple, playing the arcadian shepherd Strephon, sang:

> Take a wretched thief
> Through a city sneaking,
> Pocket handkerchief
> Ever, ever seeking:
> What is he but I

Robbed of all my chances –
Picking pockets by
Force of circumstances?
I might be as bad –
As unlucky, rather –
If I'd only had
Fagin for a father!

The song, which occurred in Act 2 after the trio 'Faint heart never won fair lady', was dropped after the opening. A second song from Act 2 was also soon cut – in which Mountararat detailed the history of someone who failed to earn recognition through the brilliance of his talents. Only when a distant relative died leaving him a millionaire was he raised to the peerage and hailed as a genius.

The Prime Minister, W. E. Gladstone, went to see *Iolanthe* within a week or so of its opening, as a guest of Sullivan, and wrote to the composer afterwards:

Nothing, I thought, could have been happier than the manner in which the comic strain of the piece was blended with its harmonies of sight and sound, so good in taste and so admirable in execution from beginning to end.

Clearly Gladstone had enjoyed the performance of *Iolanthe* as an entertainment and it seems unlikely that he recognized any possible caricature of himself – whether intended by Gilbert or otherwise – in the role of the Lord Chancellor; or, indeed, of a similarity between the Fairy Queen and Queen Victoria, of Private Willis and the Queen's servant John Brown, or Strephon and Lord Randolph Churchill – whose group of activists was currently causing problems for the other parties.

It was in the following spring that Gladstone wrote again to Sullivan offering him a knighthood. The ceremony took place at Windsor Castle on 22 May 1883 and George Grove was knighted on the same occasion. Sullivan's diary recorded:

I bowed low – then knelt down – the Queen took the equerry's sword and laid it first on right then on left shoulder – said softly 'Sir Arthur' and gave me her hand to kiss. Then I rose, bowed low again, and backed out.

Iolanthe ran for 398 performances. The music was a delight and the satire on the House of Lords was both topical and amusing at a time when the Liberals had only recently taken office in 1880 and whose reforming legislation was being impeded by the House of Lords in its right of veto. The music publishers, Chappell, sent out more than 10,000 vocal and piano scores of *Iolanthe* in just one night – the employees all staying until almost midnight to cater for the rush demand. The public loved the opera.

The Savoy Theatre now had telephones behind the scenes. Gilbert and Sullivan also had direct lines from their homes to the Savoy. Sullivan held a dinner party at his home to celebrate his forty-first birthday in May 1883. The Prince of Wales attended, as did the Duke of Edinburgh, Gilbert, Burnand and other notables. Sullivan celebrated the occasion by allowing his dinner guests to hear selections of *Iolanthe* being sung over the telephone from the Savoy – the company being engaged by Sullivan to sing the selections specially for the occasion.

Shortly after Sullivan's knighthood had been conferred the *Musical Review* commented harshly:

Some things that Mr Arthur Sullivan may do, Sir Arthur Sullivan ought not to do. Here is not only an opportunity, but a positive obligation for him to return to the sphere from which he has too long descended.

The reviewer in *Bell's Life* spoke out stridently:

Where is this topsy-turvydom, this musical and dramatic turning of ideas wrongside out, to end? . . . It seems to me that Gilbert starts out primarily with the object of bringing Truth and Love and Friendship into contempt, just as we are taught the devil does. Mr Gilbert tries to prove that there is no such thing as virtue, but that we are all lying, selfish, vain, and unworthy. In the Gilbertian world there are no martyrs, no patriots, and no lovers . . . As a moral lesson I prefer Punch and Judy to *Iolanthe*. I have much pleasure in bidding adieu to Mr Gilbert's unwholesome feeling and in calling the attention of my readers to an interesting exhibition of pictures of Venice now on view at the rooms of the Fine Art Society, New Bond Street.

Princess Ida

Gilbert had earlier written a play entitled *The Princess* that was performed at the Olympic Theatre in 1870. The play had been based on Lord Tennyson's poem 'The Princess' and Gilbert used the play when preparing the libretto for the next opera and, indeed, most of the dialogue was taken directly from it – even the blank verse was retained. He described the new opera as 'A Respectful Operatic Per-Version of Tennyson's "Princess".'

Gilbert read out the part which became Act 1 to Sullivan in February 1883. Sullivan was not particularly keen at first but almost six months later his diary recorded that he liked the piece very much as it had by then shaped out. Sullivan began to compose *Princess Ida* well enough – an enthusiastic start with two choruses and two songs on the first day of work. But he was heavily involved with the Leeds Festival by the autumn, conducting Beethoven's

Overleaf:
Scenes from the original
Princess Ida showing
King Hildebrand arriving at
Castle Adamant; and King
Gama in the inset.

KING GAMA

Missa Solemnis, and he soft-pedalled on *Princess Ida*. The applause he received at Leeds – where his conducting of Beethoven's Mass in D was regarded as the finest in the country – reminded him that the audiences were praising Sullivan the conductor, not Sullivan the composer.

Princess Ida was the only opera written in three acts and, as there were two fairly lengthy intervals to allow for scene-changing, the playing time was thought by many to be excessive; and the contrived puns and the blank verse were regarded as dated. The opera was viewed as being more serious than those which had already been produced by Gilbert and Sullivan since the score was more akin to the grand opera style than that of its predecessors. The principal subject matter of women's rights and of education for women was itself somewhat dated when the opera was produced early in 1884, since Girton and Newnham Colleges at Cambridge as well as Somerville and Lady Margaret Hall at Oxford had been founded in the 1870s. There is a recurring theme of women's superiority over men and of the folly of being overtly absorbed by one's ideals – the sub-title of the opera is 'Castle Adamant'! But there is also a subsidiary satire on the military life – the heavily-armoured sons of King Gama soon lose their fight with the poorly-equipped Hilarion and his friends.

On New Year's Day Sullivan rehearsed the orchestra before lunch and then, not being able to find a cab, walked home in a snowstorm where he composed Gama's song 'Nothing to grumble at' and Ida's 'I built upon a rock'. He collapsed at the full dress rehearsal the next day. The first night took place on 5 January 1884. Four days before the opening Sullivan had been in a weak state. He still had two songs to compose. The score, however, was ready for the first night. Sullivan was nearly unable to conduct due to exhaustion and his kidney illness. D'Oyly Carte had amended the programmes to state that François Cellier would conduct when Sullivan, doped with morphine and black coffee, managed to appear at the theatre. The performance began late and did not end until almost midnight. He managed to get through the long evening, took a bow with Gilbert and then promptly collapsed again. The public were told that he was suffering from muscular pain of the neck. With his usual characteristic immodesty he recorded later in his diary of the 'brilliant success' of *Princess Ida*. Possibly because of Sullivan's precarious state of health, Gilbert remained at the Savoy Theatre for the opening of *Princess Ida* instead of walking the streets of London in an effort to ward off the panic of first-night nerves. Gilbert did not watch the opera but sat in the Green Room reading a newspaper.

There was a fairly short prelude rather than the usual lengthy overture – but the *Observer* found this to be to the point and full of

100

spirit. An amusing incident occurred on the first night when Princess Ida, during Act 2, falls from the castle walls into the stream below. She disappeared from the view of those in the stalls effectively enough but the audience in the gallery were still able to see her bouncing on a mattress beyond the scenery.

The opera had a run of 246 performances – lasting for nine months and making it one of the shortest of the Gilbert and Sullivan runs. Not all the critics enthused, some describing the work as clumsy, tedious and dull. But the *Sunday Times* believed that:

It is the best in every way that Sir Arthur Sullivan has produced, apart from his serious works.

Perversely, *Figaro* thought that *Princess Ida* was:

from every point of view the weakest.

Perhaps the most obvious weakness of the plot of *Princess Ida* is that it has one main story element that did not allow Gilbert to diverge or to divulge much of his unique creativity. Its problem was that it was first and last a parody of a poem by someone else. Again, there were almost too many principal parts. Some of the players were on the stage for limited periods only. King Gama, for instance, did not appear at all in the very lengthy Act 2, and opportunities for detailed characterization were therefore reduced.

Jessie Bond played Melissa, Durward Lely played Cyril, George Grossmith appeared as King Gama and Rutland Barrington as King Hildebrand. Barrington believed that a major weakness of *Princess Ida* was the relatively small part afforded to King Hildebrand!

Sullivan's music was enjoyed more than Gilbert's plot. The dramatic critic Edmund Yates was scathing of the latter's efforts:

It was a desperately dull performance . . . there were not three and a half jokes worth remembering throughout three and a half hours' misery . . . We are always hearing of Mr Gilbert's wonderful stage management but the tumble of the Princess and her rescue from drowning were so ludicrously mismanaged as to evoke hisses and laughter.

Gilbert's economy in ideas and rehashing of his old stories, plays and poems, or of stories written by others, was noted constantly by the critics. In writing of *Princess Ida,* the *Musical World* commented:

As concerning the expenditure of thought, Mr W. S. Gilbert is

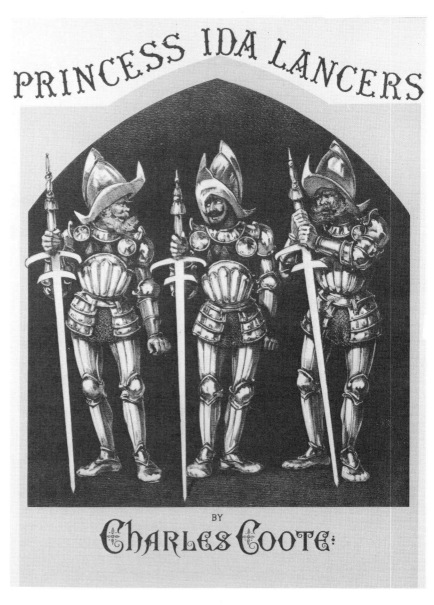

Princess Ida Lancers from an illustrated music cover.

economical. Were he a housemother in the same spirit, he would burn up all the candle-ends, well sift the cinders, save the kitchen fat and exercise his utmost ingenuity upon the cold mutton . . . He has trimmed a dish removed from the table years ago, and re-served it with sauce *à la* Sullivan.

The music of Act 2 is a succession of such rich melodies that it is often referred to as a string of pearls. George Grossmith was one of a number of principals who believed that *Princess Ida* was Sullivan's best score. The grotesquely bad-tempered and unlikeable King Gama, Gilbert confided to George Grossmith, was intended to be a portrait of himself:

I meant it for myself: I thought it my duty to live up to my reputation.

The constant blank verse was not universally appreciated. In Act 2, for instance, Lady Psyche, Professor of Humanities, muses:

> Man will swear and Man will storm –
> Man is not at all good form –
> Man is of no kind of use –
> Man's a donkey – Man's a goose –
> Man is coarse and Man is plain –
> Man is more or less insane –
> Man's a ribald – Man's a rake –
> Man is Nature's sole mistake!

Perhaps due to his poor state of health and touchiness that *Princess Ida* was not being as well-received as his other operas had been, and perhaps due to a feeling that life was passing relentlessly by and that there were other musical areas he wished to explore and needed the time to do so, Sullivan sent D'Oyly Carte a formal letter at the end of January stating that he intended to write no other music for comic opera. Probably Sullivan's decision would have been final had both he and Gilbert not agreed in legal terms in February 1883 to provide D'Oyly Carte with a further opera, on request, for a five-year period. Indeed, *Princess Ida* had been the first opera to be produced under the terms of this new contract. D'Oyly Carte insisted that this agreement was a binding one and Sullivan had no option but to accept his position.

There had been disagreement between librettist and composer during the summer of 1883 when they tried to decide on the subject-matter for the next opera. Sullivan flatly objected to Gilbert's attempt to resurrect the magic lozenge idea. Gilbert still wanted Sullivan to set the lozenge plot and revamped it in various ways hoping that Sullivan would agree. But Sullivan was resolute and a position of stalemate ensued. By the spring of 1884 attendances at the Savoy were falling off and D'Oyly Carte wrote to both Gilbert and Sullivan to inform them that a new opera would be required in six months to replace *Princess Ida*. Sullivan replied:

It is impossible for me to do another piece of the character of those already written by Gilbert and myself.

Gilbert reminded Sullivan that unless they kept to their contract they would be liable for D'Oyly Carte's losses. He was saddened that Sullivan felt unable to produce another piece – since the two of them had worked for many years together in a spirit of thorough good feeling. Sullivan felt that he had seen enough of topsy-turvy plots. He wanted a story with 'a feeling of reality about it' – and a situation in which the music could act in its own sphere, to arise and speak for itself. But Sullivan appeared to want things both ways. He wrote to Gilbert:

I hope with all my heart that there may be no break in our chain of joint workmanship.

D'Oyly Carte became anxious. Gilbert even suggested that perhaps Sullivan would like to work with a different librettist on this occasion but, paradoxically, Sullivan refused the suggestion – talking instead of Gilbert's 'matchless skill and genius'. Sullivan now wanted a totally new plot. Gilbert replied:

Anxious as I am, and have always been, to give due weight to your suggestions, the time has arrived when I must state – and I do so with great reluctance – that I cannot consent to construct another plot for the next opera.

Whereupon in May 1884 Gilbert was suddenly inspired to write the plot for *The Mikado*! Gilbert wrote again to Sullivan and Sullivan's diary recorded thankfully on 8 May 1884:

Gilbert wrote to propose piece on lines I had suggested. Wrote and accepted with greatest pleasure.

It was Gilbert who had backed down and at least Sullivan had the grace to write expressing his pleasure:

My dear Gilbert,
Your letter of today was an inexpressible relief to me, as it clearly shows me that you, equally with myself, are loath to discontinue the collaboration which has been such a pleasure and advantage to us.
    If I understand you to propose you will construct a plot without the supernatural and improbable elements, and on the lines you describe, I will gladly undertake to set it without further discussing the matter, or asking what the subject is to be.
Yours sincerely,

Arthur Sullivan

He further confided to his diary on 9 May 1884:

all unpleasantness at an end.

The *Musical Times* had reminded readers and Sullivan that:

It will look rather more than odd to see announced in the papers that a new comic opera is in preparation, the book by Mr W. S. Gilbert and the music by Sir Arthur Sullivan . . . he must not dare to soil his hand with anything less than an anthem or a madrigal; oratorio . . . and symphony must now be his line. Here is not only an opportunity, but a positive obligation for him to return to the sphere from which he has too long descended . . . to do battle for the honour of English art.

It is not difficult to see why Sullivan stayed with comic opera. He had worked productively and cordially with Gilbert, he enjoyed comedy and had a sense of humour himself and, more practically, he needed a steady income in order to pay for his foreign travel, lavish entertainment and heavy gambling. He received a fee of three hundred guineas for conducting the Leeds Festival in 1883 but he sometimes lost that amount in only one night gambling in London or Monte Carlo. High Art, he found, paid few bills.

The Mikado

Princess Ida came to the end of its run in September 1884. But there was no new opera planned in detail by Gilbert and Sullivan to replace it at the Savoy – the first time that a gap of this nature had occurred. D'Oyly Carte decided to revive both *The Sorcerer* and *Trial by Jury* as a double-bill until the next opera was written and rehearsed. Such revivals, in fact, were to come as a welcome surprise to fans of Gilbert and Sullivan. Before the days of recordings (*The Mikado* was the first of these operas to be recorded on disc but not until 1917 and it was also the first Gilbert and Sullivan opera to be filmed – in 1938) once an opera came to the end of its run it was unusual for it to appear again.

Whether or not an old Japanese executioner's sword really did crash from the wall of Gilbert's study to the floor giving him the germ of an idea is immaterial, although it provides a dramatic story. More relevantly, there was at that time a Japanese Exhibition at Knightsbridge which included displays of Japanese paintings, pottery and costumes. Liberty's was selling fabrics and dresses in Japanese styles (the store provided some of the costumes for *The Mikado*) and fashionable London was taking on an oriental aspect. So Gilbert set his next adventure in Japan.

Sullivan's stipulation had been that the plot of the next opera must be free from the supernatural and the improbable. Certainly, the probability of Gilbert's plot might be questioned, yet Sullivan appears to have set to work with gusto and composed a score that many regard as his major operatic contribution. Always a stickler

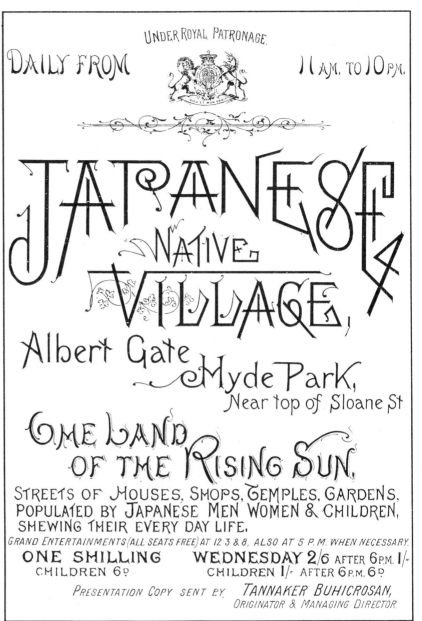

Advertisement for the Japanese Village in Knightsbridge.

for precision, Gilbert hired girls from the Japanese Exhibition to teach the performers how to walk, bow and manage a fan. George Grossmith played the comic lead, Ko-Ko, and wielded the huge sword that had hung in Gilbert's house and which reputedly had set off his train of thought for things oriental. Katisha's costume was believed to be two hundred years old, and some of the other actresses wore very old dresses. Many costumes were authentic in design.

106

As was often the case, certain numbers were written for specific actors and actresses. Gilbert knew, even before he put pen to paper, that George Grossmith would be playing the comic lead. The trio 'Three little maids from school' was written to enable the three actresses Sybil Grey, Leonora Braham and Jessie Bond – all of whom were short in stature – to work together as a concerted trio. The entrance of the Mikado in Act 2 occurred to a Japanese military march. The Mikado's song 'My object all sublime' had not pleased Gilbert during rehearsals and his last-minute decision to cut it was altered only when the company expressed to him their dismay at its possible loss.

Gilbert worked through a dozen versions of the story before he was sufficiently satisfied with the plot to begin the libretto. Perhaps one reason for the extensive changes in the preliminary plot was that on this occasion Gilbert was not working from an established plan from a Bab Ballad idea. The title was changed from *Titipu* to *The Mikado* at the last minute.

In January Sullivan was saddened by the death of his brother's widow in Los Angeles, and showed concern for the orphaned children, visiting them in the autumn. Meanwhile he worked on *The Mikado* fervently. His diary for 2 March recorded:

All these days since February 21st writing and rehearsing. No drives, parties, or recreations of any kind.

3rd March: Worked all night at Finale, 1st Act. Finished at 5am 63 pages of score at one sitting.

The author Weedon Grossmith (George Grossmith's brother) remarked that Gilbert arrived at every rehearsal with perfection in his pocket. During rehearsals Gilbert addressed Durward Lely, playing Nanki-Poo:

Very good, Lely, very good indeed, but I have come down from the back seat in the gallery, and there are one or two words which failed to reach me quite distinctly. Sullivan's music is, of course, very beautiful and I heard every note without difficulty, but I think my words are not altogether without merit, and ought to be heard without undue effort.

Gilbert seems to have been even more of a martinet than usual during these rehearsals. He was determined that not only should the words be distinctly spoken but that gestures should be correct and appropriate. Rehearsals had not proceeded smoothly. Gilbert had made the cast jumpy. George Grossmith had much to think about since Ko-Ko is a major acting part and he had problems in remembering all his lines. He was weak on the opening night in Act 1 but gained more confidence in the second act. Grossmith recalled the first night in his book, *A Society Clown*:

It must have appeared to all that I was doing my best to spoil the piece. But what with my own want of physical strength, prostration through the numerous and very long rehearsals, my anxiety to satisfy the author, and the long rows of critics rendered *blasé* by the modern custom of half-a-dozen matinées a week, I lost my voice, the little there is of it, my confidence, and – what I maintain is most valuable to me – my own individuality. In fact I plead guilty . . . a lamentable spectacle.

Grossmith became so nervous after the opening that he resorted to sedatives to calm himself.

The first night occurred at the Savoy on 14 March 1885. The audience included royalty and, as usual on such occasions, the distinguished in London society. Leonora Braham played Yum-Yum, Rosina Brandram played Katisha and Rutland Barrington appeared as Pooh-Bah. There were triple encores for both the songs 'Three little maids from school' and 'The flowers that bloom in the spring'. During the first performance Gilbert walked the Embankment:

Agony and apprehension possessed me.

The ovation at the close of the opera for composer and librettist set his mind at ease. Sullivan's diary recorded:

Seven encores taken – might have taken eleven.

Rutland Barrington sang in tune all through the first performance, an unusual occurrence for him, but, as Gilbert remarked, that was only due to first-night nerves!

The Mikado had a run of two years – with 672 performances and this was a record. The opera might have been set in Japan but it had an English theme, as a satire on pluralism and snobbery as epitomized by Pooh-Bah, on female cunning as illustrated by Katisha and on the pressures of life in the person of Ko-Ko. The libretto was witty and polished and the music, with an emphasis on English folk-songs, flowed gracefully and richly. The press, often moderate in praise, described the welcome accorded to the opera as tumultuous since the audience positively roared its approval of 'Three little maids from school'. The *Pall Mall Gazette* afforded *The Mikado* two pages in order to do justice to its account of the production – illustrated with sketches of composer and librettist as well as of scenery and characters suitably attired. G. K. Chesterton later wrote:

In this play Gilbert pursued and persecuted the evils of modern England

Interior plan of the Savoy Theatre, showing the seating arrangements.

till they had literally not a leg to stand on, exactly as Swift did under the allegory of *Gulliver's Travels*. I doubt if there is a single joke in the whole play that fits the Japanese. But all the jokes in the play fit the English.

The *Era* recorded of the opening:

Messrs Gilbert and Sullivan must be familiar with success by this time, but never in their brilliant partnership of sprightly music and fantastic fun has a more unanimous verdict of approval been passed upon their labours than when the curtain fell on Saturday last.

The *Theatre* enthused:

Nothing fresher, gayer or more captivating has ever bid for public favour than this delightful composition. The text of *The Mikado* sparkles with gems of wit, and its author's rhyming and rhythmic gifts have never been more splendidly displayed . . . *The Mikado* contains half-a-dozen numbers, each of which is sufficiently attractive, to ensure the opera's popularity.

The critic writing in the *Whitehall Review* must have lived to regret his assessment:

Sybil Grey, Leonora Braham and Jessie Bond in *The Mikado* – as three little maids from school, 1885.

Mr Gilbert was far from being his best. His libretto was written in the same satirical vein which has characterized his former works. But there was nothing really funny in it. His satire seemed to be laboriously drawn out, with neither pith nor point. Thus we do not calculate that *The Mikado* will have lasting fame.

D'Oyly Carte became so paranoid about pirate versions that he hired detectives to inform him of proposed productions in the United States. At least one pirate management sent a 'spy' to London. The opera became popular in the United States once D'Oyly Carte organised a touring company in England and had it secretly sent to America. By suddenly arriving in New York and producing a rehearsed cast, D'Oyly Carte was able to present *The Mikado* there before the major pirate versions were ready for production. He had transferred this touring company on a Cunard liner, the cast travelling under assumed names, from Liverpool to New York. It opened in August 1885 and had a New York run of

430 performances. By the following year there were believed to be one hundred and seventy pirate versions performed on a single night in America. The first pirate version in New York was described by the *New York Herald* as:

butchered, botched, mauled and mangled.

The city of Mikado in Michigan was so-named in 1886. *The Mikado* was also popular in Scandinavia and Germany. The D'Oyly Carte Company had grown so involved that at one point *The Mikado* was played by four companies in Britain, five in North America and a tenth toured in Europe, visiting Holland, France, Germany and Austria-Hungary. The touring life led by these artists literally took Gilbert and Sullivan to the people of much of the world before records and films could serve a similar function.

There was a command performance before Queen Victoria at Balmoral Castle in September 1891.

Ruddigore

Between 1885 and 1887 Sullivan was conductor of the Philharmonic Society in London, but 1886 was an especially busy time. It was, even more than usual, the year of his twin responsibilities. He composed not only the next comic opera but was also heavily engrossed in his oratorio, *The Golden Legend* – possibly his finest non-theatrical composition. The oratorio was written for the Leeds Festival held in October. The libretto was a setting of Longfellow's poem of the same name, prepared by Joseph Bennett. Sullivan was overworked:

How am I to get through this year's work? Do they think me a barrel-organ? They turn a handle and I disgorge music of any mood to order.

The *Yorkshire Post* believed that:

On no former occasion has the world-renowned Leeds chorus met together with stronger determination to achieve honour for itself, its work, and its conductor, than on the last morning of the Festival.

Sullivan and his oratorio were both cheered by the audience, and the choir and orchestra threw flowers. *The Times* reported:

The Leeds Festival may boast of having given life to a work which, if not one of genius in the strict sense of the word, is at least likely to survive till our long expected English Beethoven appears on the scene.

The *World* described the composer as 'the Mozart of England'.

Sullivan had alternated during the summer of 1886 between

Drawing of the baronets of *Ruddigore* emerging from the picture frames in the picture gallery, 1887.

composition of this serious work and the next Savoy opera. For the plot of *Ruddygore* (changed within days of its appearance to *Ruddigore*) Gilbert returned to his earlier play, *Ages Ago*, in which portraits come to life and become part of the action of the story. He developed this idea into a melodrama which poked fun at the blood and thunder of many theatrical presentations. Yet despite being overworked Sullivan managed to have the score finished a week before the opening on 22 January 1887. *The Mikado* ended on 19 January and then the final rehearsals for the new opera lasted throughout the next nights. The cast must have been utterly worn-out by the time the curtain descended on one of these first nights!

Gilbert went to town in planning the costumes. The uniforms of twenty regiments appeared on stage in the chorus of officers. They were the uniforms of regiments in the British Army as worn earlier in the century and each was an accurate representation.

Because of the expense of costumes, and the stage mechanism necessary to change portraits into real people, the opera was costly to produce. The military uniforms for the male chorus and the props cost £6,000. The settings of a Cornish coastal scene and a complex gallery in Ruddigore Castle cost £2,000 and it is significant that the opera was not revived until as late as 1920.

The appearance of a new Gilbert and Sullivan opera had become important news, and the press commented on the secrecy surrounding the rehearsals for *Ruddigore*. It cannot seriously be denied that such caution existed and yet Gilbert wrote to attempt to deny this to the *Pall Mall Gazette* on 20 December:

Sir,
You are pleased to make merry with what is supposed to be an exaggerated anxiety on the part of Sir A. Sullivan and myself lest the details of the opera now in rehearsal at the Savoy should become prematurely known to the public. So little has this consideration troubled us, that we invited to the reading of the piece, which took place three weeks before the first stage rehearsal, no fewer than forty-four ladies and gentlemen of the chorus, who are in no way concerned with the dialogue, besides a dozen personal friends. We have declined to accede to several requests which have been made to us to allow the details of the plot of the piece to be published in newspapers; and in acting thus we believe we have taken no unusual course. It is not customary for dramatic authors in this or any other country to publish their plots eight weeks before the production of their pieces. You say that so great is the fear of piracy that even the actors themselves do not know the name of the play, nor the names of the characters they are severally engaged to represent. The name of the play is at present unknown to myself and I shall be much obliged to anyone who will tell it to me.
I am, Sir, your obedient servant,
W. S. Gilbert

But despite Gilbert's protestation of not wanting secrecy to surround new productions, such secrecy had been practised previously and caution was clearly in play on this occasion. Such press speculation was good for Savoy business anyway, and Gilbert clearly knew this.

The queue for seats began at about one o'clock on the afternoon of the opening night. By six o'clock perhaps two thousand were standing outside the theatre. Many were disappointed not to receive tickets for these first-night performances. The *Country Gentleman* reported:

Many apply, but few are chosen . . . What are the essential qualifications of a first-nighter at the Savoy? Did one know one would endeavour to live up to them. Must a candidate for a stall on these august occasions be tall, or short, dark or fair? I am willing to make up either way. Must one be a

Buddhist? If so, I shall be sworn in to that faith. I am willing to applaud the performances from first to last . . . I pray that someone may enlighten me that I may be qualified for admission when next a new Gilbert and Sullivan is forthcoming.

Ruddygore had an uncertain audience reaction at first. Some hissed the opera and wanted *The Mikado* back again. People began to call the play *Bloodygore* and hence Gilbert changed its title to *Ruddigore*. He joked, tongue in cheek, that perhaps its title should be altered to 'Kensington Gore, or not so good as *The Mikado*'.

The first-night audience enjoyed Act 1 and gave the performers an ovation at its close. But Act 2 appeared to drag. Sullivan's diary noted that during the final twenty minutes the audience showed dissatisfaction. Gilbert altered Act 2 within a matter of days and, later still, cut it markedly. There was, however, also much applause on this first night. Perhaps the audience became tired of waiting for Act 2 to begin as there was an interval of thirty minutes – though they had been prepared for this since D'Oyly Carte had issued 'indulgence slips'. But Act 2, when it arrived on stage, seems to have been regarded as feeble and with a downright stupid ending in its original plot. On the opening night Sir Roderic appeared by rising from a stage trap. Gilbert later changed the method of entry. He had the ghostly ancestors come to life twice in the original version – the second time to serve as partners for the female chorus at the end of Act 2. This second resurrection was regarded as a weakness and was also soon cut out.

The *St James's Gazette* reported the opening:

Shortly after the beginning of the second act the interest of the story begins to flag, until at last the plot had seemed within an inch of collapsing.

Indeed, there was literally a collapse on this opening night when two of the frames in the picture gallery crashed to the stage! Theatre-going lovers of Gilbert and Sullivan operas were astonished to read in their newspapers of the hisses attending the first night of *Ruddygore*. The news was flashed far and wide: 'The First Flat Failure'. The critic of the *Pall Mall Budget* noted with understanding:

It is the misfortune of Messrs Gilbert and Sullivan that they are their own rivals, and every new work makes their task harder.

The *Era* soon commented:

From the first the Savoy has been nightly crowded. All the drawbacks attending the first night were speedily overcome and we have seldom seen a more finished and complete rendering of a comic opera.

Rutland Barrington played Sir Despard Murgatroyd, Jessie Bond played Mad Margaret, Leonora Braham played Rose Maybud and George Grossmith appeared as Robin Oakapple. But within days of the opening Grossmith had an operation for peritonitis. Henry Lytton, his understudy, was his replacement and this chance opening secured the latter's future at the Savoy. Lytton recalled the occasion in his book, *The Secrets of a Savoyard*:

Upon the Monday morning I was told I was to play the part – and play it that very night . . . Then the cue came and I went on. The silence of the audience was deathly. They gave me not the slightest welcome. The great Grossmith, the lion comique of his day, was not playing. Robin Oakapple was being taken by an unknown stripling. No wonder they were disappointed and chilling. First I had a few lines to speak and then I had a beautiful little duet with Miss Leonora Braham who was playing Rose Maybud. And when that duet 'Poor little man' was over, and we had responded to the calls for an encore, all my tremors and hesitation had gone. I knew things were all right . . . The applause when the curtain fell was to be unforgettable. It betokened a triumph.

Gilbert was criticised by the French because of the implied insult to the French navy in Dick Dauntless' number 'I shipped d'ye see, in a Revenue sloop' since they took offence at being referred to as 'Mounseers' and 'Parley-voos'. Gilbert intended to satirize British boasting, not French valour, and he even wrote to a newspaper in Paris assuring the French that no insult was intended. But the London correspondent of *Figaro* attacked Gilbert for supposedly insulting the French and perhaps Gilbert had been unwise to include such lines as:

> But to fight a French fal-lal
> It's like hittin' of a gal,
> It's a lubberly thing for to do.

Figaro went as far as to say:

Should the authors ever present themselves in Paris, let us wish they may be remembered in order to be hooted, and let us note, in passing, that these gentlemen have never succeeded in having any of their trash played in France, which explains to a certain extent their ridiculous revenge.

Others, similarly, complained of aspects of *Ruddigore* – including the cause of the Unionists. Gilbert lost his temper and on one occasion replied to a complainant:

Your letter is an impertinence. If there exists an idiot capable of drawing the conclusions you suggest from any incidents in my plays, I must decline to pay him the compliment of entering, directly or indirectly, into controversy with him. I have neither time nor inclination to deal with such maniacal babble.

Ruddigore had the advantage of electricity on stage whilst the earlier production of Gilbert's play *Ages Ago*, produced eighteen years before, had only gas lighting. Electricity allowed a stage to be darkened slowly and even made totally dark. This produced ghostly effects when the ancestors of the Murgatroyd family came to life from their family portraits. It was so dark at the front of the house whilst these effects were being managed that the conductor would have problems in making known his wishes to the orchestra. Phosphorescent material was tried in the conductor's baton but it was not effective, so a baton was specially made consisting of a tube of glass containing a platinum wire that was attached to batteries and which made the wire glow red.

Ruddigore ran for 288 performances. This was a low run for Gilbert and Sullivan but to those who described the opera as a failure Gilbert rejoined that he could do with a few more such failures:

Well, it ran eight months and, with the sale of the libretto, put £7000 into my pocket.

Sullivan described *Ruddigore* as a play which happened to have songs interspersed at intervals. Gilbert thought that Sullivan's music swamped his words. It seems that neither composer nor librettist was totally satisfied with the contribution of the other in this piece. Perhaps rather wickedly, Sullivan left Gilbert the score of *Ruddigore* in his will. Sullivan in places wavered close to a grand operatic style – especially in the number 'When the night wind howls in the chimney cowls'. Gilbert believed:

That music seems to my uninstructed ear to be very fine indeed, but out of place in a comic opera. It is as though one inserted fifty lines of *Paradise Lost* into a farcical comedy.

In later life Gilbert admitted that *Ruddigore* was one of his favourite operas – the other two favourites for him being *The Yeomen of the Guard* and *Utopia Limited*. *Ruddigore* contains numerous musical gems including the madrigal 'When the buds are blossoming', the ballads 'There grew a little flower' and 'To a garden full of posies' and the dramatic ghost song 'When the night wind howls'.

When Ruddigore closed there was no new opera ready to take its place. D'Oyly Carte therefore revived *H.M.S. Pinafore* from November 1887 to March 1888, *The Pirates of Penzance* from March to June 1888 and *The Mikado* from June to September 1888.

Cartoon of W. S. Gilbert
*c*1878.

8 The Later Operas: 1887-89

The Yeomen of the Guard

Sullivan went off to the Riviera for relaxation and then to Berlin where he conducted *The Golden Legend* for the ninetieth birthday of Kaiser William 1. The irony was that when the composer was presented at the palace to the German royal family a selection of tunes from *The Mikado* was played in his honour.

On his return to England, Gilbert tackled him again about his infamous lozenge plot. Sullivan wavered but within months decided against the proposal finally. It was a theme in which Gilbert had immense faith – whereby the swallowing of a magic tablet made a person into whoever he had been pretending to be before he swallowed it. But Sullivan decried the idea:

It is a puppet show, and not human. It is impossible to feel any sympathy with a single person. I don't see my way to setting it in its present form.

Gilbert tells us that the inspiration for the next opera came one morning whilst he was waiting for a train at Uxbridge Station, and he noticed a poster advertising furnishings. The firm was the Tower Furnishing Company and its poster depicted the Tower of London. This gave him the germ of an idea to place the next opera in the Tower. The urgency of the need to work in harmony once again was shown when on the morning of Christmas Day in 1887 Gilbert, Sullivan and D'Oyly Carte gathered at Sullivan's home. Sullivan, to his relief, was able to record:

Gilbert read plot of new piece (Tower of London) – immensely pleased with it. Pretty story, no topsy-turvydom, very human and funny also.

Alfred Cellier, conductor of the earlier Gilbert and Sullivan operas and himself a noted composer of comic operas.

1887 was the year of Victoria's Jubilee. She had been Queen for fifty years and so a Savoy opera with an historical subject would appeal both to Gilbert and to his audiences. Fortunately, it appealed to Sullivan too, for otherwise it is possible, once again, that the partnership at this point might have been dissolved. This new opera was to be described in the billing not as a comic opera but as 'A new and original opera' in order to emphasise a rather different departure from their previous joint efforts. The story was straightforward and moving. Gilbert, on this occasion, did not satirize any individual or any group. He visited the Tower of London frequently to try to soak in its history and its unique place in British history. He also made sketches of its warders. He attempted to work harmoniously with Sullivan to try to prevent any temperamental flareup and even provided Sullivan with alternative versions of many lyrics to help the composer with a wider option of rhythms for the words. Again, he tried to gain something of the atmosphere of Tudor London by reading some early literature.

At first his title was to have been *The Tower of London*, then *The Tower Warders* and then *The Beefeaters*. When the title was finally chosen as *The Yeomen of the Guard* this, in fact, was a descriptive error. The Yeomen of the Guard are actually the monarch's personal bodyguard and, although they wear a similar uniform to the warders at the Tower of London, they are a distinct body.

Gilbert and Sullivan had become used to tremendous runs for their operas at the Savoy. Other collaborators had usually to be content with far more modest runs. It was, therefore, professional jealousy, despair and fright that caused Sullivan to panic when Alfred Cellier's work, *Dorothy*, performed at the Gaiety Theatre, reached first its 500th performance – and actually closed after 931 shows. This run was never achieved by Gilbert and Sullivan for any of their operas. Sullivan had telegraphed Gilbert from Monte Carlo after *Dorothy* had reached its 500th performance to warn him that they had a real competitor. So while Gilbert was writing the book of the new opera in the spring of 1888 Sullivan decided that, since others were now as successful as Gilbert and himself, he would write no further operas in a light vein. Other factors were weighing heavily with Sullivan including D'Oyly Carte's plans to build a large theatre in which to produce English opera and the fact that Carl Rosa was producing grand opera at Drury Lane – a province in which Sullivan's conscience told him he should be leading the way. Gilbert replied to Sullivan's worries:

Why in the world are we to throw up the sponge and begin all over again because *Dorothy* has run 500 performances beats my comprehension. We have the best theatre, the best company, the best composer, and (though I say it) the best librettist in England working together – we are well known and as much an institution as Westminster Abbey – and to scatter this splendid organisation because *Dorothy* has run 500 nights is, to my way of thinking, to give up a gold mine. What is Dorothy's success to us? It is not even the same class of piece as ours. Is no piece but ours to run 500 or 600 nights? Did other companies dissolve because *Mikado* ran 650 nights?

As the first night approached Gilbert had fears that the opera would not meet with approval due to its serious nature. Both author and composer wanted last-minute alterations and neither wanted to give way. Sullivan wrote in his diary that at a complete dress rehearsal there was:

a regular flare-up. He worried everyone and irritated me beyond bearing – in one of his worst moods. I can't stand it any longer, and get as angry and irritable as he is. Eventually we made it up.

The opera opened on 3 October 1888. The overture was written in symphonic form, and the opening scene showed, not the usual rousing chorus, but the solitary figure of Jessie Bond playing Phoebe sitting by a spinning wheel – and singing sadly. There were other fairly serious numbers early in Act 1 and the audience had not expected such a departure from the traditional format. This opera was much more serious and its characters more real and given more interesting personalities by Gilbert than was usually the case. Indeed, the character of the jester Jack Point is often played so sadly when he loses his love that the tragedy of his loss is felt so keenly by the audience that his broken heart in the finale has sent audiences away blinking with damp and sympathetic eyes.

Courtice Pounds first appeared at the Savoy in this production playing Colonel Fairfax, George Grossmith played Jack Point and Geraldine Ulmar played Elsie Maynard. Grossmith and Ulmar sang the duet 'I have a song to sing, O' so well that it was encored three times.

The Yeomen of the Guard was a departure from Savoy traditions but audiences liked its colour and its songs and it ran for 423 performances. The opera opened on a Wednesday rather than on the customary Saturday for Savoy first nights. Gilbert was so nervous that he managed to unnerve everyone in sight. Jessie Bond, due to open the opera alone on the stage, had to beg Gilbert to get off the stage during the overture before he succeeded in reducing her to a quivering mass.

Richard Temple played Sergeant Meryll and on opening night Gilbert, suffering from nerves and gout, wanted Sullivan to cut Temple's song 'A laughing boy but yesterday'. It remained for that night but was soon deleted to help make a rather lighter sequence of songs. On this first night Gilbert, for a change, went off to Drury Lane and watched the play being performed there before returning round the corner to the Savoy for yet another ovation. Sullivan's diary recorded of the first night:

I was awfully nervous and continued so until the duet 'Heighday' which settled the fate of the opera. Its success was tremendous . . . After that, everything went on wheels, and I think its success is even greater than *The Mikado*.

A major source of ideas for Gilbert was an historical novel entitled *The Tower of London* written by Harrison Ainsworth in 1840. The plot of *The Yeomen of the Guard* was thought by many to

Overleaf:
The Graphic in an issue from October 1888 illustrated its front page with these scenes from *The Yeomen of the Guard*. In the main picture the condemned Fairfax is greeted by the Lieutenant of the Tower, Sir Richard Cholmondeley – the only true historical character in any of the Gilbert and Sullivan operas.

121

Phœbe Meryll (Miss Jessie Bond) and
Wilfred Shadbolt (Mr. W. H. Denny)
"Were I thy Bride"

Phoebe Meryll
(Miss Jessie Bond)

Sergeant Meryll
(Mr. Richard Temple)

be too close to that of a popular opera by William Wallace entitled *Maritana* (1845). *Punch* renamed the new Savoy opera 'The Beefeater's Bride, or The Merryman and his Maritana' – by the unknown team of Sulbert and Gillivan. But Gilbert also used one of his Bab Ballads, 'Annie Protheroe', where a girl was in love with a headsman who had his favourite notices pasted into a book.

The opera received many appreciative press notices. The *Morning Advertiser*, writing of the song Sullivan mentioned above – 'I have a song to sing, O' – believed:

Sir Arthur Sullivan has never written anything more delicately melodious and elegant.

The *Daily Telegraph* reported of Sullivan:

We place the songs and choruses of *The Yeomen of the Guard* before all his previous efforts of this particular kind. Thus the music follows the book to a higher plane, and we have the genuine English opera, forerunner of many others, let us hope.

Gilbert cannot have been pleased by the comment in *The Times*:

Mr Gilbert is in his way a man of genius, and even at his worst is a head and shoulders above the ordinary librettist. In the present instance he has not written a good play but his lyrics are suave and good to sing and, wedded to Sir Arthur Sullivan's melodies, they will no doubt find their way to many a home where English song is sung . . . Sullivan's score is fully equal to previous achievements, and the success of the piece will no doubt be largely due to it.

Sullivan believed *The Yeomen of the Guard* to be his best joint work with Gilbert; and Gilbert, as already noted, thought that this opera was one of the three best that he had produced in collaboration with Sullivan. Neither librettist nor composer had found this opera especially easy to write. It had taken Gilbert five months to write the words. Sullivan found some of the verses very difficult to set, and yet some of the music shows Sullivan at his most inventive. In Phoebe's song 'Were I thy bride', and Jack Point's 'I've wisdom from the east and from the west', Sullivan provided the singer with one melody and the orchestra with another and very different one and the result was sparkling. The songs of Act 2 are so fine that they might be described as Sullivan's second string of musical pearls. The walls of the Norman keep were authentically represented on stage as were both the uniforms and the accoutrements of the warders.

Following a Royal Command performance of *The Golden Legend* at the Albert Hall, Queen Victoria had urged Sullivan to write a grand opera. He viewed the suggestion as a command in itself, and he knew that in such a situation the composer would be the dominant partner.

D'Oyly Carte and Sullivan were always much closer in terms of friendship than either was with Gilbert. Sullivan was D'Oyly Carte's best man when he married Helen Lenoir at the Savoy Chapel in 1888. D'Oyly Carte's first wife had died about three years before. On his re-marriage to his secretary and business associate, he settled in Adelphi Terrace in an Adam house where he installed that almost unheard of luxury – a lift. When D'Oyly Carte built the Savoy Hotel, opening it in 1889, adjoining the Savoy Theatre – there was a connecting study between the two buildings for the impresario – Sullivan became a director of the hotel, but not the playwright. It was Sullivan whom D'Oyly Carte involved in his vision to plan a new theatre for performances of grand opera. The triumvirate was not seen by Gilbert as having equal balance. He felt left out and his relationship with Sullivan

The Royal English Opera House was opened by Richard D'Oyly Carte in 1891 as a home for English grand opera, but it was sold in 1892 and became the Palace Theatre of Varieties.

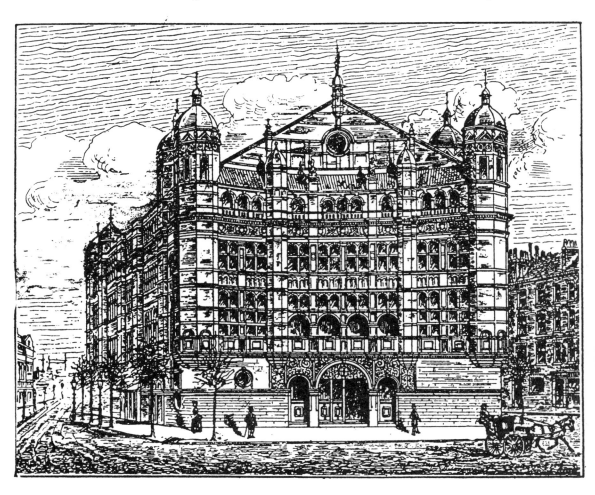

was always formal. They always addressed each other on surname terms and, astonishingly, it appears that they were never photographed together.

Late in 1888 Helen D'Oyly Carte laid the first stone of D'Oyly Carte's new grand theatre – the Royal English Opera House in Cambridge Circus which opened in 1891. Gilbert, Sullivan and D'Oyly Carte were all present on this occasion. The latter wanted Sullivan to write a grand opera for its opening and for Gilbert to write the book but Gilbert demurred firmly. He wrote to Sullivan in February 1889 that their real successes had been the more comic of their operas:

Such a subject as *The Yeomen* is far more congenial to my taste than the burlesque of *Iolanthe* or *The Mikado* – but I think we should be risking everything in writing more seriously still.

D'Oyly Carte would soon need a new opera for the Savoy since ticket sales for *The Yeomen of the Guard* dropped in the early part of 1889. It was Gilbert's idea that Sullivan should work with a more serious librettist on a grand opera – even suggesting Julian Sturgis with whom Sullivan, taking up the suggestion, eventually worked on *Ivanhoe*, but that at the same time Sullivan should write the next Savoy opera with himself. But Sullivan was in one of his moods of not wanting to write any further comic operas and the collaborators corresponded in an increasingly heated fashion, and long-distance at that since Sullivan was in the Mediterranean with the Prince of Wales. As before, each thought that the work of the other took too great a share in the production. Gilbert's stance became as firm as Sullivan's:

If you are earnest when you say that you wish to write an opera with me in which the music shall be the first consideration . . . there is most certainly no 'modus vivendi' to be found that shall be satisfactory to both of us. You are an adept in your profession, and I am an adept at mine. If we meet, it must be as master and master – not as master and servant.

The Gondoliers

The next and twelfth opera in the total collaboration was *The Gondoliers* set in Venice and this is regarded by many as their firm favourite. It was an opera which very nearly did not get completed. Gilbert had begun the planning of this opera in his plot-book but stopped work abruptly on the project when he read a letter that Sullivan had written to D'Oyly Carte demanding more of a voice in how the musical parts of the operas were presented on stage. Sullivan had said that the operas were pieces written by Gilbert with music added on by himself. Gilbert then wrote to Sullivan telling him that his letter teemed with unreasonable

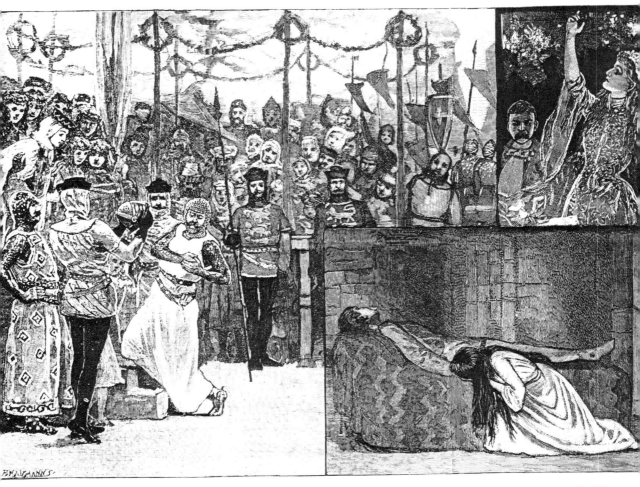

Scenes from the new opera of *Ivanhoe*.

demands and groundless accusations. D'Oyly Carte met Sullivan in Paris and told the latter of Gilbert's next plot set in Venice. This idea interested Sullivan who had recently been to Venice; and so Sullivan found himself agreeing to write the grand opera *Ivanhoe* to open D'Oyly Carte's new theatre and, at the same time, to set the next Savoy opera. In May 1889 Gilbert and Sullivan shook hands and buried the hatchet, and within a few days Sullivan wrote to his collaborator:

I understand from Carte that you had some subject connected with Venice and Venetian life, and this seemed to me to hold out great chances of bright colours and taking music. Can you not develop this with something we can both go into with warmth and enthusiasm, and thus give me a subject in which – like *The Mikado* or *Patience* – we can both be interested?

Sullivan composed the music of *The Gondoliers* during the

126

summer and also that for *Ivanhoe* at the same time. Gilbert, realising that the composer was under stress, even suggested having the opening of this next Savoy opera delayed if necessary, and he was as helpful as he was able to be:

Dear Sullivan – will this do? If it don't, then send it back and I'll try again.
Yours very truly, WSG

Sullivan was far from well – often arriving home exhausted, sleeping for only an hour and sometimes feeling too tired and ill to attend rehearsals. But he knew that he had the work to complete and, however tired he was at night, he managed to compose such gems as 'Try we lifelong we can never straighten out life's tangled skein', 'Dance a cachucha' and 'When a merry maiden marries' without a hint in the music of his low physical condition at the time.

Sullivan's insistence that the music had to be more prominent on this occasion resulted in the opening of Act 1 being free from dialogue for almost twenty minutes. Hence, *The Gondoliers* has the longest vocal score in the series and few of the pages in the libretto are of dialogue. Sullivan had demanded more of a share for the music and Gilbert saw to it that he got just that, but Sullivan, ironically, soon complained:

There is a good deal more work in it than there was in *The Yeomen* for nearly all the numbers are rapid. You will hear very little slow music in it. Of course the result is that there are more pages in the score. Two minutes *Allegro* means perhaps twenty pages, but with an *Andante* movement you would only use about six.

Eight musical numbers from *The Gondoliers* had to be re-set by Sullivan before they were regarded as acceptable.

Since *The Yeomen of the Guard* continued to attract good houses, there was no rush for *The Gondoliers*. Indeed, Gilbert took almost five months to finish the libretto and Sullivan wrote the music during an extended period in the summer of 1889. It is likely that each spent longer on this opera than on any of those already produced. Final preparations, however, were as rushed as usual. The first rehearsal for the orchestra occurred only five days before the opening, after which Sullivan worked during the night until three o'clock in the morning to write the overture. At this stage librettist and composer had not even decided on the title for the opera. The dress rehearsal itself took an astonishing seven hours.

The Gondoliers is an amusing satire on republicanism and social snobbery in its various forms. But this opera was also, in reflection, a tale about Gilbert and Sullivan themselves – the two

Overleaf:
The Gondoliers was given a command performance at Windsor Castle in March 1891 – the first occasion on which Victoria had permitted a dramatic entertainment in the castle since the death of her husband thirty years earlier.

gondoliers ruled jointly and in unison and this, similarly, was the only way in which the partners as creators found true fulfilment in their stage work.

George Grossmith had left the company in August 1889 to renew his career in music halls, and so Frank Wyatt played the comic lead as the Duke of Plaza-Toro. Courtice Pounds and Rutland Barrington played the gondoliers Marco and Giuseppi; and Rosina Brandram, Geraldine Ulmar and Jessie Bond played, respectively, the Duchess of Plaza-Toro, Gianetta and Tessa. W. H. Denny played Don Alhambra and eighteen-year-old Decima Moore appeared in one of the leading parts as Casilda:

I was in a whirl. I walked on, took one look at the audience and gulped. Then I saw Sullivan's face beaming up at me from the conductor's stand, and my confidence returned.

The Gondoliers opened on 7 December 1889. The *Sunday Times* reported the opera as a 'Great Success':

May it go forth to the world that the distinguished collaborators to whom the present generation is indebted for some of its most delightful entertainment have scored a great triumph.

The *Daily Telegraph* said it all when it announced:

The Gondoliers conveys an impression of having been written *con amore*.

Interestingly, the *Echo* attempted an explanation of the tremendous appeal which these operas held for audience after audience:

It is not an opera or play; it is simply an entertainment – the most exquisite, the daintiest entertainment we have ever seen.

Indeed, neither Gilbert nor Sullivan seemed at times quite sure what to call these Savoy pieces. They used the term comic opera rather than operetta but the descriptive billing varied from 'An entirely original grotesque opera' (*Thespis*); 'A novel and entirely original dramatic cantata' (*Trial by Jury*); 'An entirely original nautical comic opera' (*H.M.S. Pinafore*); 'A new and original melo-dramatic opera' (*The Pirates of Penzance*); 'A new and original aesthetic opera' (*Patience*); 'An original fairy opera' (*Iolanthe*); 'A new and original supernatural opera' (*Ruddigore*).

The critic of *Punch* disagreed with most other assessments:

While admiring the composer's skill, I feel constrained to call attention to the poverty of the plot and the miserable dullness of the dialogue.

There would not be a chance for the opera had the authors' names been Smith and Brown. But British cant in excelsis converts the auditorium of the Savoy into a kind of conventicle, where people sit and follow the book as if at church. I noticed more eyes fixed on the books than on the stage. It was like a congregation following the singing of Hymns Ancient and Modern. I suppose the hymns sung on this occasion were not exactly ancient but they were not so modern that they had not been employed by Sir Arthur before.

Nonetheless, Gilbert was pleased and relieved that *The Gondoliers* was generally so well-received and he wrote to Sullivan:

I must thank you for the magnificent work you have put into this piece. It gives one the chance of shining right through the twentieth century with a reflected light.

Sullivan, equally delighted, responded:

A drawing which appeared in the *Graphic* in December 1889 illustrating the quintet from Act 1 of *The Gondoliers*.

Don't talk of reflected light. In such a perfect book as *The Gondoliers* you shine with an individual brilliancy which no other writer can hope to attain.

Some costumes in the opera of *Ivanhoe*.

In 1890 Gilbert sold his home in Kensington and moved to a mansion at Harrow Weald which was to be his final home. It had been called Graeme's Dyke – but he promptly renamed it Grim's Dyke. It was a large house with spacious gardens and in them he dug out a large lake.

The Gondoliers had a lengthy run of 554 performances, until the summer of 1891. There had been a Command Performance at Windsor Castle in March 1891. Queen Victoria's diary recorded:

132

The music, which I know and am fond of, is quite charming throughout and was well acted and sung.

D'Oyly Carte's new theatre opened with *Ivanhoe* on 31 January 1891. The opera ran for six nights every week and two casts of principals were prepared to allow for this continuous run. The opera had 155 performances – an astonishing number for a grand opera. Perhaps D'Oyly Carte was at fault in not encouraging and planning further ahead for other viable ventures to follow it, for his Royal English Opera House did not long succeed but was turned into a music hall – as the Palace Theatre – in 1892. Gilbert's hostile attitude to D'Oyly Carte's new theatre had created problems for the latter, for it is likely that part of his plan had been to produce the Gilbert and Sullivan operas, as well as grand operas, at the Royal English Opera House and perhaps lease the Savoy Theatre. D'Oyly Carte had invested lavishly for *Ivanhoe*, providing Sullivan with a magnificent theatre, an orchestra of over sixty players and accomplished singers. One song especially – 'Ho! Jolly Jenkin' – became a favourite of Victorians for many years. Some critics enthused about *Ivanhoe* but others felt that Sullivan's true vocation lay with the Savoy.

Gilbert and Sullivan had already been at loggerheads again when *Ivanhoe* opened. Sullivan wrote to Gilbert that morning:

Let your presence at the theatre tonight be an intimation that you are as ready and willing as I am to think no more of what has happened . . . the enclosed stalls are not what I should have liked to send you, but the Royalties have taken two boxes out of six.

Gilbert did not attend the opening. He felt too aggrieved with Sullivan although he did go to see *Ivanhoe* a month later. What had happened to sully relations this time was nominally about the expense of a carpet for the Savoy but, even though Gilbert was technically correct, in reality the disagreement had more to do with Gilbert's precise mind and exaggerated sense of wounded pride. Gilbert had returned with his wife from a cruise to India and was astonished and angry to discover that £4,500 had gone on expenses including £500 on carpets for the front of the Savoy; though, in truth, the carpet of which Gilbert complained so bitterly was really only £140. He attacked D'Oyly Carte with such verbal force that matters seemed to be hopelessly estranged. Gilbert's position was that a carpet was not a repair and that the partners were not responsible for wear-and-tear. The controversy raged. Gilbert wrote to Sullivan in May 1890 to let him know that he had informed D'Oyly Carte that he was not to produce any of his libretti after Christmas 1890:

In point of fact after the withdrawal of *The Gondoliers*, our united work will be heard in public no more.

It angered Gilbert that Sullivan appeared to support D'Oyly Carte in this controversy. When Gilbert took the matter to court, Sullivan was distressed at 'seeing our names coupled in hostile antagonism over a few miserable pounds'. Their audiences were amazed to read in the press that they were quarrelling about a mere carpet when composer and librettist had each made £90,000 during the previous eleven years of the partnership. It was Helen D'Oyly Carte whose tact and perseverance eventually brought Gilbert and Sullivan together again for two final operas, but it was three more years before they worked together on the penultimate opera.

9 The Last Two Operas: 1893-96

Utopia Limited

Gilbert was not the man easily to forget a grudge and letters of accusation and counter-accusation continued to fly across London, but time works wonders and he cooled down once D'Oyly Carte had admitted that some of his charges in the accounts had been unintentional errors. Sullivan wrote to Gilbert:

Let us meet and shake hands. We can dispel the clouds hanging over us by setting up a counter-irritant in the form of a cloud of smoke.

They did meet and discussed plans for the next opera, although Sullivan was committed for a while with other work, but suggestions that Sullivan should work with Arthur Conan Doyle and J. M. Barrie did not bear fruit. Instead Sullivan composed the music for Sydney Grundy's opera *Haddon Hall* – not comic as the Savoy operas written with Gilbert had been, and yet not grand opera either. Gilbert had worked with Alfred Cellier on *The Mountebanks* – and so was able, at last, to present his beloved idea of a lozenge plot to the theatrical world. It was produced at the Lyric Theatre and had a successful run.

Sullivan was far from well. In the early months of 1892 he became seriously ill at Monte Carlo. The Prince of Wales ordered his personal surgeon to travel to France to examine Sullivan, and D'Oyly Carte also made the journey. An operation was impracticable since he was very weak and so injections of morphia had to suffice. On his return to England he stayed at Sandringham with the Prince and Princess of Wales.

Since the next opera was not ready in time, D'Oyly Carte

W. S. Gilbert reading the libretto of *Utopia Limited* to the Savoy Company in the Savoy Theatre. François Cellier, Arthur Sullivan, Helen and Richard D'Oyly Carte, as well as stars of the Company such as Rutland Barrington, Rosina Brandram, Nancy McIntosh and Walter Passmore, can all be identified.

mounted *The Nautch Girl* by George Dance and with music by Edward Solomon in 1891 – the first time that a work of main billing that was not by Gilbert and Sullivan had appeared at the Savoy. It was followed in 1892 by a revival of *The Vicar of Bray* (Grundy/Solomon). Then by *Haddon Hall* (Grundy/Sullivan) later that year.

It was at his final home, Grim's Dyke, that Gilbert sat down to write *Utopia Limited*. Perhaps the recent success of *The Gondoliers* encouraged him to place the new opera even further afield geographically. He chose a South Sea island that was visited by typical Victorian officials who accompanied a returning princess whose education at Girton College, Cambridge, was now over.

The satire was in the folly of attempting to transport English systems and ideas to this idyllic, sunny spot. Sullivan was recovering slowly from the illness which could well have killed him. He took the story for *Utopia Limited* with him on his return to the Riviera in search of sunshine and Gilbert visited him in France, in the villa which he rented, to discuss this next opera further. From France, early in 1893, Gilbert wrote home to his wife:

Dearest Kits,
. . . the reading went off *most successfully* – both Sullivan and Grove enthusiastic – declaring it's the best plot I've done. We have arranged all business matters on a satisfactory footing. This is a pleasant house standing in an orange garden close to the sea – everything very nice and comfortable and informal. A.S. extremely pleasant and hospitable and much disappointed that I leave as soon as Sunday . . . Probably be home Thursday evening. I'll wire to Guerany to have a fly ready, so don't trouble to send. Goodbye, old lady – no end of love from
Your affectionate
Old Boy

Sullivan returned home, but premature ageing, weariness and illness had all taken their toll. The two partners had not worked together in harness for three years. They had problems with this opera but both appeared genuinely to want their joint efforts to succeed. Each demanded the right to inject additions and to make changes and, had they both not tried to remain cool on this occasion, drama would easily have been sparked. Gilbert wrote to Sullivan:

I will come on Thursday as you suggest. I assume that you are not averse to standing a bit of bread and cheese and a drop of beer to a pore working man wots bin out of work for some years?

One source of disagreement was the role in the opera of Lady Sophy – the governess to the princesses. Sullivan objected firmly that her role was that of another ageing predatory woman at whom Gilbert delighted to poke fun. The finale was another problem area. Eventually, Gilbert asked Sullivan to compose a finale before he had written the words! He then wrote words that fitted the music, telling Sullivan:

It is mere doggerel – but words written to music are sure to be that. You may chop this about just as you please.

But Gilbert proved to be correct in his assessment and so within days of the opening the finale was dropped. Sullivan then set music to words which Gilbert provided in their usual way of working and the new finale was much more satisfactory.

Gilbert's gout bothered him so badly that during rehearsals he appeared at the theatre using crutches. The production at the Savoy was lavish and the bill totalled about £7,200 – probably the highest sum expended on any Savoy production. The opera ran for 245 performances and this was not a lengthy run by Savoy standards. Sullivan complained about the high cost of the production. For instance, there were to be four Gentlemen at Arms. Gilbert replied:

Dear Sullivan
. . . you must remember that these four people must be dressed *somehow*, they can't go naked (unless you insist on it), and if they are put into good uniforms they will cost at least £50 apiece.

Neither composer nor librettist simply wrote these operas and then left others to produce them. They remained intimately involved with all stages – before, during and after the first night.

Unusually, a public rehearsal to which the press were invited was held on the evening before the first performance. The theatre was crowded and neither Gilbert nor Sullivan stopped the flow on many occasions to make suggestions. Gilbert had long believed that various poor press criticisms for some previous operas were caused by an imperfect appreciation of the operas after seeing only one performance. When this full dress rehearsal was finished, Gilbert spoke to the audience of his pleasure in working once more with the company. Those on stage then gave him three cheers. Sullivan spoke next and D'Oyly Carte listened – thankful that opera number thirteen was proceeding so well.

Utopia Limited was first performed on 7 October 1893. People queued for admittance from the morning right through the day. This was the first new Gilbert and Sullivan opera to be presented

The imported Flowers of Progress in *Utopia Limited* were seated across the stage like Christy Minstrels.

to the public in four years and interest was enormous. The casting of the opera demanded several very accomplished singers and a number of these were comedy roles.

Gilbert was no longer in any physical condition to walk the pavements of the Embankment on first nights:

I have an effective method of dealing with first nights which I can strongly recommend. As the curtain rises on Act 1, I leave the theatre and do not return until 11.15. I usually spend the interval at some other theatre – if possible – where there is a dull and highly unoriginal comedy, with plenty of platitudinarian dialogue and a violent plot. This cheers me and puts me on good terms with myself.

On the first night of *Utopia Limited* a number of old Savoyards were in the audience, including Jessie Bond and George Grossmith. Sullivan received a long ovation when he entered the auditorium to conduct the orchestra. The scene was emotional and charged with sentiment and excitement, and the audience was well-pleased with *Utopia Limited*. After the first night's show was completed, Gilbert and Sullivan appeared on stage from opposite sides to a storm of applause – Gilbert managing without his crutches – and they shook hands before their adoring public.

Nancy McIntosh appeared as Princess Zara. Gilbert had heard her singing at a party and he asked Sullivan to audition her. She was later adopted by the Gilberts and lived with them at their home. Rutland Barrington appeared as King Paramount and Rosina Brandram as Lady Sophy. Walter Passmore played Tarara, the Public Exploder, and he was to become a worthy successor to George Grossmith in the comic lead parts.

The actors and actresses at the Savoy in these later years had to play a wide variety of parts – and not only in the Gilbert and Sullivan operas. After *The Gondoliers* ended, for instance, the company played roles in the pieces written by others. The D'Oyly Cartes were eager to keep the company intact even when there was no new Gilbert and Sullivan opera to stage. Rutland Barrington, Courtice Pounds, Jessie Bond, Frank Wyatt and W. H. Denny played in *The Nautch Girl* in 1891. Rutland Barrington, Courtice Pounds, Rosina Brandram and W. H. Denny all appeared in *The Vicar of Bray* in 1892; and the same four appeared in *Haddon Hall* later in 1892. Rutland Barrington, Walter Passmore, Rosina Brandram and Decima Moore appeared in *Jane-Annie* in 1893. The libretto for this piece had been written by J. M. Barrie and Arthur Conan Doyle, and the music was by Ernest Ford.

It appears that Gilbert's infatuation with the American Nancy McIntosh ran deep. She was a singer but not an actress – despite being tutored in the latter area by Gilbert himself. The libretto seems to have been prepared in such a way that she was afforded too much of a star role. Other characters, in comparison, King Paramount apart, received scant attention and their roles are less than satisfactory because they are ill-developed.

The set had been designed by Hawes Craven, one of Henry Irving's designers from the Lyceum Theatre. The throne-room in Act 2 had arches and many lights on the walls and others hung down from fixtures that appeared to be strings of diamonds. The view through open doors to the moon and the sea was described by one critic as the most beautiful scene ever put on a London stage. The costumes and uniforms were colourful and impressive.

Gilbert enjoyed his jibes at political parties in the words he gave to Princess Zara:

No political measures will endure because one Party will assuredly undo all that the other Party has done; inexperienced civilians will govern your Army and your Navy; no social reforms will be attempted because out of vice, squalor and drunkenness no political capital is to be made; and while grouse is to be shot, and foxes worried to death, the legislative action of the country will be at a standstill. Then there will be sickness in plenty, endless lawsuits, crowded jails, interminable confusion in the Army, and in short, general and unexampled prosperity!

The *Daily Telegraph* described these words as 'the bitterest speech Mr Gilbert has ever penned'. Gilbert promptly cut some of the more controversial parts in the above passage. He did not view himself as an out-and-out rebel but as an entertainer of audiences. Gilbert told one reporter that the opera was only political in a very general sense and that it had:

nothing of a party character. It doesn't do to divide the house.

It has been suggested that Gilbert overshot the mark in parodying the English Court – referring to customs 'of the Court of St James's Hall', the latter being an entertainment of minstrels; and that the Royal Family were irritated by such clowning. But it is improbable that any annoyance was actually aroused.

Many of the critics were generous in praise of the new opera. The socialist George Bernard Shaw, who was the critic for *The World*, described *Utopia Limited* as the most enjoyable of the Savoy operas. Shaw went out of his way to praise D'Oyly Carte (more than Gilbert or Sullivan) for his major role in effecting changes in theatrical management. But the dramatic critic of the *Pall Mall Gazette*, a leading Tory paper, found the opera perhaps the most depressing of all the Gilbert and Sullivan collaborations. A correspondent for *Vanity Fair* remarked:

Everybody went to the Savoy Theatre on Saturday last predetermined in

Rosina Brandram as Lady Sophy in *Utopia Limited* with the two young princesses played by Emmie Owen and Florence Perry.

favour of a huge success. On every face there was a smile. In every heart there echoed an encore.

The *Daily News* noted of Act 1 – which had lasted for over one hundred minutes:

It was recognised that the first act could be better for being shortened.

The *Pall Mall Gazette* was even more forthright:

It is always a melancholy business when a writer is driven to repeat himself. *Utopia Limited* is a mirthless travesty of the work with which Gilbert's name is most genuinely associated. The quips, jests, the theory of topsy-turvy, the principle of paradox, the law of the unlikely, seem to have grown old in a single night.

141

But another paper referred to the prosperous restoration of the historic triumvirate of Gilbert, Sullivan and D'Oyly Carte. Not all the critics praised Sullivan's music – speaking of a dearth of fetching tunes and one critic was even more to the point:

It would be altogether unreasonable to expect the musician of more than a dozen comic operas to go on producing strains new in character and expression.

The cost of mounting this opera had been so high that the Savoy Theatre lost money in the production. It was now 1894 and many years had elapsed since Gilbert and Sullivan had given the theatre-goers of London *Thespis* in 1871. Public tastes were changing and D'Oyly Carte, writing to Gilbert about the limited run of *Utopia Limited*, felt:

There is no doubt in my mind that what the public want now is simply 'fun' and little else.

The Grand Duke

Two more years were to go by before *The Grand Duke*, the fourteenth and final Gilbert and Sullivan opera, appeared at the Savoy. In the meantime, Sullivan worked again with Burnand and they produced the comic opera *The Chieftain*, about a band of brigands in Spain. This was a reworked expansion of their much earlier work *The Contrabandista*. D'Oyly Carte then let the Savoy for a season to the Carl Rosa Opera Company after which it was closed for several months. *The Mikado* was revived towards the end of 1895 and ran for 127 performances – a longer run than that of *The Grand Duke* which followed it. Indeed, there were six matinée performances of *The Mikado* during the run of *The Grand Duke* as well as a further revival of *The Mikado* (with a run of 226 performances) after *The Grand Duke* had been withdrawn.

In 1871 Gilbert and Sullivan had written their first joint opera, *Thespis*, about a company of actors who changed roles with the gods on Mount Olympus and within a year had turned the world upside down. That opera had been moderately well-received. Twenty-five years later in 1896 their last joint venture, *The Grand Duke*, had a rather similar plot in which a band of theatrical players attempted to take over the running of a kingdom. Also each opera had a Greek scene. This last opera, like *Thespis*, had only a moderate success.

In August 1895 Gilbert read the plot of the new opera to Sullivan and Sullivan soon wrote to him:

My dear Gilbert,
I have studied the sketch plot very carefully and like it even more than I

did when I heard it first on Thursday. It comes out as clear and bright as possible. I shall be very pleased to set it, and am prepared to begin (as soon as you have anything ready for me) and have written to Carte to tell him so.

Helen D'Oyly Carte had been instrumental in getting Gilbert and Sullivan to work together for just one more opera. Her energy was even more necessary as the production went forward to rehearsal for D'Oyly Carte was not well, Sullivan was in agony from his long-standing kidney problem and Gilbert had a severe attack of gout. In 1894 Gilbert, then only fifty-eight, had written:

I am a crumbling man – a magnificent ruin, no doubt, but still a ruin – and like all ruins I look best by moonlight. Give me a sprig of ivy and an owl under my arm and Tintern Abbey would not be in it with me.

It appears that Gilbert knew that *The Grand Duke* would be his last effort in collaboration with Sullivan. Perhaps surprisingly, in view of all that Sullivan had said over the years, it was not to be Sullivan's last comic opera. Gilbert was becoming weary of devising plots. The twist at the end of *The Grand Duke* was contrived and hardly funny. The complexity of the story-line shows that the old Gilbert was no more; his creativity had become stilted, and his plot was mechanical and complex.

When rehearsals commenced in January 1896 Gilbert's gout was so troublesome that he had to be carried to the stage. A great deal of re-writing occurred after rehearsals had commenced. Once George Grossmith had decided to leave the company it seems that Gilbert decided to cut down the part of the Grand Duke Rudolph to a minor role, for it is clear that he had originally written the part specifically for George Grossmith to play. Richard Temple and Jessie Bond decided not to appear in the new opera. In her memoire Jessie Bond explains that her forthcoming marriage was not regarded by Gilbert as a good enough reason for her leaving the company:

When I told Gilbert he was so angry that I don't think he ever quite forgave me; he would not accept my health as an excuse, he was unreasonable as, alas, he often was!
'You are a little fool!' he said . . . Neither he nor Arthur Sullivan sent me a wedding present.

It seems that Gilbert was so irritated by Jessie Bond's sudden decision to leave the Savoy that he wrote his anger into the story when he finalised the libretto. He made Julia Jellicoe in the plot abandon her engagement to Ernest and, as a professional obligation, play the Grand Duchess instead. In the words Gilbert gave to the Notary:

Though marriage contracts – or whate'er you call 'em – are very solemn,
Dramatic contracts (which you all adore so) are even more so.

Despite the tired plot, Sullivan was able to write some beautiful pieces including the quintet in Act 1 'Strange the views some people hold'; the procession that opens Act 2 'As before you we defile'; the 'Brindisi' for Baroness von Krakenfeldt and the 'Roulette Song' for the Prince of Monte Carlo. Yet many of his other melodies in this opera were commonplace.

D'Oyly Carte had worked hard to produce striking scenery and costumes. The company was accomplished – including Rutland Barrington, Walter Passmore (who played the comic lead of the Grand Duke Rudolph), C. H. Workman, Rosina Brandram and Ruth Vincent. A Hungarian singer, Ilka von Palmay, played the English heroine – her accent providing a useful contrast between that spoke by the citizens of Pfennig-Halbpfennig and that of the English Julia Jellicoe whose part she played. Scott Fishe played the Prince of Monte Carlo. As with the role of Inez in *The Gondoliers*, he did not need to go on stage until near the end of the opera. Indeed, he did not appear on stage until about eleven o'clock on the opening night, so he spent time earlier in the evening at his club. People who saw him there assumed that Gilbert had had a fit of anger and had dismissed him from the cast! Charles Kenningham played the theatrical manager, Ernest Dummkopf. Kenningham had been in *Ivanhoe* at D'Oyly Carte's other theatre and so was an unusual singer in that he had managed a foot in each of Sullivan's and D'Oyly Carte's camps.

Gilbert did with the libretto of *The Grand Duke* precisely what he had done with *Utopia Limited* when he had extended the part of Princess Zara for Nancy McIntosh. The new agreement banned Nancy McIntosh from appearing in *The Grand Duke* because of her limited acting ability. Hence, Gilbert looked round and found Ilka von Palmay singing at Drury Lane Theatre. Strangely, she was the cause of an injunction several years previously brought by D'Oyly Carte when the Royal Court Theatre in Berlin wanted her to appear in *Der Mikado* in the male role of Nanki-Poo! On this occasion Gilbert introduced the part of Julia Jellicoe especially for Ilka von Palmay – the part was not even envisaged in the original outline – and several numbers (an aria, a recitation and three duets) were hastily prepared for her to sing. This late introduction of the character of Julia Jellicoe served merely to provide Ilka von Palmay with a major part. It added little to an already confused story-line but rather interrupted its flow.

The opera opened at the Savoy on 7 March 1896. Sullivan recorded, as usual after a first night: 'success great and genuine' but, though the audience was enthusiastic, this was a forlorn hope

144

of a successful run rather than a description of reality. Gilbert was more practical in his assessment and wrote of *The Grand Duke*:

I'm not at all a proud Mother, and I never want to see the ugly misshapen little brat again!

The *Court Circular* was kindly in its comment:

Once more Mr Gilbert and Sir Arthur Sullivan have added to the gaiety of the nation.

Musical Standards reported:

It is absurd, of course, to expect a mine to be workable for ever, and it is equally absurd to pretend that one can observe no falling-off in the quality of the precious stones brought to the surface . . . In Mr Gilbert's libretto one of the characters, for the sake of rhyme, pronounces ghost as ghoest, and we may be pardoned if we call *The Grand Duke* a ghoest of a Gilbert and Sullivan opera.

The *Manchester Courier* reported accurately:

This theatre has now achieved such a position that a first night success is a foregone conclusion, and does not of necessity mean that the piece is either remarkably good or sure of lasting popularity.

The *Sketch*, writing of Sullivan's contribution, noted:

The music, it may be said, hardly clings to the ears, the melodies are somewhat elusive.

But the *Times* was forthright in its criticism of *The Grand Duke*:

Signs are not wanting that the rich vein which the collaborators and their followers have worked for so many years is at last dangerously near exhaustion. This time the libretto is very conspicuously inferior to the music. There are still a number of excellent songs, but the dialogue seems to have lost much of its crispness.

The critic on the *Pall Mall Gazette* was perhaps poking vicious fun at Gilbert's complexity of plot in this opera rather than at Sullivan's music when he wrote in equally complex terms:

The musically described secret sign of the Sausage Roll has broad elements of the most laughable burlesque, combined with so rare a refinement that one's laughter is ever upon the edge of gravity, yet ever rebutting and defeating gravity so victoriously that laughter here attains a responsibility which belongs to it rarely in the range of humour.

After the opening, Sullivan went off to Monte Carlo, writing to his friend, the librettist Burnand:

I arrived here dead beat and feel better already. Another week's rehearsal with WSG and I should have gone raving mad. I had already ordered some straw for my hair.

He travelled next to Lucerne and had a brief romance with twenty-one year old Violet Zillah Beddington with whom he went so far as to propose marriage.

The Grand Duke had the briefest run of any Gilbert and Sullivan opera, except for *Thespis*. Musical tastes were undergoing changes. Musical comedies became the rage in the 1890s, and *The Grand Duke* was produced at the time of such popular pieces as *Geisha* at Daly's Theatre.

In the aftermath of the recent disagreements, a new contract now allowed D'Oyly Carte to produce revivals of the Gilbert and Sullivan operas at the Savoy once again. *The Grand Duke* ran for a mere 123 performances. When it was withdrawn *The Mikado* was revived, followed by *The Yeomen of the Guard*, *The Gondoliers*, *The Sorcerer* with *Trial by Jury*, *H.M.S. Pinafore*, *The Pirates of Penzance* and *Patience*. It was during the last of these revivals that Sullivan died on 22 November 1900. Richard D'Oyly Carte followed him within a few months on 3 April 1901. Gilbert survived much longer – until 29 May 1911.

10 Separate Ways, Revivals and Demises

From 1896 Sullivan kept going his round of social visiting including royal associations, his visits to race meetings and his interest in gambling, although he suffered from pain for much of the time. It is likely that he understood that he had possibly now a short time left to live, and his thoughts turned again to serious music. He agreed to write a ballet for the Alhambra Theatre which was to be presented to celebrate Victoria's Diamond Jubilee, and at the beginning of 1897 he began to write this ballet in Monte Carlo at his usual winter villa and so *Victoria and Merrie England* was created. It was well-received and contained much the sort of music that Sullivan had written for the Savoy operas.

He left for Germany, travelled to Bayreuth and enjoyed *Die Meistersinger*, describing it as the best comic opera ever devised but he did not enthuse about Wagner's *The Ring*.

In the autumn of 1879, back in England, Sullivan considered writing a new opera for the Savoy with libretto by J. W. Comyns Carr assisted by Arthur Wing Pinero. He struggled to complete this opera, *The Beauty Stone*, but he found the libretto to be a mass of involved sentences and the practical problems were increased when the librettists adamantly refused to come to his aid by assisting with alterations that would have eased his musical difficulties. The opera was performed from the end of May 1898 but it had a run of only fifty nights – a bitter disappointment for all concerned. The complex dialogue had not helped the piece but the fact that the opera was not a comedy (but rather an opera comique in the French style with long musical scenes joined by bridging dialogue) did not seem to go down well with the audiences who expected, by long tradition, to see *comic* operas at the Savoy.

Arthur Sullivan in the 1890s, showing signs of strain and ill-health, seated at his desk holding a quill.

In October 1898 Sullivan conducted the Leeds Festival, and this was to be his last. The programme included a new work, Elgar's *Caractacus*. Sullivan's illness was now so pronounced that two other conductors were on standby in case he should be unable to appear.

Despite his weak condition, he planned another comic opera. Probably his friendship with D'Oyly Carte and the failure of the latter's other theatre made Sullivan feel partly responsible for helping to ensure that the Savoy Theatre continued to run as a viable enterprise. Later in 1898 Sullivan met Basil Hood and they decided to work together on a comic opera called *Hassan* which was to have an oriental flavour. Sullivan liked the libretto but influenza struck and he went first to the Riviera and then to

Switzerland and it was there that Hood travelled to meet him in mid-1899. The opera was started at that time but not completed until November when it was produced under the amended title *The Rose of Persia*. It became a box-office success and made more money for D'Oyly Carte than any Savoy offering since *The Gondoliers*. There were those who described the work as Sullivan's best. It ended its run of 213 performances in June 1900, the cast including Henry Lytton, Walter Passmore, Rosina Brandram, Decima Moore and many chorus members of very long standing.

When *The Rose of Persia* was taken off, the Savoy produced revivals of *The Pirates of Penzance* and *Patience*. At the end of 1899 Sullivan spent the winter – unusually – in London, but he travelled to Monte Carlo in February 1900 and yet he soon returned home again. In May he attempted to write a *Te Deum* of Thanksgiving for performance at St Paul's Cathedral to celebrate the conclusion of the Boer War. In June, Basil Hood delivered to Sullivan the outline for a new opera to be set in Ireland and called *The Emerald Isle*. Sullivan completed the *Te Deum* in July and this was his last finished work, and included his tune 'Onward Christian Soldiers' in the last chorus. In August and September he composed in Switzerland much of the music for *The Emerald Isle* but he was weary and ill and near the end. He returned to London in mid-September and for the next few months deteriorated still further. He was unable to attend the opening of the revival of *Patience* on 7 November and his absence from the Savoy on this occasion prompted a kindly letter from Gilbert. The latter must have gained some comfort from sending this letter, since the last occasion on which Gilbert and Sullivan are believed to have met was in the previous June but the meeting was a sad one in which they did not speak. Neither had they spoken, even on stage, at the first night of the revival of *The Sorcerer* and *Trial by Jury* on 22 September 1898, but had merely bowed to their audience from opposite ends of the stage. Sullivan's diary had recorded of that occasion:

Opera went very well. Call for Gilbert and self. We went on together but did not speak to each other.

Sullivan, now terminally ill with his recurring complaint, had also to contend with bronchitis. It had been Mrs D'Oyly Carte's idea to have Gilbert, Sullivan and her husband all appear on stage to take a bow for the revival of *Patience* in November 1900 – and that all three should appear in bath-chairs! Sullivan was too ill to attend but he wrote:

Pray tell Gilbert how very much I feel the disappointment. Good luck to you all. Three invalid chairs would have looked *very well* from the front.

Only Gilbert and D'Oyly Carte walked on stage at the end of the performance – each holding a walking-stick and looking a little like Chelsea pensioners. A week or so before Sullivan died he received the following letter from Gilbert who was preparing to travel abroad for the sake of his health:

My dear Sullivan
I would be glad to come up to town to see you before I go, but unfortunately in my present enfeebled condition, a carriage journey to London involves my lying down a couple of hours before I am fit for anything, besides stopping all night in town. The railway journey is still more fatiguing. I have lost 60 lbs in weight, and my arms and legs are of the consistency of cotton-wool. I sincerely hope to find you alright again on my return, and the new opera running merrily.
Yours very truly,
W. S. Gilbert

Sullivan had a heart attack on 22 November 1900 and this killed him. He was fifty-eight. By a quirk of fate it was St Cecilia's day – the patroness of music. Sullivan's nephew Herbert and his valet and housekeeper were present at his death. Mrs Ronalds arrived too late by cab. When Sullivan died, Gilbert and his wife were by then travelling in Egypt with Nancy McIntosh and they read of his death in the newspapers. Gilbert wrote to Herbert Sullivan from abroad:

My dear Sullivan,
I did not hear of your uncle's terribly sudden death until three days since, or I should have written to express my personal sorrow, and my sympathy with you in the great loss you have sustained. It is a satisfaction to me to feel that I was impelled, shortly before his death, to write to him to propose to shake hands over our recent differences, and even a greater satisfaction to learn through you that my offer of reconciliation was cordially accepted. I wish I had been in England that I might have had an opportunity of joining the mourners at his funeral.

Sullivan was buried in the crypt of St Paul's Cathedral despite his wish that he should be buried alongside his parents and brother in Brompton Cemetery. Indeed, the grave in Brompton Cemetery had actually been opened. The first part of the funeral was held in the Chapel Royal, St James's Palace. Sullivan's funeral procession travelled along the Embankment and Richard D'Oyly Carte, so ill at home that the news of Sullivan's death had been kept from him, chanced to look from his window in the Adelphi and saw the procession and somehow knew that he was saying farewell to his old friend. In St Paul's Cathedral the Band of the Scots Guards

Sir Arthur Sullivan's funeral at St Paul's Cathedral on 27 November 1900. The occasion was almost that of a state funeral by order of Queen Victoria. Flags on public buildings were flown at half-mast.

played, Victoria sent a wreath and the choir consisted of the Savoy Theatre company conducted by Alfred Cellier.

Edward German completed Sullivan's task and wrote the music for the outstanding section of *The Emerald Isle*. It was Sullivan's last work and this splendid piece, by way of a posthumous epitaph, was acclaimed when it appeared at the Savoy from April 1901 – achieving over 200 performances.

A memorial to Sullivan by Sir William Goscombe John was erected in the Embankment Gardens very close to the Savoy Theatre. It was unveiled in 1903. The inscription below the bust of Sullivan reads:

> Is life a boon?
> If so, it must befall
> That Death, whene'er he call
> Must call too soon!

151

The memorial to Sullivan in St Paul's Cathedral, designed by William Goscombe John.

The words are by Gilbert and come from *The Yeomen of the Guard*. When Gilbert was asked if he could select something from their joint works he wrote to Sullivan's nephew:

It is difficult to find anything quite fitted to so sad an occasion, but I think this might do.

In the north transept of St Paul's Cathedral there is another memorial to Sullivan, also designed by Sir William Goscombe John, including a medallion with Sullivan's head.

In his will Sullivan left personal bequests including those to Gilbert, Richard D'Oyly Carte and Mrs Ronalds; Herbert Sullivan was his residual legatee. In 1900 Sullivan left £54,000. In 1901 Richard D'Oyly Carte left £240,000. In 1911 Gilbert left £112,000. In 1913 Helen D'Oyly Carte (by then remarried) left £117,000.

Sullivan was sorely missed. He had been invariably courteous and kindly and rehearsed patiently, even when suffering physically. Henry Lytton, in his book *A Wandering Minstrel*, told the tale of a young singer who arrived early for an audition only to find no one about but a man sitting at a piano. The young singer admitted to the stranger that he was very nervous about meeting Sullivan; so the stranger suggested that he practised his songs there and then before Sullivan arrived. This they did together. Sullivan, of course, was the man at the piano and the singer got the job.

Richard D'Oyly Carte followed Sullivan to the grave remarkably quickly. He died a matter of months after Sullivan on 3 April 1901. He was fifty-six. A memorial window to him was designed by E. J. Priest for the Savoy Chapel and unveiled by Sir Henry Irving in 1902. The Savoy Theatre closed on four occasions in mourning – for the death of Sullivan and then again for his funeral, for the death of Queen Victoria in 1901 and for the death of Richard D'Oyly Carte. The Opéra Comique was now demolished and times were changing. By the 1899 revival of *H.M.S. Pinafore* only Richard Temple, playing Dick Deadeye, remained as a long-standing principal.

Helen D'Oyly Carte ran the Savoy Theatre single-handed after her husband's demise. She saw to the production of *The Emerald Isle*, after which there was a revival of *Iolanthe*. Then the theatre was let for several years to William Greet who produced Edward German's *Merrie England* there in 1902. Mrs D'Oyly Carte took over the running of the Savoy again in December 1906, when Gilbert personally supervised the stage direction of a revival of the Gilbert and Sullivan operas – Gilbert receiving £5,000 for performance rights for five years together with a rehearsal fee of

£200 for each opera produced.

In his mock-Tudor mansion on Harrow Weald, which had been his home since September 1890, Gilbert enjoyed being a gentleman landowner. He had a staff of forty looking after the house and grounds. He was appointed a Justice of the Peace in 1893 and was also made Deputy Lieutenant of the County of Middlesex. After the turn of the century he was free of gout, from 1902, and had nearly a decade more to live. He enjoyed keeping cats, dogs, monkeys, a donkey, a fawn and lemurs in his garden and home, and also had an interest in photography and conjuring. Dinner parties were held regularly at Grim's Dyke. Gilbert admired attractive women and delighted in amusing them. At his dinner parties it was frequently the men who were asked to withdraw after the meal – contrary to the usual custom – leaving Gilbert with the female guests! He journeyed to the Crimea to see the place which had fascinated him in his younger days. He began to visit the cinema and then bought an American Locomobile steam-car in 1902 in which he had his first motoring accident:

Grim's Dyke, Harrow Weald, was Gilbert's home from 1890 until 1911.

I made my début by spoiling a parson, who came round a dead wall on a bicycle. He was pretty badly hurt. The car was turned over at a ditch. I

153

was pitched over the dash-board onto my head . . . and my wife was pitched very comfortably into a hedge, where she looked like a large and quite unaccountable bird's nest.

Gilbert had written a libretto which Sullivan was unable to set in 1894 as he was considering other avenues, and this was set by Osmond Carr and appeared as *His Excellency* in October 1894 with Nancy McIntosh in the cast. But Carr was not a Sullivan and the opera suffered accordingly. *The Grand Duke* had been more than simply the end of the Gilbert and Sullivan partnership; for Gilbert did not work on a fully original piece for the Savoy again.

Gilbert's burlesque of *Hamlet* had appeared in 1891 as *Rosencrantz and Guildenstern* and was produced at the Vaudeville Theatre. His comic opera *The Mountebanks* for the Lyric, with music by Alfred Cellier, had a run of over two hundred performances. Gilbert also collaborated with George Grossmith (Junior) who wrote the music for his operetta *Haste to the Wedding*. Gilbert's play *The Fortune Hunter* opened in Birmingham in 1897 after which it moved on to Edinburgh where Gilbert kept an eye on the production. Whilst in Scotland he gave an interview to the *Evening Dispatch* of Edinburgh in which he admitted that his personal favourites amongst his own works were the two plays – *Gretchen* and *Broken Hearts* and the opera *The Yeomen of the Guard*. He said that he deplored French plays produced in England and had various comments to make about certain famous actors of the age, including Irving, Tree and Alexander, unwisely saying that they spoke blank verse dully and monotonously. The content of his interview with this reporter quickly reached London and the *Era* protested:

Mr Gilbert's abnormal self-esteem has with advancing years developed into a malady. In his own estimation he is a kind of Grand Llama or Sacred Elephant of dramatic literature. The mildest criticism of his work, the most gentle disapproval of one of his plays, is a crime of lèse-majesté for which, if it were in his power, he would punish the culprit severely . . . his real kindliness and good nature have simply been obscured by the abnormal protruberance of his bump of self esteem.

Gilbert took one look at this attack and demanded £1,000 in a lawcase during which he entertained the court with a display of his intelligence and humour. He told the court that he preferred to read hostile criticism because he knew how good he was, but he didn't know how bad he was. When asked to name a current bad play he mentioned the pantomime at Drury Lane. Counsel suggested to him that the pantomime only went on for a short time in the year – to which Gilbert retorted that it went on for a long time in the evening. When he was asked whether he was cool and calm on the particular occasion, he replied that he was calm and deliberate but that he didn't know his temperature at the time! The judge summed up:

The plaintiff, while objecting to criticism, has not been sparing in his criticism of others.

The jury could not agree amongst themselves and each side paid its own costs.

In 1898 Gilbert had taken an American journalist to court, claiming that she had misrepresented his views. Losing the case, he later wrote:

The Garrick Theatre was built by W. S. Gilbert and opened in 1889.

The Judge summed up like a drunken monkey – he is in the last stage of senile decay and knew absolutely nothing about the case.

In 1904 Gilbert produced his burlesque *The Fairy's Dilemma* for

the Garrick Theatre. He then had the satisfaction of seeing the Gilbert and Sullivan operas produced once again in an important series of revivals at the Savoy. When this 1906 season of revivals began in December Mrs D'Oyly Carte provided tea for those waiting in the queue, and the doors of the pit and gallery were opened earlier than usual. The *Observer* noted:

For to say that *The Yeomen of the Guard* was revived last night is to announce not the mere revival of a play, but the re-establishment of a national institution.

This time it was Gilbert and Helen D'Oyly Carte who received the ovations. It had been decided to produce *The Yeomen of the Guard*, *The Gondoliers* and *The Mikado* in London but the last of these was not staged and *Patience* was substituted. Prince Fushimi of Japan was to visit London and the Lord Chamberlain had decided that, in deference to Japanese feelings, *The Mikado* should not be presented in London, although it ran in the provinces. It was found that time was available for the performance of a fourth opera and the audience voted for *Iolanthe*.

Audiences were quickly drawn to these revivals but behind the scenes the productions were marred by severe disagreements between the ageing Gilbert and Helen D'Oyly Carte. He was angered that the musical director François Cellier and Mrs D'Oyly Carte engaged for the principal parts people who were singers first rather than people with acting ability who would have been Gilbert's first choice. Yet for this series of revivals he was powerless and had no right of veto. Relations between Gilbert and Mrs D'Oyly Carte worsened. He wrote to her in 1909:

You are not a free agent or you would never have treated me with the gross insolence and black ingratitude which have characterized the Savoy methods during the last 2½ years . . . the operas have been insulted, degraded and dragged through the mire . . . and people have been engaged whom the call boy would have told you were ridiculously unsuitable.

However, in 1910 Gilbert sold the performing rights to Mrs D'Oyly Carte for a second term. A second season had been held at the Savoy from April 1908 until the following March when *The Mikado*, *H.M.S. Pinafore*, *Iolanthe*, *The Pirates of Penzance*, *The Gondoliers* and *The Yeomen of the Guard* were all produced and Richard Temple and Rutland Barrington returned. Mrs D'Oyly Carte then ceased to manage the Savoy. She remarried and her death occurred in 1913.

The D'Oyly Carte Company toured the provinces but did not return to London until 1919 – to the Princes in Shaftesbury

Charles Herbert Workman as Ko-Ko in *The Mikado* during the second season of revivals in 1908-9. From March 1909 Workman took over the running of the Savoy Theatre from Helen D'Oyly Carte.

Avenue. The subsequent history of the Company lies beyond the scope of the present volume but, in a nutshell, its management was taken over by Rupert D'Oyly Carte, second son of Richard D'Oyly Carte – by his first marriage. In June 1929 the Savoy was rebuilt internally and the D'Oyly Carte Opera Company, as it had now become known, began its first London season for twenty years at the new Savoy in October 1929 – in a season which lasted for five months! Lady Gilbert sat in a box for the opening and Henry Lytton from the curtain announced:

I can only say how glad we are to be back in our old home. It's like fairyland.

Rupert D'Oyly Carte died in 1948 and the administration now sat on the shoulders of his daughter Bridget D'Oyly Carte who ran the Company until its demise, due to lack of funds, in 1982. The D'Oyly Carte Opera Company was re-formed, not altogether unexpectedly, in 1988 in large part due to a bequest in Bridget D'Oyly Carte's will, as well as to sponsorship by British Midland and individual donations.

Gilbert was knighted in 1907. It was always a source of irritation to him that Sullivan had received this accolade as far back as 1883. He must have been honoured, however, even though he described it as a commuted old age pension! Indeed, it was the first such knighthood to be awarded purely to a dramatic author.

Sir W. S. Gilbert's last libretto for an opera was produced at the Savoy from December 1909. This was *Fallen Fairies* (based on his much earlier fairy comedy *The Wicked World*). The music was written by Edward German and Nancy McIntosh was in the leading role. The manager, C. H. Workman, dismissed this actress within a week. Gilbert was furious and took action at law but the opera was not popular and only lasted a matter of weeks. Workman had so incurred Gilbert's wrath over this matter that the former was not given permission to revive *Ruddigore* – the next work to have been once more produced.

Gilbert believed that 1909 was to be his last year on earth – having been informed by a palmist that he would die on 10 July. Indeed, in the same year he had the strange experience of reading a headline in one evening paper – 'Death of W. S. Gilbert in great agony'. A journalist interviewed Gilbert at Grim's Dyke wanting details of his life and work for an eventual obituary to appear in the *Times*, and Gilbert, amused by the situation, complied willingly. He still walked six or seven miles a day and had never worn spectacles. He remarked of old age:

It is the happiest time in a man's life; the worst of it is there's so little of it.

Gilbert's last literary work was to re-write *The Mikado* in story form for children but this did not appear in print until 1921 due to war-time difficulties over the production of books.

He continued to travel and had holidays in the Azores and Constantinople in 1910. His final play was called *The Hooligan* and was produced at the Coliseum in February 1911. It had a surprisingly serious flavour, illustrating the last hours of a prisoner held in a condemned cell.

Sir W. S. Gilbert died on 29 May 1911. He had a busy day, visiting Chelsea in the morning, then calling on a sick friend before lunching in a club. That afternoon he had arranged to teach two young women to swim in the lake at Grim's Dyke. One of the women was soon in a state of panic and Gilbert quickly swam out to her, but the strain of the sudden exertion was too much for his heart. He sank and was dead when he was pulled from the lake. He had long ago said that a pleasing way to die would be on a day in summer in his own garden. He was seventy-four.

He was cremated at Golders Green and his remains were buried in Great Stanmore churchyard. A memorial to Gilbert was erected on the Embankment, fairly close to that of Sullivan. It is on a wall directly opposite the Embankment Underground Station and was unveiled in 1915. Gilbert's memorial was designed by Sir George Frampton who also produced the memorial to Edith Cavell just off Trafalgar Square, and the Peter Pan statue in Kensington Gardens. Figures of comedy and tragedy are placed on either side of Gilbert's likeness. The initial idea for the inscription was suggested by Anthony Hope – author of the novel, *The Prisoner of Zenda* – and the adapted inscription reads: 'His Foe Was Folly and His Weapon Wit.' Lady Gilbert had a memorial tablet with a portrait of her husband erected in Harrow Weald Church. Gilbert's wife, Kitten, outlived him for many years, dying in 1936.

Despite the sadness of the hostility and personal recrimination between the two partners in the latter years, Gilbert mellowed sufficiently to be generous in his praise of his former partner after Sullivan's death:

I remember all he has done for me in allowing his genius to shed some of its lustre upon my humble name.

It is a source of gratification to me to reflect that the rift that parted us for a time was completely bridged over, and that, at the time of Sir Arthur Sullivan's lamented death, the most cordial relations existed between us.

11 Gilbert: A Librettist at Work

In a typically Gilbertian sense it has become almost traditional for biographers to describe Gilbert in affable terms. They also tend to point, almost as an aside, to a number of anecdotes which supposedly illustrate in an amusing way his superior wit and intellect when he was involved in problematic situations with others. Little of this description, however, stands up to much scrutiny. Gilbert was a complex character and the amazing dimension is that his partnership with Sullivan survived, on and off, for twenty-five years and fourteen operas without floundering and collapsing earlier. Certainly, there were numerous occasions on which this could well have occurred. Sullivan, gentle soul though he was by nature, dug in his toes on a number of vital issues and this clearly infuriated Gilbert almost beyond that which he was capable of bearing.

The evidence is legion that Gilbert was a most difficult and peculiar person. He was a man who went to a revival of his first play, *Dulcamara*, and sat in the audience and hissed. He was a man who puzzled over the attitude of an acquaintance:

I never could understand his hostility . . . until I remembered that thirty-seven years ago I introduced him to the woman who is now his wife.

George Grove, having spent time alone with Gilbert in 1893 when they were both staying with Sullivan near Monte Carlo, declared him:

a hard cynical man of the world – a bitter, narrow, selfish creature.

A caricature from *The Ludgate Magazine* showing a benign Gilbert seated comfortably in an armchair with his feet on a stool – a favourite writing position in his library at Grims Dyke.

It was Gilbert himself who once wrote: 'I am an ill-tempered pig, and I glory in it.' But he was more than that. There are numerous instances in which he was selfish, hysterically angry, mentally cruel, unfeeling when hurting others, extremely rude, boastful of his own successes in clashes with others, authoritarian in demeanour, sensitive to what he regarded as insults to himself, obstinate, aggressive, extremely conceited and egocentric in the extreme. His personality was abnormal in that he appeared to obtain enjoyment from belittling and wounding those with whom he came into contact.

It is necessary only to relate a number of instances in order to illustrate Gilbert at his worst. In 1877 he waged a war of pamphlets with the actress Henrietta Hodson who was the lessee of the Royalty Theatre. It was not a pamphlet war which he began but it was one which he lost – after which he wrote to implore her not to publish his formal apology since that would mean that he could not show his face again. She related:

He told me that, somehow or other, he had invariably quarrelled with everyone with whom he had been professionally connected, and I took the greatest pains to prevent giving him any cause to quarrel with me. I agreed with him in all that he said, and I concurred with him in all his opinions. When he complained that Shakespeare had statues elevated to him, whereas he, who was in every way Shakespeare's superior, had none, I went so far as to console him with the assurance that, if only he would be patient, there could be no doubt that he too would live to see his own statue . . . When he said that Miss Robertson had ventured, at a dinner party, to observe that she did not like one of his plays, in which she was acting, and that, before he forgave her, he had forced her to cry and humbly sue for pardon, I merely replied that anyone who questioned his great ability must be insane . . . The last rehearsal was going on [the play was *Ought We To Visit Her?*] when suddenly Mr Gilbert jumped up, and commenced pulling his hair and dancing like a maniac . . . 'Do, pray,' I said, 'let the rehearsal go on quietly, and if anything goes wrong, make a note of it, and we will go all over it again.' On this he put on his hat and, without a word, walked out of the theatre.

Subsequently, despite Gilbert's efforts, Henrietta Hodson appeared in a revival of his play *Pygmalion and Galatea* at the Haymarket. At rehearsals he would sit on stage and talk and laugh with a companion (who appears to have changed daily) whenever Miss Hodson appeared and rehearsed her part. Similar treatment had earlier been meted out to Madge Robertson who had first played Galatea and who had annoyed him with her views on performance. He sat in a box and talked and laughed loudly with friends – turning his back on the stage when this actress was performing.

Gilbert could be extremely abusive and child-like. During the carpet quarrel with Sullivan and D'Oyly Carte he screamed at them in the latter's office at the Savoy that he would beat them yet and called them 'bloody sheenies'. A recording of Gilbert speaking made in 1906 showed that he had, perhaps surprisingly, a fairly high tenor voice and not a deep-throated one. It appears that he often became, verbally, very excitable. P. G. Wodehouse recalled that he once spoilt a joke that Gilbert was telling in company by laughing too soon and that Gilbert's eyes seared him like a flame, giving him a glare of pure hatred.

Seymour Hicks, related to Gilbert by marriage, told of a rehearsal when Gilbert was having trouble with a well-known actor on stage. The part had been gone over and over until the actor rebelled. A verbal slanging was ended abruptly and cruelly by Gilbert who told the actor that the difference between them both was that he himself was an extremely clever man. Hicks further remarked that Gilbert seemed incapable of geniality, particularly with men. He was an imposing, domineering figure who stood six feet four inches tall.

Violent death interested Gilbert enormously. He attended Crippen's trial in 1910 and when writing his final play – *The Hooligan* – he managed somehow to visit the condemned cell in Pentonville Prison where Crippen had recently been hanged. When in 1891 stage props were auctioned at the Savoy – during a period of quarrelling when the operas were not being presented at all – Gilbert bought, of all things, the executioner's axe and block from *The Yeomen of the Guard*.

The real Gilbert, he himself remarked more than once, appeared in his blank verse plays; and also in the Savoy opera in the person of Jack Point in *The Yeomen of the Guard*. It was Point who died in sadness of a broken heart, having lost his ideal love. Gilbert made Jack Point – essentially himself on the stage – say the words:

> When a jester
> Is outwitted,
> Feelings fester,
> Heart is lead!
> Food for fishes
> Only fitted,
> Jester wishes
> He was dead!

Human genius, it is often said, is seldom bestowed without exacting its price; and bearing in mind Gilbert's passion for purity of relationships and of ideal love, it seems more than possible that he was a man who was sexually impotent. If so, in the words of Phyllis in *Iolanthe* 'that would account for a good many things'. It would explain his continuing interest in young women at the level of love in the imagination but without the occurrence of serious emotional developments. It would explain his abiding passion for what might be termed the 'princess plot' in many of his plays and operas. He developed a stereotyped story-board whereby he chose to set a plot in a tranquil place that was often remote from normal, everyday life and sexual love and where women decided to live without men – although the latter eventually intruded on the scene and this often resulted in problems that were caused by the intruders. The ending came with some form of resolution to the problem – whether of marriage (reluctant or otherwise) or the expulsion of the intruders. Gilbert made frequent use of the princess plot from 1870 when he adapted Tennyson's work and produced his play *The Princess*. His other works in which he made use of this pattern of plot included *The Wicked World, Broken Hearts, Gretchen* and *Fallen Fairies*. This general pattern was discernible, at least in part, in a number of the Gilbert and Sullivan operas – *Thespis, The Sorcerer, The Pirates of Penzance, Patience, Iolanthe* and *Princess Ida*. Then Sullivan at this point demanded something different but the typical princess plot appeared again in *Utopia Limited*. This would also explain that Gilbert (as played by Jack Point) failed in love because he did not know or practise the appropriate techniques of wooing; it would explain why he attempted to keep at bay actual sexual relations in those around him; it could account for his lack of children; and it would explain his incredible over-reaction when attempting to protect and shield overtly female members of the Savoy cast from amorous encounters with members of the public and with the male cast. At the Savoy, actors and actresses had their dressing-rooms on different sides of the stage and interaction was banned except in the communal atmosphere of the Green Room. Jessie Bond, when playing in *Patience*, was sent a note by young men attending the opera and Gilbert was so irritated, having asked to see the note, that he over-reacted in his dealings with the young men – telling them that there were three ways of dealing with them. He was prepared to go before the curtain and explain to the audience what had happened and that Miss Bond refused to continue whilst they were in the theatre; they could leave voluntarily or Gilbert would have them carried out by attendants – the choice was up to them. The bewildered young men took the second option but the gibe soon followed that Gilbert was running not simply a theatrical group but the Savoy Boarding School!

Anyone who doubts the complexity of Gilbert's inner mind and his fertile imaginings needs only to read through the opera synopses at the end of this book. His treatment of ageing females is a matter in itself. It is common to describe Gilbert's lack of feeling for the characters of lonely middle-aged women in the Savoy operas and of their desperate attempts to attract a mate. Certainly, Sullivan felt that he had seen enough of such characters by the time that the planning stage of *Utopia Limited* was reached and he wrote to Gilbert about the characterization of Lady Sophy:

Cartoon of Gilbert by 'Spy' published in *Vanity Fair* in May 1881.

If there is to be an old or middle-aged woman in the piece at all, is it necessary that she should be very old, ugly, raddled, and perhaps grotesque, and still more is it necessary that she should be seething with love and passion (requited or unrequited) and other feelings not usually associated with old age? I thought that 'Katisha' was to be the last example of that type.

The literary Gilbert turned his wrath in these operas on elderly women who were in love. He appeared to resent a woman of mature age who showed an interest in sexual love – even in a plot which he himself had written! But in order to try to keep the record balanced it must be stressed that a contralto role had simply become as much a part of the pattern of the operas as that of the baritone comic lead and that of the tenor and soprano who fall in love. It is nonsensical to describe Gilbert's portrayals of the elderly contralto characters solely in terms of hopeless creatures in love and as figures of fun. Rather did most of them manage to do quite well by the ends of the respective plots by making suitable matches. It is true that Ruth in *The Pirates of Penzance*, Katisha in *The Mikado* and Lady Jane in *Patience* are portrayed by Gilbert in comic tones – but even in these instances the latter two characters marry Ko-Ko and the Duke respectively and, traditionally, Ruth gets the Sergeant of Police. Lady Blanche in *Princess Ida* is unusual in remaining alone. The Duchess of Plaza-Toro in *The Gondoliers*, unusual for a contralto role, was already married.

There had been a gap of several years between *Thespis* (1871) and *Trial by Jury* (1875) and then the further gap before *The Sorcerer* (1877). But from *The Sorcerer* onwards the collaborators produced a succession of fresh Gilbert and Sullivan operas almost to order – practically a new opera each year or so from 1877 to 1889 and two more followed after that. It became part of the regular expectation of London theatre-goers to anticipate the next one in the series; and, of course, these were days before gramophone recordings, and so there might be a considerable delay – perhaps of many years – before a particular opera appeared as a revival and an audience had the opportunity of seeing a favourite work again.

Gilbert and Sullivan wrote in interdependence. They needed one another, although it seems that Gilbert needed Sullivan rather more than the composer needed Gilbert. The works they each produced for the musical stage but working with other collaborators have not endured as have the Gilbert and Sullivan operas. Each artist was highly successful but pre-eminently so only when working with the other. Such interdependence can cause resentment in an artist; and Sullivan supposedly wanted to concentrate on grand opera whilst Gilbert grumbled and believed that his words were made subordinate to Sullivan's music. There was certainly professional irritation on the part of each man as one realised how much he needed and was indebted to the other. 'There is no Sullivan without a Gilbert' commented Sullivan in 1898. In eight years he had tried working with six new librettists without finding an effective partner although his eventual collaboration with Basil Hood produced success in *The Rose of Persia* and *The Emerald Isle*. Similarly, 'A Gilbert is no use without a Sullivan and I can't find one,' Gilbert wrote to a friend in 1903.

Fascinating insights are available into Gilbert's methods of working. He kept thick plot books in which he jotted down ideas for future plays or operas. He often leafed through these leather-bound books when he was searching for starting-points for a new libretto. A specific story-line would then be developed, changed and expanded in the plot book until he reached a point where he had sufficient detail and confidence to begin writing out the outline plot straight through from start to finish. Even at this stage changes occurred, various characters might even be abandoned and names of surviving characters might be altered. At the planning stage of *Iolanthe*, for instance, various roles including the Attorney-General and the Admiral of the Fleet disappeared. The Fairy Queen, once called Varine, eventually did not have a name and Corydon (later Strephon) was a shepherd employed by a beautiful young shepherdess.

The next stage was for Gilbert to attempt to write some of the dialogue and then the lyrics. Eventually, the final libretto was written out in full in the plot book. Gilbert usually wrote at his desk from about eleven o'clock at night until two or three in the morning. He explained to a portrait painter:

My usual writing dress would hardly do for exhibition, consisting as it does of a night-shirt and dressing-gown, for I only write after 11pm when everyone has gone to bed. Then you have absolute peace. The postman has done his worst and no one can interrupt you unless it be a burglar.

In the *New York Tribune* in August 1885 Gilbert explained in astonishing detail how the Savoy operas progressed from vague ideas to finished pieces. His account shows that, just as Sullivan worked hard and selflessly to complete the music, Gilbert, similarly, was tireless in writing and re-writing. Gilbert's methods of preparing a new opera were so well thought-out that the progressive detail in this published account is worth quoting at some length:

Very few people have any idea of the amount of earnest thought that a dramatic author must bestow upon his original work before it is in a condition to be presented to the very exacting audiences that fill a good London theatre on the occasion of the first performance of a new play. I do not mean to say that original dramatic composition involves necessarily a high order of literary ability. On the contrary, I believe the chief secret of success is to keep well within the understanding of the least intelligent section of the audience. The dramatic author is in a position of a caterer, who has to supply one dish of which all members of every class of society are invited to take part . . . It does not call for a very high order of merit on the part of the chef, but it requires a good deal of practical skill nevertheless.

Gilbert went on to narrate how *The Mikado* developed from an initial idea to a finished piece and his account serves as a model of methodology for all the other operas:

In May, 1884, it became necessary to decide upon a subject for the next Savoy opera. A Japanese executioner's sword hanging on the wall of my library – the very sword carried by Mr Grossmith at his entrance in the first act – suggested the broad idea upon which the libretto is based. A Japanese piece would afford opportunities for picturesque scenery and costumes, and moreover, nothing of the kind had ever been attempted in England. There were difficulties in the way. Could a sufficient number of feminine Japanese dresses in good condition be procured in London? How would the ladies of the chorus look in black wigs? Could they be taught to wear the Japanese costume effectively? However, none of these difficulties appeared to be insuperable, and the scheme of a Japanese opera was decided upon. Then it became necessary to fit the company with parts, and this was not so easy a matter as it may at first sight appear to be. We had written six operas for practically the same company, and in this, our seventh, it was of course necessary to steer clear of everything that we had already done, and yet to fit our company with parts to which they could do justice, and which would do justice to them. The accident that Miss Braham, Miss Jessie Bond, and Miss Sybil Grey, are short in stature and all of a height, suggested the advisability of grouping them as three Japanese schoolgirls who should work together throughout the piece . . . The next thing was to decide upon two scenes, which should be characteristic and effective. The respective advantages of a street in Nagasaki, a Japanese market-place, wharf with shipping, a Japanese garden, a seaside beach and the courtyard of a Japanese palace, were duly weighed; and the courtyard and the Japanese garden were finally decided upon. The story of the piece had to be drawn up in narrative form, and this I find was done in eleven different ways, each presumably an improvement upon its immediate predecessor. The story is next divided into two acts, and the sequence of events in each act is decided upon, with the exits and entrances sketched out, the purport of the various dialogues suggested, and the musical situations arranged. I had to make a dozen shots at the 'scenario' (that is the technical name for the piece in its skeleton form), before a course of action was finally decided upon.

The plot having reached this stage, I read the story and the scenario to Sir Arthur Sullivan. He approved of the story; made some valuable suggestions bearing chiefly on the musical situations, and after three or four hours of careful deliberation the chain of events was finally determined, and a twelfth and last version of the story, varying in no great degree from its immediate predecessor, was prepared the next day and then the libretto was begun. The libretto in its first full form is simply the scenario reduced to dialogue of the baldest and simplest nature, leaving the songs to be written afterwards. No attempt at a joke is to be found in the dialogue; it merely carries on the action in the fewest possible words. Having roughly sketched out the dialogue it was put aside for a time, that I might devote myself to the words of the songs. My usual practice is to furnish Sir Arthur Sullivan with the songs of the first act, and while he is setting them I proceed with the songs of act two. When these are practically finished I revert to the dialogue, elaborating and polishing the crude suggestions contained in the first version of the libretto, while he composes the music, and so it comes to pass that the pianoforte score and the libretto are usually completed at about the same date. The libretto is then set up in type and read to the company. This is always a nervous affair, for by this time the jokes have lost their point, the situations their novelty, and the author is generally at a loss to see where the laughs will come in. I have often seen it stated that actors and actresses form a dispiriting audience at such a ceremony, and that they care little for the story or the dialogue in the abstract, their attention being concentrated on the parts which they believe they are destined to play. I am bound to say that my own experience is to the contrary effect. As a body they are keenly alive to such merits as the piece may possess, and I am sorry to say that I have often had occasion to wish that my play had gone with the audience half as well as it did when it was read to the company.

Then comes the actual business of putting the piece upon the stage. Hitherto, it has existed only in manuscript – henceforth it is to live as an aggregate of fifty human beings. As the piece is an opera, the company must have the music before they begin to study the dialogue and action. The music rehearsals usually last a fortnight, during which the author occupies himself, partly in getting the rhythm of the musical numbers into his very unmusical head, partly in arranging details of scenery with the scenic artist, partly in arranging details of the costume, but chiefly with determining 'stage management' of the piece, so that when the first 'stage rehearsal' takes place he shall be in a position to announce a clear and distinct policy to his company. To this end facsimile models of the scenes, on a scale of half an inch to the foot, are supplied to me, by the scenic artist, and on the miniature stages the piece is duly rehearsed, by the aid of blocks of wood three inches and two and a half inches in length representing men and women respectively. The details which are obtained by these means are committed to paper, and, at the very first rehearsal, the piece begins to take a definite and distinct form. While these matters are occupying me, Sir Arthur Sullivan is busy with the music rehearsals.

Gilbert and Sullivan controlled all aspects of stage management. Gilbert explained to the noted theatre critic, William Archer:

Of course, I plan out the whole stage-management beforehand . . . I know exactly what groupings I want – how many people I can have on

168

this bank, how many on that rostrum, and so forth. I have it all clear in my head before going down to the theatre; and there the actors and actresses are good enough to believe in me and to lend themselves heartily to all I require of them. You see I have the exact measure of their capabilities and take good care that the work I give them should be well within their grasp.

In preparing the Savoy operas for production, Gilbert took a positive lead in illustrating precisely how he wished the acting to be carried out. George Grossmith related that Gilbert would stand beside an actor on the stage and repeat the words and gestures many times until they were delivered as he desired them. Decima Moore, playing Casilda, described how Gilbert taught her dialogue:

He would read a line out clapping his hands between the words to emphasise their rhythm thus: 'I've no patience (clap) with the presumption (clap) of persons (clap) in his plebeian (clap) position (clap).'

Rutland Barrington, a very experienced Savoyard by the time of *The Gondoliers*, irritated Gilbert by putting in some of his own gags. Gilbert complained to D'Oyly Carte:

It must be played exactly as I wrote it.

In 1889 Gilbert wrote directly to the actor who was playing the leading comedy role in a touring company:

I find on enquiry that Mr Carte's grievance does not refer to your altering the dialogue but to the introduction of *inappropriate, exaggerated* and *unauthorised* business . . . no actor will ever find his way into our London Company who defies authority in this respect.

Gilbert regarded the chorus as an important aspect of the total scene – not as a means of filling the stage in a decorous manner but as a lively part of the plot. Consequently, he gave them considerable thought at the planning-stage and during rehearsals insisted that each member of the chorus played the part of a necessary and real character. Whether the curtain rises on involved jurymen in *Trial by Jury*, sailors scrambling over the ship in *H.M.S. Pinafore*, Venetian girls making bouquets in *The Gondoliers* or rapturous maidens swooning with passion in *Patience* the chorus members were not merely part of an animated back-drop but provided lively characterisations in their own right. For practical purposes, once the story-line proceeded, Gilbert tended to group the chorus in fairly formal patterns – whether semi-circular or straight-line arrangements and particularly when the entire company of perhaps fifty actors and actresses were represented on stage. He found that this formality was necessary in order to give the principal players a reasonable space for acting. But whilst for much of the action in an opera the chorus was grouped to provide a participating background to the principals, and to enable the audience to focus their primary interest on the action of these principals, it was not his intention that the chorus should remain stationary for extended periods. Gilbert trained his chorus to react to the continuing drama of the unfolding story. His prompt-books show the detailed way in which he instructed the chorus in movements, aside speaking and display of feelings. But this is not the same as a stereotype movement for all, as might be followed by adhering to an automatic set of mechanical gestures. In *Iolanthe*, for instance, during Tolloller's song, 'Spurn not the nobly born', Gilbert's notes read:

Chorus exhibit in action the sentiments expressed by the singer – during the ballad Peers sit and stand grouped in attitudes of despair – at the end Peers stand with arms extended in imploring attitudes.

Since author and stage-director were one and the same individual, the impression of a stage character which was conveyed to the audience was invariably a reflection both of Gilbert's initial conception and of his continuing intention. A contemporary theatrical manager, John Hollingshead, described Gilbert thus:

He was somewhat of a martinet in his stage management, but he generally knew what he wanted, was more often right than wrong and was consequently an able director of his own pieces.

Towards the end of the Gilbert and Sullivan partnership William Archer believed that:

The victory of Gilbertian extravaganzas over *opéra-bouffe* as adapted for the London market, is the victory of literary and musical grace over rampant vulgarity and meretricious jingle.

Many years earlier Archer had written in his book about contemporary English dramatists (1882) that:

The wall which divides the stage of the Opéra Comique from that of the Globe, for years divided humour from inanity, wit from horse-play, refinement from vulgarity, literature from the lowest form of literary hackwork.

It was Gilbert, perhaps alone amongst English authors, who had sufficient strength of character and mastery of stagecraft to impose his ideas on others in the theatre. Archer further described Gilbert as:

The most striking individuality, the most original character our theatre of today can boast . . . The very fact that he is personally by no means popular in the theatrical world is not without its significance. This may arise partly from adventitious circumstances, such as his severity as a stage-manager – a severity which produces admirable results – and may be partly due to absolute faults of character . . . in such a world as that of the London theatres no one can be thoroughly popular who is not either an accomplished Philistine or an accomplished hypocrite.

12 Sullivan: A Composer at Work

An operetta may be defined as a fairly light piece having a romantic or sentimental story-line, with songs, perhaps dances and spoken dialogue and also orchestral music. Its structure is basically that of an opera. But operetta is a term that neither Gilbert nor Sullivan used to describe their joint endeavours. It was used in the nineteenth century to indicate satiric or farcical stage plays with music, following the lead of Jacques Offenbach with such works as *Orpheus in the Underworld* (1858) and *La Belle Hélène* (1864). In the 1870s Offenbach's operettas were popular in London, and *Trial by Jury* was produced for an Offenbach season. Sullivan's operas became popular in Britain and America and *The Mikado* was performed in Germany but they did not reach the international repute afforded to the works of Offenbach. Gilbert's plots were geared to English social and topical satire and Sullivan's music did not quite have the lightness of Offenbach or even of Strauss.

The works of Gilbert and Sullivan were perhaps neither opera nor operetta. They stood alone: they were pieces by Gilbert and Sullivan and simply a highly developed form of entertainment. George Bernard Shaw described Savoy opera as a *genre* in itself — although, paradoxically, he believed that *Haddon Hall* (Grundy and Sullivan) was its highest expression.

Sullivan's style was eclectic and perhaps because of this he sometimes strayed into areas where he floundered for his more serious music often lacked emotional depth. The music of *Ivanhoe* and *The Golden Legend* was episodic since Sullivan found difficulty in attempting to sustain musical ideas in large structured programmes.

Arthur Sullivan approaching fifty years of age.

Sullivan always claimed that the music of his Savoy operas played second fiddle to Gilbert's words. When he settled down to set Gilbert's words to music, Sullivan usually stressed the accentuation of these words, and when he discovered a satisfactory rhythm he composed a suitable melody to fit in with the rhythm. The system sounds convoluted and time-consuming and yet, for him, it worked well and the resulting music was sparkling and fresh. Part of Sullivan's unique inspiration lay in his gift of melody. A catalogue of his tunes is unnecessary. He wrote hundreds that have already endured for a century and more:

Oh, foolish fay (*Iolanthe*)
When a merry maiden marries (*The Gondoliers*)
Ida was a twelve-month old (*Princess Ida*)
For he's going to marry Yum-Yum (*The Mikado*)
Never mind the why and wherefore (*H.M.S. Pinafore*)
So go to him and say to him (*Patience*)
In sailing o'er life's ocean wide (*Ruddigore*)

– this handful merely represents the wealth and richness of the tuneful songs in Sullivan's operatic music.

Sullivan read over Gilbert's verses, searching for rhythms that might strike him beyond the immediacy of the superficial metre. It was the accentuation of syllables that interested him. He made notes on a number of possible rhythms with various time signatures and would later choose one of these. The melody later began to take shape – perhaps not for days – and he wrote out the tune at some speed, attempted a sketchy harmony and an initial instrumental coverage.

Sullivan was aware that Gilbert's words needed to be heard (and equally aware that Gilbert would demand that they should be!). He became expert at placing a word on just that right beat of a bar to give it correct emphasis and to provide a phrasing with deeper and more poignant meaning. Sullivan had an almost uncanny knack when it came to successful word-setting. He had long practice in the technique over many years and he made even accents that appear unexpected seem acceptable at the very least but more usually highly worthwhile and natural in the finished piece. Long before he began to cope with Gilbert's irregular metres, he had the daunting experience of setting words such as the following from *Kenilworth* (and then only in his early twenties):

> Look, how the floor of heaven
> Is thick inlaid with patines of bright gold,
> There's not the smallest orb which thou behold'st
> But in his motion like an angel sings,
> Still quiring to the young-eyed cherubins;
> Such harmony is in immortal souls.

His skill was consummate, whether setting such heavy blank verse or amusing blank verse for Gilbert:

> Young Fred'ric!
> Who calls?
> Your late commander!
> And I, Your little Ruth!
> Oh, mad intruders, how dare you face me?
> (*The Pirates of Penzance*)

or sensitive verse for Gilbert which demanded very much a professional touch:

> You'll sit and mope
> All day, I hope
> And shed a tear

Upon the life
Your little wife
Is passing here.
And if so be
You think of me
Please tell the moon:
I'll read it all
In rays that fall
On the lagoon:
You'll be so kind
As tell the wind
How you may be,
And send me words
By little birds
To comfort me
(*The Gondoliers*)

Several of the tunes Sullivan produced for Gilbert's lyrics appear to fit badly (including, for instance, 'Oh, happy the lily' from *Ruddigore*) and it seems that, on occasions, he resorted to setting pre-prepared tunes if inspiration did not arrive quickly; and it is true that he was always working frenetically towards a fast-approaching deadline.

Sullivan's use of harmony relied on the conventions of many other composers – Donizetti and Auber, Mendelssohn and Schumann, Gounod and Bizet – even Wagner and Parry. His eclecticism developed patterned and predictable habits. It is possible that Sullivan was not fully aware of the extent of his debt to other composers believing, rather, that each had only the same seven notes to work with. But he was quick enough to point out the debts owed by other musicians. On his return to Leipzig his diary shows an apparent disapproval of plagiarism:

Ran over to Dresden . . . saw Wagner's *Rienzi*, which was a great disappointment – a mixture of Weber, Verdi and a touch of Meyerbeer. The whole very commonplace, vulgar and uninteresting.

Sullivan seemed to be more confident and settled when working in the major. Rarely did he produce good pieces entirely in the minor – though these do include:

Go away, madam (*Iolanthe*)
Oh fool, that fleest my hallow'd joys (*The Mikado*)
When the night wind howls (*Ruddigore*)
The funeral march from *The Yeomen of the Guard*

By the time that Sullivan began to score *Ruddigore* (1887) he had had the experience of working on *The Golden Legend*. The

175

harmonic wealth in such songs as Mad Margaret's 'Never doubting, never doubting' and Sir Roderic's 'When the night wind howls' shows a mature richness of musical skills. This richness continued in *The Yeomen of the Guard* but there was to be no steady progression towards empyrean heights. Sullivan's last complete opera, *The Rose of Persia*, was inconsistent, exhibiting elements of coarse musical comedy. In his later operas, Sullivan's somewhat limiting style was forced to rely on earlier harmonic devices.

He was an adept at writing a fugue although in the Savoy operas such counterpoint was seldom utilized. Noted examples of his fugal style are the entrance of the Lord Chancellor in *Iolanthe* and the entry of the Learned Judge in *Trial by Jury*.

Sullivan's primary concern (incorporating his specialism and abiding interest) was with the orchestral potentiality of a song rather than with its vocal possibility. The only significant pieces of unaccompanied chorus in the Savoy operas occur with 'Hail Poetry! thou heav'n born maid' (*The Pirates of Penzance*) and 'Eagle high in cloudland soaring' (*Utopia Limited*). More usually, the chorus members were accompanied by music of vivacious vitality.

His soloists had their work cut out to achieve the technical range he demanded of them – whether the bass-baritone Pish-Tush in *The Mikado*, the coloratura Mabel in *The Pirates of Penzance* or the tenor Frederic in the same opera. Tenors tended to be given only one major song, although several tuneful ballads were allocated to them.

Sullivan's natural courtesy and decency, his tactful avoidance of trouble and his patience were essential ingredients in the continuing Savoy partnership. Eventually he was at times required to make do with what Gilbert was prepared to produce – as with the finale of the first act of *Utopia Limited* which consists only of a succession of comic songs and afforded Sullivan little climactic potential. On other occasions he bowed to Gilbert's desire for a change of tune – as with the song 'Is life a boon?' from *The Yeomen of the Guard*. Only the third attempt by Sullivan to set this song was acceptable to Gilbert who did not wish repetitions to impede the flow of his words. He rejected the setting in six-eight time and Sullivan, irritated beyond belief, agreed to begin with the song again. This was most unusual since Sullivan invariably planned the rhythm and then worked on the melody. But on this occasion, in order to keep the peace, he changed to a different rhythm in the new setting.

Sullivan explained his usual methods of working to Arthur Lawrence, an early biographer:

An engraving from *The Illustrated London News*, 23 October 1886, of the Leeds Musical Festival. Sullivan is seated whilst conducting.

The first thing I have to decide upon is the rhythm, and I arrange the rhythm before I come to the question of melody . . . Five out of six treatments are commonplace and my first aim has always been to get as much originality as possible in the rhythm, approaching the question of melody afterwards . . . It is only after I have decided the rhythm that I proceed to the notation. My first work – the jotting down of melodies – I term 'sketches'. They are hieroglyphics which, possibly, would seem undecipherable. It is my musical shorthand, and of course it means much to me. When I have finished these sketches the creative part of my work is completed.

Sullivan prepared a skeleton score next – with vocal parts but not yet with accompaniment or any instrumental work, and when these voice parts were written out rehearsals could begin. Orchestration commenced only when stage rehearsals were well advanced.

Sullivan explained in an interview the lengthy process of setting a comic opera:

People generally think that I can rattle off one of these Savoy pieces without the least difficulty in a very short space of time. I can assure you that my comic operas – light and airy as they may seem, give me far more trouble and anxiety than a cantata like 'The Golden Legend'. In this latter case, you see, I am quite irresponsible. I have no one to consider but my band and my singers. There is no stage business to worry about. It is all straightforward and simple. But when I do an opera for the Savoy it is very different. A quantity of the music has invariably to be re-written – and very often more than once. Either singers are not quite suited, or else I find the situation, when it takes shape upon the stage, requires something different to what I had anticipated. For these reasons, too, I am only able to begin the orchestration when these rehearsals are well advanced.

Sullivan usually composed the more difficult choruses first. Then he turned his attention to the quartets and trios. Next came the duets and finally the solo songs.

A former messenger-boy working for Chappell remembered the procedure when the score of *Patience* was being prepared for printing:

I used to take the proofs with me, and catch a horse-bus to Victoria Street. Mr Sullivan worked in the semi-basement. The Butler would let me in. It was a plainly furnished room. There was a piano, but I don't recollect ever seeing Sullivan playing it. He wrote most of his music at his desk, smoking cigarettes and sipping weak gin-and-water. Very often he would say to me: 'Now you call back tomorrow morning, my boy, and I'll leave the MS with the Butler for you.' I knew this meant he was going to work through the night.

Sullivan appeared not to be distracted unduly by interruptions during the writing of the music. His diary recorded on 20 April 1881 during the final preparations for *Patience*:

Rehearsal at 12, then home to write Tenor Song, afterwards cut out. Duke of Edinburgh came to see me, stayed while I wrote and dined. Went to the theatre at 7.30 to dress-rehearsal. Came home late. Second Tenor Song and sketched-out Overture. To bed at 5.30am. Finished all scoring of the Opera.

His nephew, Herbert Sullivan, recalled that when people entered the room where Sullivan was composing:

It did not spoil the sequence of his thoughts, nor destroy his mood.

While he worked, he even talked to his nephew if he were about – and usually smoked cigarettes using a long holder. Sullivan did not use a piano when composing his operas as that would have imposed restraints on the total effect he sought to obtain. Frequently, whilst composing in pain he lay on a sofa in his library.

During the music rehearsals, Sullivan sat at a piano on the Savoy stage. Gilbert – who was distinctly unmusical – continually made notes, listened to the music and then finalised stage movements. The latter's prompt-book was an exercise book with the printed libretto pasted on the right-hand pages only and with notes and details of positions on stage and movements of actors written in on the left-hand pages.

In later rehearsals Gilbert sat in the stalls and from there he instructed the cast. Sullivan conducted an orchestra of about thirty players for his comic operas, including strings, oboe, two flutes, two clarinets, one or two bassoons, two horns, two cornets, two trombones and one percussionist. Hence his operas were scored for a fairly small orchestra. His orchestration was seldom written for strings alone – apart from a few numbers such as 'Ah, leave me not to pine' (*The Pirates of Penzance*) and 'He loves! if in the bygone years' (*Iolanthe*). For strings he used first violins, second violins, violas, cellos and a double-bass – perhaps with a total of ten musicians playing strings. Sullivan was a practical musician; apart from being a pianist, he was able to play the clarinet, the flute, the trombone and trumpet. He possessed an intimate understanding of the technical and practical problems involved in playing these instruments. His strings were given added colour and strength by doubling with woodwind: first violins with a flute, second violins with a clarinet and violas with a bassoon. The orchestra was complemented by a company of perhaps fifty singers. Probably due to his frequently debilitated

Part of Sullivan's library at Queen's Mansions showing his desk and chair.

physical condition, Sullivan conducted an orchestra whilst seated on a chair – a style of performance that was at times criticised by those who felt that a more flamboyant stance was much more effective and theatrical.

On tour usually only a small group of orchestral players accompanied the singers round the country. At each performing venue these regular players would be reinforced by employing local musicians, although such freelance assistance might utilize limited playing ability. The conductor worked (as conductors invariably still do) from a vocal score marked with many additions and corrections. Sullivan's full orchestral score of *The Mikado* was the only one to be published – and that within his lifetime, but in Leipzig in Germany in 1898, and not in England. The full score of *The Mikado* was left by Sullivan in his will to the Royal Academy of Music, *The Yeomen of the Guard* to the Royal College of Music, *Iolanthe* to Richard D'Oyly Carte, *Ruddigore* to W. S. Gilbert and *Patience* and *The Pirates of Penzance* to François Cellier. Others were left to Herbert Sullivan. Various of these autograph scores were held for many years by Coutts Bank in the Strand. In a 1966 auction at Sotheby's of some of these original manuscripts, several went to the USA and three others remained in England and were bought as the result of an appeal fund.

The present whereabouts of Sullivan's autograph manuscript scores is as follows. *Thespis* is lost in all forms. *Trial by Jury* is at the Pierpont Morgan Library, New York. *The Sorcerer* is in the John Wolfson Collection, New York. *H.M.S. Pinafore* is in the A. A. Houghton Jnr. Collection, New York. *The Pirates of Penzance* is at the Pierpont Morgan Library, New York. *Patience* is at the British Library Reference Division, London. *Iolanthe* was held by Dame Bridget D'Oyly Carte until her death in 1985 when it passed to the Savoy Hotel Group. *Princess Ida* is in the Bodleian Library, Oxford. *The Mikado* is owned by the Royal Academy of Music, London. *Ruddigore* is owned by the Savoy Theatre, London. *The Yeomen of the Guard* is owned by the Royal College of Music, London. *The Gondoliers* is held by the British Library Reference Division, London. *Utopia Limited* was given by Herbert Sullivan in 1915 to a sale for the Red Cross held at Christie's. The score was sold for fifty guineas to a Mr Hudson and then disappeared. Its whereabouts are at present unknown. *The Grand Duke* is part of the John Wolfson Collection, New York.

Many discrepancies exist between the full autograph scores and the vocal scores – and even between libretti and the prompt books used by stage managers; discrepancies that range from minor matters such as accents on notes to more pertinent matters such as different notes given by different sources, to even more serious differences such as added orchestral parts and entire verses of songs. Even reliable band parts have not always been easily obtainable by amateur societies. Only in recent years have some of the discrepancies in these different sources been partially reconciled as a result of the patient study of enthusiasts. Definitive performances of Sullivan's musical intent are still far on the horizon with regard to most productions, but a start was made in establishing a clear stance in the musical direction of *Iolanthe* and *The Yeomen of the Guard* – the first two operas that were produced by the re-formed D'Oyly Carte Opera Company in 1988, for the musical director – most unusually in over one hundred years of performances – had access to the autographed scores in preparing both these productions. Gilbert's libretti also need to be studied with a view to obtaining authentic renderings. His papers are deposited at the British Library in London and include plot-books, manuscripts, diaries, letters and photographs. The remainder of his papers were bought by the Pierpont Morgan Library in New York and the Beinecke Library, Yale University.

It is therefore the more surprising that the musical standards of the D'Oyly Carte Opera Company were maintained at such a high level – though one varying in accuracy and authenticity – over so many years. In this connection, it needs to be borne in mind that

Sullivan's ornate bedroom at 1 Queen's Mansions, 58-60 Victoria Street – the flat he leased from 1881 for the remainder of his life, and which he shared with his valet, a French housekeeper and a parrot named Polly. His secretary, Walter Smythe, lived at 2 Queen's Mansions.

Sullivan provided a demanding range of musical items for his chorus and principals to perform – including the innovation of having various vocal themes competing one with the other at the same time. The musical jollity includes such numbers as in *The Pirates of Penzance* chorus 'When the foeman bares his steel' sung against the counter theme for sopranos 'Go, ye heroes, go to glory'; the trio 'My brain it teems' for Ko-Ko, Pooh-Bah and Pish-Tush, from *The Mikado*; and 'In a contemplative fashion' – the quartet that breathes fire, venom and then tranquility in *The Gondoliers*. This musical device the composer claimed to have invented as his own.

13 The Gilbert and Sullivan Operas: summary and synopses

Thespis

Sub-title
The Gods Grown Old

Descriptive billing
An entirely original Grotesque Opera in 2 Acts

Date and theatre of first performance
26 December 1871, Gaiety Theatre, London

Length of original run
64 performances

Overture
Lost, but almost certainly written by Sullivan

Setting
Act 1   Ruined temple on Mount Olympus
Act 2   The same with ruins restored, a year later

Time
Classical

Cast list and performers in first London season

Jupiter	John Maclean
Apollo	Frederic Sullivan
Mars	Frank Wood

Jupiter displaying his powers to the mortals in the first production of *Thespis*.

Diana	Mrs H. Leigh
Mercury	Ellen Farren
Venus	Miss Jolly
Thespis	J. L. Toole
Sillimon	J. G. Taylor
Timidon	Mr Marshall
Tipseion	Robert Souter
Preposteros	Henry Payne
Stupidas	Fred Payne
Sparkeion	Mlle Clary
Nicemis	Constance Loseby
Pretteia	Rose Berend

Daphne   Annie Tremaine
Cymon   Miss L. Wilson
Chorus of Stars

Songs and choruses
Act 1   Throughout the night (Stars)
        Oh, I'm the celestial drudge (Mercury)
        Oh incident unprecedented (Mercury, Mars, Apollo, Diana)
        Here far away from all the world (Sparkeion, Nicemis)
        Climbing over rocky mountain (Chorus)
        I once knew a chap who discharged a function (Thespis)
        So that's arranged – you take my place (Jupiter, Mercury, Apollo,
            Diana)
        When mighty Jove goes down below (Thespis)
        Phoebus am I, with golden ray (Sparkeion)
        I am the moon, the lamp of night (Nicemis)
        Mighty old Mars, the God of War (Timidon)
        When as the fruit of warlike deeds (Daphne)
        The Muse of Fame (Chorus)
        We will go, down below (Gods)
        Here's a pretty tale for future Iliads and Odysseys (Chorus)

Act 2   Of all symposia (Chorus)
        To work and think, my dear (Sillimon)
        Little maid of Arcadee (Sparkeion)
        Olympus is now in a terrible muddle (Mercury)
        You're Diana, I'm Apollo (Sparkeion, Daphne, Nicemis, Thespis)
        Oh rage and fury (Jupiter, Apollo, Mars)
        We can't stand this (Jupiter, Apollo, Mars)
        Jupiter, Mars and Apollo have quitted the dwellings of men (All)
        Now here you see the arrant folly of doing your best to make
            things jolly (Thespis with Chorus)

Synopsis

Act 1
Olympus – the mountain of the gods – is in a shambles. The buildings
and grounds are in ruins and the gods themselves are the worse for wear
despite their immortality, having to rely heavily on hair-dyes, cosmetics
and pills stolen from the mortals on earth. These deities, led by Jupiter,
are worried because they cannot understand why their popularity has
dwindled over the centuries. Their peace is shattered as the sacred
mountain suddenly swarms with mortals preceded by two young lovers,
Sparkeion and Nicemis. It is their wedding day and they are glad to get
away from the rest of the party, despite being jealous of previous
relationships each other has had. The mortals are all members of a
theatrical troupe led by their manager, Thespis, and having caught up
with the two lovers in the ruins of the Temple of the Gods they pause for a

185

picnic. The gods, hidden from sight, listen to their bickering conversations with mounting frustration until, irritated with this intrusion of their privacy, they reveal themselves with as much splendour as they can muster and Jupiter scares the mortals away by displaying his powers. But Thespis approaches Jupiter and introduces himself, and the latter, recognising Thespis as a manager of obvious influence, questions him as to why the popularity of the gods has dwindled on earth. Thespis suggests that the gods should descend to earth and find out at first hand the reasons for their lack of popularity since this would place them in a stronger position to effect improvements in their standing. The manager offers to lend his troupe to take the places of the gods on Olympus whilst they are away and Jupiter agrees, leaving Mercury behind to assist and to check on the mortals' progress.

Act 2

A year has passed and on the surface everything on Mount Olympus appears to be satisfactory. The temple has been repaired with theatrical props and now looks magnificent. But the reality is a different matter. The roles of the gods have been unevenly distributed to the actors and their management has been weak, resulting in a series of major problems. Nicemis, for instance, plays the moon goddess Diana, discharging her duties at night but, as she gets cold and frightened when in the dark alone, her lover Sparkeion accompanies her. But Sparkeion is playing Apollo – the sun god – and so the sun now shines at night. The role of Cupid is played by a youth who has an eye for pretty girls to such an extent that he fires arrows only at the girls and forgets all about the men. The time has come for the annual heavenly court where all the complaints of mortals everywhere are discussed. Mercury calls the court to order and this is presided over by Thespis. Jupiter, Apollo and Mars have returned in disguise to Olympus. They are shocked by the changes they see, tackle Mercury and Thespis and remain in disguise – unrecognised by the rest of the actors. A long list of grumbles is read out to the court. Athens has experienced a foggy Friday in November every day for the last six months because Thespis forgot to turn off the rain. Grapes now contain only ginger beer since Tipseion, the new god of wine, has taken the pledge. But as the catalogue of disasters is presented, the fury of the gods is aroused and they reveal themselves, and depose the actors who are banished back to earth. Their punishment is to become a troupe of tragedians whom no one ever goes to see, whilst the gods begin to sort out the problems which the actors have left behind.

186

Trial by Jury

Sub-title
None

Descriptive billing
A novel and entirely original Dramatic Cantata

Date and theatre of first performance
25 March 1875, Royalty Theatre, London

Length of original run
131 performances

Overture
None

Setting
A courtroom

Time
1875

Cast list, performers in first London season and voices

The Learned Judge	Frederic Sullivan	Bar
Counsel for Plaintiff	J. Hollingsworth	Bar
Defendant, Edwin	Walter H. Fisher	Tenor
Foreman of the Jury	C. Kelleher	Bass
Usher	B. R. Pepper	Bar
Plaintiff, Angelina	Nellie Bromley	Sop

Chorus of Bridesmaids and Gentlemen of the Jury

Songs and choruses
Hark, the hour of ten is sounding (Chorus)
Now, Jurymen, hear my advice (Usher)
When first my old, old love I knew (Defendant)
All hail great Judge (Chorus)
When I, good friends, was called to the bar (Judge)
Oh, will you swear by yonder skies (Usher, Jury)
Comes the broken flower (Bridesmaids)
O'er the season vernal, time may cast a shade (Plaintiff)
With a sense of deep emotion (Counsel for Plaintiff)
Oh, gentlemen, listen, I pray (Defendant)
That seems a reasonable proposition (Judge, Counsel for Plaintiff)
A nice dilemma we have here (Judge, Counsel for Plaintiff, Defendant, Plaintiff)
I love him – I love him – with fervour unceasing (Plaintiff, Defendant)
The question, gentlemen, is one of liquor (Judge)
Oh, joy unbounded (All)

A benefit matinée held at the Theatre Royal, Drury Lane in 1906 of *Trial by Jury*. Gilbert is dressed as an Associate and Rutland Barrington is the Learned Judge.

Synopsis

The time is ten o'clock and the court is preparing for the first case of the day. The jurymen, barristers and members of the public enter to hear the case of Angelina who is suing Edwin for breach of promise of marriage. The Usher directs everyone to their places and then advises the jury of the need for bias-free decisions. Edwin enters and when it is realised that he is the defendant he is forced to endure a torrent of abuse from the members of the court – despite the advice on impartiality given by the Usher. Edwin proceeds to cite his side of the story. His case is that having developed a youthful adoration for Angelina he grew bored with her and eventually fell in love with someone else. But the jurymen are clearly in no mood to sympathize with Edwin. The Learned Judge arrives and receives a rapturous welcome. He relates how he reached the exalted rank of judge and tells the court that as a lowly barrister he had furthered his career by promising to marry the elderly ugly daughter of a wealthy attorney. The delighted attorney had helped him in his career and when he became successful he dropped the attorney's daughter, and so he believes he is now in an excellent position to try the current breach of promise of marriage case. The Judge finishes his tale and the Usher swears in the jury and then calls for the plaintiff. Her bridesmaids enter first, suitably attired for a church ceremony – and even carrying posies! The bridesmaids affect the members of the court and not least the Judge who sends a note to the leading bridesmaid, but when the lovely Angelina enters the Judge recalls his note and sends it to the plaintiff instead. The jury pour scorn on Edwin until the court is called to order, and counsel for the plaintiff then puts Angelina's case. Edwin's callous behaviour is emphasised and the plaintiff's case is further strengthened when Angelina faints in court – much to the concern of everyone but Edwin. When Edwin begins to give his defence he meets with a hostile audience. Undeterred, he likens his love to that of nature and he explains that, as nature is constantly changing, his feelings of love are entitled to do likewise. But he suggests a remedy by which he is prepared to marry Angelina that day and also his new love the next day, a scheme which is greeted warmly by the Judge until he is reminded that this is contrary to the law. Angelina stresses her great love for Edwin and demands suitably high damages in compensation. Edwin retorts that she cannot possibly love him because he smokes and drinks to excess and also has a dreadful temper. The Judge suggests that it would be interesting to get the defendant drunk to see if he is telling the truth and whether he really would thrash and kick Angelina but, not surprisingly, she objects. An impasse is reached until the Judge, tired of the proceedings, remedies the situation by announcing his intention of marrying Angelina himself; an idea that is readily accepted by Angelina, the jurymen, the rest of the court and also by the bridesmaids.

The Sorcerer

Sub-title
None

Descriptive billing
An entirely new and original Modern Comic Opera in 2 Acts

Date and theatre of first performance
17 November 1877, Opéra Comique, London

Length of original run
178 performances

Overture
Probably written by Alfred Cellier (possibly by Hamilton Clarke) with alterations by Sullivan

Setting
Act 1   Exterior of Sir Marmaduke's Mansion, midday
Act 2   The same, at midnight

Time
1877

Cast list, performers in first London season and voices

Sir Marmaduke Pointdextre	Richard Temple	*Bass*
Alexis, his son	George Bentham	*Tenor*
Dr Daly, the rector	Rutland Barrington	*Bar*
Notary	Fred Clifton	*Bass*
John Wellington Wells, a sorcerer	George Grossmith	*Bar*
Lady Sangazure	Mrs Howard Paul	*Con*
Aline, her daughter	Alice May	*Sop*
Mrs Partlett, a pew-opener	Helen Everard	*Con*
Constance, her daughter	Giulia Warwick	*Sop*
Chorus of Villagers		

Songs and choruses

Act 1　Ring forth, ye bells (Chorus)
　　　　Constance, my daughter (Mrs Partlett, Constance)
　　　　When he is here I sigh with pleasure (Constance)
　　　　Time was when Love and I were well acquainted (Dr Daly)
　　　　Sir Marmaduke – my dear young friend, Alexis (Dr Daly, Sir
　　　　　　Marmaduke, Alexis)
　　　　With heart and with voice (female chorus)
　　　　Oh, happy young heart (Aline)
　　　　My child, I join in these congratulations (Lady Sangazure)
　　　　Welcome joy, adieu to sadness (Sir Marmaduke, Lady Sangazure)
　　　　All is prepared for sealing and for signing (Notary, Chorus)
　　　　Love feeds on many kinds of food, I know (Alexis)
　　　　My name is John Wellington Wells (Wells)
　　　　Sprites of earth and air (Wells)
　　　　Let us fly to a far-off land (Aline, Alexis)
　　　　Now to the banquet we press (Chorus)
　　　　Eat, drink and be gay (Sir Marmaduke)
　　　　Oh love, true love (Alexis, Aline)
　　　　Oh, marvellous illusion, oh, terrible surprise (All)

Act 2　'Tis twelve, I think (Alexis, Aline, Wells)
　　　　Why, where be oi (Chorus)
　　　　Dear friends, take pity on my lot (Constance)
　　　　Oh joy, oh joy, the charm works well (Alexis, Aline)
　　　　Thou hast the power thy vaunted love (Alexis)
　　　　I rejoice that it's decided (Alexis, Aline, Sir Marmaduke, Mrs
　　　　　　Partlett, Dr Daly)
　　　　Oh, I have wrought much evil with my spells (Wells)
　　　　Hate me! I drop my H's – have through life (Lady Sangazure,
　　　　　　Wells)
　　　　The fearful deed is done (Aline)
　　　　Oh, my voice is sad and low (Dr Daly)
　　　　Alas! that lovers thus should meet (Aline, Dr Daly)
　　　　Or I or he must die (Wells, All)
　　　　Now to the banquet we press (All)

Synopsis

Act 1

Alexis Pointdextre, an officer serving with the Grenadier Guards, is celebrating his betrothal to Aline Sangazure with a banquet on the lawns of his family mansion. The villagers of nearby Ploverleigh have been invited to attend by his father, Sir Marmaduke Pointdextre. These include a humble pew-opener, Mrs Partlett, and her love-lorn daughter Constance, who is infatuated by the village rector, Dr Daly. The latter accepts his advancing age and regards himself as a resigned bachelor and so Mrs Partlett's subtle hints on her daughter's behalf fall on unreceptive ground. Aline arrives accompanied by her mother, Lady Sangazure, who had been a childhood sweetheart of Sir Marmaduke and, despite the passing years, the two are still fond of one another. Alexis is so deliriously happy at the prospect of his forthcoming marriage that he wants everyone to share in his good fortune so he decides to consult a London firm of family sorcerers on the subject of love potions. The sorcerer, John Wellington Wells, arrives at the mansion, agrees to provide a suitable potion which has an effect only on unmarried people and suggests that it could be easily administered to the guests in cups of tea. He casts the spell accompanied by the cries of invisible spirits and later, unaware of the teapot implications, Dr Daly brews the tea and passes it out to the guests. The potion does not take long to work and, watched closely by Alexis, Aline and the sorcerer, the villagers soon succumb to its effect and fall into a deep sleep.

Act 2

Pleased with the progress of the plan, Alexis, Aline and Wells eagerly await midnight when the potion will cause the sleepers to awaken and those who are unattached will then fall in love with the first person they see. Midnight arrives and the unattached villagers pair off. Constance forgets about Dr Daly when she meets and falls in love with the elderly deaf Notary and soon only Dr Daly remains without a partner. Alexis insists that both he and Aline should now take the potion to assure their abiding love, but Aline angrily refuses and is hurt at his lack of faith in the strength of her love. An argument is prevented by the intervention of Dr Daly who is perplexed that the whole village has suddenly decided to get married – even Sir Marmaduke has been smitten. Alexis, assuming the recipient of his father's affection to be Lady Sangazure, resumes his composure but loses it again with the arrival of his father arm-in-arm with the comely Mrs Partlett. Wells has also been experiencing discomfort – for Lady Sangazure, having woken up under the influence of the sorcerer's magic, is desperate to find someone to love. Wells is the first person she encounters and the horrified sorcerer, having tried various excuses to deter her, resorts to the ploy of telling her that he is already engaged. Aline reconsiders Alexis's plea, takes the potion and rushes off to meet him, but she inadvertently bumps into the elderly Dr Daly and falls in love with him. The furious Alexis, having lost Aline, confronts Wells and demands that the spell should be broken. There is only one way for this to happen – either Alexis or Wells must die. The obvious candidate is Wells since it is his spell that has caused all the problems. As he perishes in smoke and fire the power of the potion is cancelled, allowing the villagers to revert to normality and to their former loves. Aline returns to Alexis, Lady Sangazure gets Sir Marmaduke, Constance hooks Dr Daly and the Notary gets Mrs Partlett.

H.M.S. Pinafore

Sub-title
The Lass that Loved a Sailor

Descriptive billing
An entirely original Nautical Comic Opera in 2 Acts

Date and theatre of first performance
25 May 1878, Opéra Comique, London

Length of original run
571 performances

Overture
Sullivan scored the opening and sketched other parts. The remainder was probably written by Hamilton Clarke or Alfred Cellier.

Setting
Act 1   Quarter-deck of *H.M.S. Pinafore* off Portsmouth, at noon
Act 2   The same, at night

Time
1878

Cast list, performers in first London season and voices

The Rt Hon Sir Joseph Porter, First Lord of the Admiralty	George Grossmith	*Bar*
Captain Corcoran	Rutland Barrington	*Bar*
Ralph Rackstraw, able seaman	George Power	*Tenor*
Dick Deadeye, able seaman	Richard Temple	*Bass*
Bill Bobstay, boatswain's mate	Fred Clifton	*Bar*
Bob Becket, carpenter's mate	Mr Dymot	*Bass*
Tom Tucker, midshipmite	Master Fitzaltamont	*Silent*
Josephine, the captain's daughter	Emma Howson	*Sop*
Hebe, Sir Joseph's first cousin	Jessie Bond	*MS*
Little Buttercup, a bumboat woman	Helen Everard	*Con*

Chorus of Sir Joseph's Sisters, Cousins and Aunts; Sailors and Marines

Songs and choruses

Act 1   We sail the ocean blue (Sailors)
I'm called little Buttercup (Buttercup)
The nightingale sighed for the moon's bright ray (Ralph, Chorus)
I am the Captain of the *Pinafore* (Corcoran, Chorus)
Sorry her lot who loves too well (Josephine)
Over the bright blue sea (Chorus)
I am the monarch of the sea (Sir Joseph, Chorus)
When I was a lad I served a term (Sir Joseph, Chorus)
A British tar is a soaring soul (Ralph, Becket, Bobstay, Chorus)
Refrain, audacious tar (Josephine, Ralph)

Act 2   Fair moon, to thee I sing (Corcoran)
Things are seldom what they seem (Buttercup, Corcoran)
The hours creep on apace (Josephine)
Never mind the why and wherefore (Sir Joseph, Corcoran, Josephine)
Kind Captain, I've important information (Dick Deadeye, Corcoran)
Carefully on tiptoe stealing (Chorus)
Farewell, my own (Ralph, Josephine, Sir Joseph, Bobstay, Dick Deadeye, Hebe, Buttercup, Chorus)
A many years ago (Buttercup)
Oh joy, oh rapture unforeseen (Josephine, Ralph, Hebe, Dick Deadeye)
For he is an Englishman (All)

Synopsis

Act 1

On the quarter-deck of *H.M.S. Pinafore* – a fighting ship of the line – the sailors leave their various tasks to buy wares from a Portsmouth bumboat woman named Little Buttercup but are interrupted by the appearance of two characters – Dick Deadeye, an unattractive sailor whom no one has any time for, and Ralph Rackstraw, a handsome sailor obviously known to Buttercup. Ralph explains that he is in love with the captain's daughter but is sad because she is far above his own station in life. The crew are welcomed on deck by the commanding officer, Captain Corcoran, who reveals that he rules by politeness rather than tough discipline. The captain tells Buttercup that his daughter, Josephine, is sought in marriage by the First Lord of the Admiralty, Sir Joseph Porter, KCB. Josephine is anything but enthusiastic about the proposed union, and the captain's fears are realised when Josephine tells him that she is in love with a humble sailor aboard *Pinafore*, but as she is the captain's daughter she decides to accept her fate. Sir Joseph arrives accompanied by his many sisters, cousins and aunts. Having described how he reached his exalted position, he hands out to the crew one of his own musical compositions for use by the Royal Navy. The crew sing it and then depart leaving Ralph to meet Josephine. He attempts to win her love but, although she obviously loves Ralph, she spurns him. He announces to the crew that he is going to kill himself and prepares the pistol but he is stopped by Josephine who rushes to him to tell him that she does love him. They decide to steal away that night and marry.

Act 2

It is now evening and the moon shines over *H.M.S. Pinafore*. Captain Corcoran sings of his worries concerning Josephine and is joined by Buttercup. She tells of her ability to read destinies, foretells that the captain is in for a major change and warns him to be prepared for it. Sir Joseph is perplexed that Josephine shows no welcoming response to his attentions. The captain advises him that she could be overawed by his high rank and so Sir Joseph attempts to reassure her that love is a platform on which all ranks can meet. Little does he know that he has pleaded his unknown rival's case admirably and this helps Josephine to confirm her commitment to Ralph. However, the planned elopement is revealed to the captain by Dick Deadeye. They listen in on the events and intervene only as the couple prepare to depart. Ralph declares to the captain his love for Josephine which he justifies by proclaiming himself a proud Englishman. Sir Joseph emerges from his cabin just in time to hear the captain utter 'Damme it's too bad' and, without allowing Corcoran an explanation, sends him to his cabin. When Sir Joseph learns the truth he immediately has Ralph escorted to the dungeon. The situation is then dramatically reversed by Buttercup who explains that, many years before, she had looked after both Ralph and the captain as babies, but unfortunately she had mixed them up. Now it seems that Ralph is really the captain and Corcoran a lowly seaman. The two return on deck suitably attired – presumably in one another's clothes. Ralph claims Josephine, Corcoran proposes to Buttercup and Sir Joseph turns to his first cousin Hebe for solace.

The Pirates of Penzance

Sub-title
The Slave of Duty

Descriptive billing
A new and original Melo-Dramatic Opera in 2 Acts

Dates and theatres of first performance
30 December 1879, Royal Bijou Theatre, Paignton, Devon
31 December 1879, Fifth Avenue Theatre, New York
3 April 1880, Opéra Comique, London

Length of original London run
363 performances

Overture
Written by Sullivan and Alfred Cellier – with assistance from W. S. Gilbert and Frederic Clay. A shortened version was re-arranged by Geoffrey Toye in 1919.

Setting
Act 1   A rocky coastline in Cornwall
Act 2   A ruined chapel by moonlight

Time
1879

Cast list, performers in first London season and voices

Major-General Stanley	George Grossmith	*Bar*
Pirate King	Richard Temple	*Bass*
Samuel, his lieutenant	George Temple	*Bar*
Frederic, a pirate apprentice	George Power	*Tenor*
Sergeant of Police	Rutland Barrington	*BBar*
Mabel, Stanley's daughter	Marion Hood	*Sop*
Edith, Stanley's daughter	Julia Gwynne	*Sop*
Kate, Stanley's daughter	Lilian la Rue	*MS*
Isabel, Stanley's daughter	Neva Bond	*MS*
Ruth, pirate maid	Emily Cross	*Con*

Chorus of Pirates, Police, and General Stanley's Daughters

Songs and choruses

Act 1   Pour, oh, pour the pirate sherry (Pirate Chorus, Samuel)
When Frederic was a little lad (Ruth)
Oh, better far to live and die (Pirate King)
You told me you were fair as gold! (Frederic, Ruth)
Climbing over rocky mountain (Female Chorus)
Oh, is there not one maiden breast (Frederic)
Poor wandering one (Mabel)
How beautifully blue the sky (Female Chorus)
I am the very model of a modern Major-General (Stanley, Chorus)
These children whom you see (Stanley, Pirates)
Hail, Poetry, thou heaven-born maid (All)
Pray observe the magnanimity (All)

Act 2   Oh, dry the glistening tear (Female Chorus)
Dear father, why leave your bed (Mabel)
When the foeman bares his steel (Sergeant, Police)
When you had left our pirate fold (Ruth, King, Frederic)
With falsehood foul he tricked us (King, Ruth, Frederic)
Stay, Frederic stay! (Mabel, Frederic)
Ah, leave me not to pine (Mabel, Frederic)
Though in body and in mind (Sergeant, Police)
When a felon's not engaged in his employment (Sergeant, Police)
With cat-like tread (Pirates, Police)
Sighing softly to the river (Stanley, Chorus)
Poor wandering one (All)

Contemporary drawing
showing the singing of the
paradox trio from the original
production of *The Pirates of
Penzance*, from the *Illustrated
Sporting and Dramatic News*.

D.H.FRISTON   ACT.II.

Synopsis

Act 1

The infamous pirates of Penzance have come ashore to celebrate the coming of age of Frederic, one of their band. Years before, Frederic had been apprenticed to the pirates due to an error made by his nurserymaid, Ruth. She inaccurately heard her master's instructions and apprenticed the boy to a pirate instead of to a pilot. Realising her mistake, she had stayed on as one of the crew. For Frederic, freedom from his indentures is to be a happy release for he loathes the idea of piracy. He insists that, once free, he intends to exterminate the pirates despite their lack of success which he knows is caused by them being too tender-hearted to those they capture since they never rob orphans. At the turn of the tide the pirates depart leaving Frederic and Ruth in the cove. Ruth attempts to woo her ward, but they are interrupted by a party of beautiful young girls. Frederic spurns the elderly Ruth and rushes to hide. But he is soon forced to disclose himself as the girls begin to remove clothing for a paddle. They are shocked and refuse his entreaties of love, except for Mabel who takes pity on him – though her sisters are sure that his beauty is all that really attracts her. Frederic attempts to warn them about the pirates but suddenly the girls are surrounded by pirates who contemplate mass-marriage. They do not anticipate the sudden arrival of the girls' father, Major-General Stanley, who is annoyed to hear of the pirates' intentions. He evades the dilemma by deceit – telling the Pirate King that he is an orphan. The pirates, saddened at his plight, immediately return his daughters.

Act 2

Major-General Stanley is filled with remorse at the lies he told the pirates. He feels that he has brought dishonour on his ancestors by purchase, even though he only bought his baronial castle a year before. Meanwhile, Frederic has organised an expedition to destroy the pirates. This consists of a patrol of nervous police constables and a worried Sergeant of Police. As they leave to prepare for the terrifying encounter, Frederic is left alone. His musings are interrupted by the Pirate King and Ruth who have arrived at the castle to share with him a strange paradox. It seems that Frederic was born in a leap year on 29 February and therefore – despite being twenty-one years old – in birthdays he is only five-and-a-quarter. His apprenticeship agreement states that he is under contract until his twenty-first birthday and so he is technically still a pirate and it is his duty to return to the pirate band. He is also forced to reveal the ploy by which Major-General Stanley deluded the pirates. The Pirate King is enraged and decides to attack the castle that very night to seek revenge. The police, now without Frederic, go out to arrest the pirates, but after a brief fight they are defeated. The Sergeant, however, now turns the tables by commanding the pirates to yield in the name of Queen Victoria which they do instantly. All seems lost for them until Ruth reveals that they are really noblemen who have gone astray. The Major-General encourages them to resume their former responsibilities and gives them his consent to marry his many daughters.

Patience

Sub-title
Bunthorne's Bride

Descriptive billing
A new and original Aesthetic Opera in 2 Acts

Date and theatre of first performance
23 April 1881, Opéra Comique, London, transferred to Savoy Theatre on 10 October 1881

Length of original run
578 performances, both theatres

Overture
Written by Sullivan

Setting
Act 1   Exterior of Bunthorne Castle
Act 2   A Glade

Time
1881

Cast list, performers in first London season and voices

Reginald Bunthorne, a poet	George Grossmith	*Bar*
Archibald Grosvenor, a poet	Rutland Barrington	*Bar*
Colonel Calverley	Richard Temple	*BBar*
Major Murgatroyd	Frank Thornton	*Bar*
Lieut. The Duke of Dunstable	Durward Lely	*Tenor*
Bunthorne's Solicitor	George Bowley	*Silent*
Lady Angela	Jessie Bond	*MS*
Lady Saphir	Julia Gwynne	*MS*
Lady Ella	May Fortesque	*Sop*
Lady Jane	Alice Barnett	*Con*
Patience, a dairymaid	Leonora Braham	*Sop*

Chorus of Rapturous Maidens and Officers of the Dragoon Guards

Songs and choruses
Act 1   Twenty love-sick maidens we (Chorus of Maidens)
        I cannot tell what this love may be (Patience, Maidens)
        The soldiers of our Queen (Chorus of Dragoons)
        If you want a receipt for that popular mystery (Colonel, Dragoons)
        In a doleful train (Chorus)
        When I first put this uniform on (Colonel, Dragoons)
        Am I alone and unobserved? (Bunthorne)
        If you're anxious for to shine in the high aesthetic line (Bunthorne)
        Long years ago, fourteen, maybe (Patience, Angela)
        Prithee, pretty maiden (Patience and Grosvenor)

Let the merry cymbals sound (Chorus of Maidens)
Your maiden hearts, ah, do not steel (Duke)
True love must single-hearted be (Patience, Bunthorne)
Now is not this ridiculous (Chorus of Dragoons)

Act 2   Silvered is the raven hair (Jane)
Turn, oh, turn, in this direction (Chorus of Maidens)
A magnet hung in a hardware shop (Grosvenor)
In a doleful train (Jane)
Love is a plaintive song (Patience)
So go to him and say to him (Bunthorne, Jane)
It's clear that medieval art alone retains its zest (Duke, Colonel, Major)
If Saphir I choose to marry (Duke, Colonel, Major, Angela, Saphir)
When I go out of doors (Bunthorne, Grosvenor)
After much debate internal (Duke, Bunthorne, Chorus)

Synopsis

Act 1

Bunthorne Castle is besieged by lovesick maidens weeping despondently for the love of Reginald Bunthorne, an aesthetic poet. But they love in vain for – as Lady Jane, an elderly spinster, explains – Bunthorne is already in love with Patience, the village milkmaid. Patience, naive in the ways of love, cannot understand why the maidens are all so unhappy. But she feels sure that the news she brings will restore their spirits for the 35th Dragoon Guards, to whom the maidens were all engaged the previous year, have just returned to the village. To the astonishment of Patience, the maidens are unmoved at this news and the Dragoons are equally shocked to discover the maidens' obsession, especially when they see Bunthorne, and they quickly leave in disgust. Once he is alone, Bunthorne is revealed as a sham – he is acting as an aesthetic merely for the attention it creates. His love for Patience is not returned and she is perplexed by the poet. Feeling concerned at her lack of knowledge in love, Patience seeks guidance from Lady Angela who explains that love is the only genuine feeling that is unselfish. So Patience decides that it would be selfish to deny her love and, rushing off, she encounters Archibald Grosvenor, a newcomer, who proceeds to woo her. When she finds that this young poet is her old childhood friend, Patience gives him her heart, but Grosvenor is loved by all women because of his great beauty and Patience realises that to love him would be a selfish act, and the two part unhappily. Bunthorne, meanwhile, despondent at losing Patience, decides to raffle himself, although before the draw can be held Patience interrupts and informs Bunthorne that, since loving him would not be selfish, she has decided to accept him. Bunthorne is overjoyed and leaves the other maidens who return to their old loves – the Dragoons – only to be confronted with Grosvenor with whom they all instantly fall in love, much to the poet's horror and the annoyance of the Dragoons.

Act 2

Lady Jane remains devoted to Bunthorne, expecting him at any time to lose interest in Patience and return her true devotion. Meanwhile, Grosvenor is desperately unhappy. He dreams of Patience but is pestered by the adoring maidens who beseech him to read out his poetry. Bunthorne is angry as he is shocked at the maidens' betrayal and at Patience's obvious regard for Grosvenor and he decides to confront his rival. The Dragoons, also bewildered at the turn of events, attempt to win back their loves and three of them dress as poets assuming, with some difficulty, the aesthetic posture, much to the maidens' amazement. They win a promise that the maidens will return to them should Grosvenor fail to choose one of their number. Bunthorne and Grosvenor meet and bicker. The former, arguing that the village is too small for two poets, threatens the other with a curse unless he renounces his aestheticism and dresses in ordinary clothes. Grosvenor relents and agrees to do this and is relieved that he now has the excuse he has been looking for to effect a change in his demeanour. Bunthorne is overjoyed and also decides to change by becoming more amiable and cheerful, but this renders him perfect. Patience decides that, because of this perfection, she cannot love him and Grosvenor who is now commonplace claims her. Bunthorne is left with faithful Jane but, as the Dragoons reclaim their loves, one of them – the Duke of Dunstable – decides out of fairness to take a plain wife, and calls on Jane. The spinster, dazzled by the prospect of being a duchess, deserts Bunthorne who remains the only single person in the plot.

Iolanthe

Sub-title
The Peer and the Peri

Descriptive billing
An original Fairy Opera in 2 Acts

Date and theatre of first performance
25 November 1882, Savoy Theatre, London

Length of original run
398 performances

Overture
Written by Sullivan

Setting
Act 1   An Arcadian landscape
Act 2   Palace Yard, Westminster

Time
1882

Cast list, performers in first London season and voices

The Lord Chancellor	George Grossmith	*Bar*
Earl of Mountararat	Rutland Barrington	*Bar*
Earl Tolloller	Durward Lely	*Tenor*
Private Willis	Charles Manners	*Bass*
Strephon, a shepherd	Richard Temple	*Bar*
Queen of the Fairies	Alice Barnett	*Con*
Iolanthe, a fairy and		
Strephon's mother	Jessie Bond	*MS*
Celia, a fairy	May Fortesque	*Sop*
Leila, a fairy	Julia Gwynne	*MS*
Fleta, a fairy	Sybil Grey	*MS*
Phyllis, a shepherdess	Leonora Braham	*Sop*

Chorus of Dukes, Marquises, Earls, Viscounts, Barons and Fairies

Songs and choruses

Act 1   Tripping hither, tripping thither (Chorus of Fairies)
        If you ask us how we live (Leila)
        Iolanthe! (Fairy Queen and Fairies)
        Welcome to our hearts again (Chorus of Fairies)
        Good morrow, good mother (Strephon, Chorus of Fairies)
        Fare thee well, attractive stranger (Fairy Queen and Fairies)
        Good morrow, good lover (Phyllis)
        None shall part us from each other (Phyllis, Strephon)
        Loudly let the trumpet bray (Chorus of Peers)
        The Law is the true embodiment (Lord Chancellor, Chorus)
        Of all the young ladies I know (Tolloller, Mountararat, Phyllis,
           Chorus)
        Spurn not the nobly born (Tolloller, Peers)
        When I went to the Bar as a very young man (Lord Chancellor)
        When darkly looms the day (Strephon, Phyllis, Tolloller,
           Mountararat, Peers)
        In babyhood (Strephon)
        For riches and rank (Phyllis)
        Go away, madam (Lord Chancellor, Fairies, Peers)
        With Strephon for your foe (All)

Act 2   When all night long a chap remains (Private Willis)
        Strephon's a Member of Parliament (Chorus of Fairies, Peers)
        When Britain really ruled the waves (Mountararat, Fairies, Peers)
        In vain to us you plead (Leila, Celia, Fairies)
        Oh, foolish fay (Fairy Queen, Fairies)
        Though p'r'aps I may incur your blame (Tolloller, Mountararat,
           Phyllis, Willis)
        When you're lying awake with a dismal headache (Lord Chancellor)
        If you go in (Lord Chancellor, Mountararat, Tolloller)
        If we're weak enough to tarry (Strephon, Phyllis)
        He loves! If in the bygone years (Iolanthe)
        Soon as we may, off and away! (Phyllis, All)

Synopsis

Act 1

Fairyland is in a state of sadness because of the protracted banishment of Iolanthe, a former member of the fairy band. In marrying a mortal twenty-five years previously, she had broken a strict fairy law, the punishment for which was death; but her sentence had been reduced to penal servitude for life. Surprised at Iolanthe's choice of residence – with the frogs at the bottom of a dark, damp stream – the Fairy Queen is persuaded to summon Iolanthe and pardon her. Iolanthe explains that she wanted to be near her son, Strephon. Presently, Strephon, a shepherd, arrives and exclaims that he is to be married to Phyllis, a ward in Chancery. When the fairies leave, Phyllis greets Strephon. They discuss their wedding plans and decide that a delay would be dangerous. The members of the House of Lords enter with much splendour and are followed by the Lord Chancellor. It appears that Phyllis is much loved by the Lords, and she is summoned but declines their proposals and announces that her heart is already given to Strephon. The Lord Chancellor is enraged and, when Strephon appears, refuses to give his consent to the proposed marriage. Later, while Strephon is being comforted by his young-looking mother, Iolanthe, the Lords, accompanied by Phyllis, jump to the wrong conclusion. Phyllis accuses Strephon of being unfaithful and offers her love to the wealthiest Lords – Tolloller and Mountararat. Strephon, in despair, summons the fairies to his aid. They reprimand the Lords and attempt to put right the misunderstanding. However, when ridiculed, the Fairy Queen reveals her identity and wreaks vengeance by threatening to enter Strephon into Parliament with supernatural powers to carry any bill.

Act 2

Outside Parliament, Private Willis of the Grenadier Guards ponders on life at Westminster. The Lords are irritated with Strephon's ability, despite their opposition, to carry any bill he chooses. In addition, Tolloller and Mountararat are having difficulties in deciding who should claim Phyllis. The Lord Chancellor has also fallen in love with Phyllis but he is in no position to approach his own ward. Strephon, in low spirits despite leading both Houses, encounters Phyllis and confesses that his mother is a fairy. This leaves Phyllis astounded but, realising her earlier mistake, she at once embraces him. The two lovers beg Iolanthe to plead their cause with the Lord Chancellor, but Iolanthe makes the startling confession that the Lord Chancellor is none other than her husband and that by fairy law she is bound not to disclose herself to him. The Lord Chancellor approaches and the two lovers flee, leaving Iolanthe who veils herself in his presence. He is cheerful, having persuaded himself that he might marry Phyllis after all. Iolanthe appeals on Strephon's behalf but the Lord Chancellor is adamant and Iolanthe has no option but to tell him that she is his wife. The punishment for this fairy crime is death and the Fairy Queen duly arrives to give judgement. However, she finds to her horror that the whole fairy troupe has married the Lords – they are now fairy duchesses, marchionesses, countesses, viscountesses and baronesses – and she must therefore kill them all. The Lord Chancellor comes to the rescue by offering to change the law so that it now reads that a fairy *must* marry a mortal or suffer death. The Fairy Queen agrees, sets her cap at Private Willis who sprouts wings, and everyone flies off to Fairyland.

Princess Ida

Sub-title
Castle Adamant

Descriptive billing
A respectful Operatic Per-Version of Tennyson's 'The Princess' in a Prologue and 2 Acts

Date and theatre of first performance
5 January 1884, Savoy Theatre, London

Length of original run
246 performances

Overture
Written by Sullivan. Illness probably prevented him from completing this overture and it remains a fairly brief introduction.

Setting
Act 1   Pavilion in King Hildebrand's Palace
Act 2   Gardens of Castle Adamant
Act 3   Courtyard of Castle Adamant

Time
Indeterminate

Cast list, performers in first London season and voices

King Hildebrand	Rutland Barrington	*BBar*
Hilarion, his son	Henry Bracy	*Tenor*
Cyril, Hilarion's friend	Durward Lely	*Tenor*
Florian, Hilarion's friend	Charles Ryley	*Bar*
King Gama	George Grossmith	*Bar*
Arac, his son	Richard Temple	*BBar*
Guron, Gama's son	Warwick Grey	*BBar*
Scynthius, Gama's son	William Lugg	*BBar*
Princess Ida, Gama's daughter	Leonora Braham	*Sop*
Lady Blanche, professor	Rosina Brandram	*Con*
Lady Psyche, professor	Kate Chard	*Sop*

Melissa, Blanche's daughter	Jessie Bond	*MS*
Sacharissa, student	Sybil Grey	*Sop*
Chloe, student	Miss Heathcote	*Sop*
Ada, student	Miss Twyman	*MS*

Chorus of Soldiers, Courtiers and Students

Songs and choruses

Act 1   Search throughout the panorama (Chorus)
Now hearken to my strict command (Hildebrand, Chorus)
Ida was a twelvemonth old (Hilarion)
We are warriors three (Arac, Guron, Scynthius)
If you give me your attention I will tell you what I am (Gama)
Perhaps if you address the lady (Gama, Hildebrand)
Expressive glances (Hilarion, Cyril, Florian)
For a month to dwell (Arac, Guron, Scynthius, Chorus)

Act 2   Towards the empyrean heights (Chorus)
Man will swear and man will storm (Psyche)
Oh, goddess wise (Ida)
Come, mighty Must (Blanche)
Gently, gently (Hilarion, Cyril, Florian)
I am a maiden cold and stately (Hilarion, Cyril, Florian)
The world is but a broken toy (Ida, Hilarion, Cyril, Florian)
A lady fair, of lineage high (Psyche)
The woman of the wisest wit (Psyche, Melissa, Hilarion, Cyril, Florian)
Now wouldn't you like to rule the roast (Melissa, Blanche)
Merrily ring the luncheon bell (Chorus)
Would you know the kind of maid (Cyril)
Oh! joy, our chief is saved (Chorus)
Whom thou hast chained must wear his chain (Hilarion, Chorus)
Some years ago (Hildebrand)
Though I am but a girl (Ida, Chorus)

Act 3   Death to the invader! (Chorus)
I built upon a rock (Ida)
Whene'er I spoke sarcastic joke (Gama)
When anger spreads his wing (Chorus)
This helmet, I suppose (Arac, Guron, Scynthius)
This is our duty plain towards (Chorus)
With joy abiding (Ida, Hilarion, Chorus)

Synopsis

Act 1

The court of King Hildebrand is awaiting the arrival of King Gama – a neighbouring monarch – and his daughter, the Princess Ida, who in infancy had been betrothed to Hildebrand's son, Hilarion. Hildebrand has issued instructions for the reception of Gama, depending on whether or not he honours the agreement and brings Princess Ida. Gama arrives accompanied by his three warrior sons – strong in arm but weak in brain – named Arac, Guron and Scynthius. Gama is an ugly, twisted monarch who enjoys being spiteful and insulting and yet is unable to understand why everyone despises him. He has not brought the princess because she has shut herself away in a country castle where she rules a women's university in which men are renounced as inferior and unnecessary. Hilarion decides to gain access to this university and win Ida's love, and his two friends, Cyril and Florian, accompany him. Hildebrand, meanwhile, keeps Gama and his sons locked away as hostages.

Act 2

The students at Princess Ida's university – Castle Adamant – have been lectured by Lady Psyche, the professor of humanities, on the theme that man is nature's sole mistake. They are then addressed by Lady Blanche, who is Princess Ida's deputy and professor of abstract science. She also administers the punishments for such crimes as drawing a perambulator and bringing chessmen – 'men with whom you give each other mate' – into the university, where even the crowing each morning is done by an accomplished hen! Finally, Princess Ida comes to lecture the students on the superiority of women over men. When all is quiet, Hilarion, Cyril and Florian climb over the castle wall. Finding discarded undergraduate robes, they clad themselves in them and in this disguise they approach Princess Ida and are admitted into the university as three young ladies. However, their scheme is discovered first by Lady Psyche who happens to be Florian's sister and then by Lady Blanche's daughter, Melissa, who – never having seen men before – is extremely curious. Both women agree to keep the secret. Lady Blanche realises that something is amiss when she hears the new students speaking with gruff voices. But Melissa plays on her mother's ambitions by persuading her that, if Hilarion succeeds with his plan, Ida will leave the university and transfer power to Lady Blanche – who already believes that she should be in charge anyway. Lunchtime comes and Cyril gets drunk. Ida, on finding that the new students are men, reels backwards and falls into the river, and Hilarion dives to the rescue and saves her from drowning. Despite this, she has the three men arrested only to find that the castle is being besieged by King Hildebrand's troops and that her father and brothers are held as hostages.

Act 3

Princess Ida is resolute. She refuses to yield to the attacking troops and holds the castle in defiance of their threats. But her students are apprehensive of the coming battle and they gradually back down leaving Ida to stand alone. King Gama, however, suggests that the outcome of the battle ought to be decided by combat between his three sons against Hilarion, Cyril and Florian. The fight takes place and Gama's sons are defeated. Ida relents, seeing the futility of further struggle and, realising at last that marriage is necessary to provide for future generations, she gives herself willingly to Hilarion. Hildebrand is pacified and the two factions are reconciled.

George Grossmith as King Gama in *Princess Ida*.

The Mikado

Sub-title
The Town of Titipu

Descriptive billing
An entirely original Japanese Opera in 2 Acts

Date and theatre of first performance
14 March 1885, Savoy Theatre, London

Length of original run
672 performances

Overture
Written by Hamilton Clarke who followed Sullivan's instructions on the numbers to be included and their ordering

Setting
Act 1   Courtyard of Ko-Ko's official residence
Act 2   Ko-Ko's garden

Time
Indeterminate

Cast list, performers in first London season and voices

The Mikado of Japan	Richard Temple	*BBar*
Nanki-Poo, his son	Durward Lely	*Tenor*
Ko-Ko, Lord High Executioner	George Grossmith	*Bar*
Pooh-Bah, Lord High Everything Else	Rutland Barrington	*BBar*
Pish-Tush, a noble lord	Frederick Bovill	*Bar*
Yum-Yum, ward of Ko-Ko	Leonora Braham	*Sop*
Pitti-Sing, Yum-Yum's sister	Jessie Bond	*MS*
Peep-Bo, Yum-Yum's sister	Sybil Grey	*MS*
Katisha, an elderly lady	Rosina Brandram	*Con*
Chorus of Schoolgirls, Nobles, Guards and Coolies		

Songs and choruses
Act 1   If you want to know who we are (Male Chorus)
        A wandering minstrel I (Nanki-Poo, Chorus)
        Our great Mikado, virtuous man (Pish-Tush, Chorus)
        Young man, despair (Pooh-Bah, Nanki-Poo, Pish-Tush)
        Behold the Lord High Executioner (Male Chorus)
        As some day it may happen that a victim must be found (Ko-Ko, Chorus)
        Comes a train of little ladies (Female Chorus)
        Three little maids from school are we (Yum-Yum, Peep-Bo, Pitti-Sing, Chorus)

So please you, Sir, we much regret (Yum-Yum, Peep-Bo, Pitti-
Sing, Pooh-Bah, Chorus)
Were you not to Ko-Ko plighted (Yum-Yum, Nanki-Poo)
My brain it teems (Ko-Ko, Pooh-Bah, Pish-Tush)
With aspect stern (Pooh-Bah, Pish-Tush, Chorus)
Oh fool, that fleest (Katisha, Chorus)
The hour of gladness (Katisha)
Ye torrents roar (Katisha, Chorus)

Act 2   Braid the raven hair (Pitti-Sing, Chorus)
The sun, whose rays are all ablaze (Yum-Yum)
Brightly dawns our wedding day (Yum-Yum, Pitti-Sing, Nanki-
Poo, Pish-Tush)
Here's a how-de-do (Yum-Yum, Nanki-Poo, Ko-Ko)
Miya sama, miya sama (Chorus)
From every kind of man (Mikado, Katisha, Chorus)
A more humane Mikado (Mikado, Chorus)
The criminal cried, as he dropped him down (Ko-Ko, Pitti-Sing,
Pooh-Bah, Chorus)
See how the Fates their gifts allot (Pitti-Sing, Katisha, Pooh-Bah,
Mikado, Ko-Ko)
The flowers that bloom in the spring (Nanki-Poo, Ko-Ko, Yum-
Yum, Pitti-Sing, Pooh-Bah)
Alone! and yet alive! (Katisha)
On a tree by a river a little tom-tit (Ko-Ko)
There is beauty in the bellow of the blast (Katisha, Ko-Ko)
For he's gone and married Yum-Yum (Pitti-Sing, Ko-Ko, Yum-
Yum, Nanki-Poo, Chorus)

Rutland Barrington as Pooh-
Bah in *The Mikado*. (D'Oyly
Carte Archive.)

Synopsis

Act 1

Nanki-Poo, a wandering minstrel, approaches a group of noblemen in
the town of Titipu in Japan and questions them about the whereabouts of
Yum-Yum, a ward of the cheap tailor, Ko-Ko. Nanki-Poo had fallen in
love with Yum-Yum but as she was engaged to Ko-Ko he had left Titipu
brokenhearted. He has now heard that Ko-Ko has been condemned to
death for flirting, so he has returned to find Yum-Yum. Pish-Tush, a
noble lord, tells him that Ko-Ko has since been released from jail and
raised to the post of Lord High Executioner. This is an attempt to thwart
the Mikado's new flirtation laws, since Ko-Ko cannot cut off anyone
else's head until he has cut off his own! Pooh-Bah, Lord High Everything
Else, tells Nanki-Poo that the wedding preparations have commenced.
Shortly after Ko-Ko's arrival, Yum-Yum and her two sisters, Peep-Bo
and Pitti-Sing, return from school. Yum-Yum is less than enthusiastic
when she sees Ko-Ko but overjoyed to meet Nanki-Poo again who
confides to her that he is the son of the Mikado but that he cannot reveal
himself because his father has ordered him to marry an elderly lady at

court named Katisha. Ko-Ko now receives a letter from the Mikado demanding an execution within a month. Ko-Ko, Pooh-Bah and Pish-Tush decide that a victim must be found. Conveniently, Nanki-Poo, distressed at losing Yum-Yum, has decided to hang himself. Ko-Ko pleads with him to be executed instead and Nanki-Poo agrees on condition that he is allowed to marry Yum-Yum for one month. Ko-Ko accepts reluctantly. Katisha arrives and tries to expose Nanki-Poo as the Mikado's son. She is thwarted but leaves threatening revenge.

Act 2
The wedding preparations of Nanki-Poo and Yum-Yum are marred by the reminder that, in one month, Nanki-Poo is to die. But Ko-Ko now brings worse news. According to the law, if a man is executed then his wife must be buried alive. The situation seems hopeless and Nanki-Poo threatens suicide there and then. Ko-Ko fears the repercussions if an execution is not carried out but he is afraid to execute Nanki-Poo – never having performed such a deed before – so he decides on a new plan. Yum-Yum and Nanki-Poo are to get married and go away quickly. Ko-Ko will pretend that he has killed Nanki-Poo and fake an execution certificate. These arrangements are just completed when the Mikado and his court enter the town. Ko-Ko lies to him and explains that an execution has taken place and, with Pooh-Bah and Pitti-Sing, he gives a graphic description of the macabre event. The Mikado is impressed but explains that he has arrived for an entirely different reason; he is searching for his son. When he realises that the man who has been executed was his son and heir, the Mikado explains that the punishment is death for killing the heir to the throne and so the executions of Ko-Ko, Pooh-Bah and Pitti-Sing must take place after lunch. There seems no answer to the problem until Nanki-Poo promises to come back to life once Katisha is engaged and cannot claim him. Ko-Ko is forced to woo Katisha but much against his will. He is successful and this allows Nanki-Poo to re-appear with his bride. Everyone is now satisfied except for Ko-Ko who has to contend with the force of Katisha's anger at his deception.

Ruddigore

Sub-title
The Witch's Curse

Descriptive billing
A new and original Supernatural Opera in 2 Acts

Date and theatre of first performance
22 January 1887, Savoy Theatre, London

Length of original run
288 performances

Overture

Written by Hamilton Clarke. Geoffrey Toye wrote a revised overture for the revival in 1921 as some of the numbers in the original overture had by then been cut from the performance.

Setting

Act 1   The fishing village of Rederring in Cornwall
Act 2   The Picture Gallery in Ruddigore Castle

Time

Early in the nineteenth century

Cast list, performers in first London season and voices

MORTALS

Sir Ruthven Murgatroyd, disguised as the young farmer Robin Oakapple	George Grossmith	*Bar*
Richard Dauntless, his foster-brother	Durward Lely	*Tenor*
Sir Despard Murgatroyd, a wicked baronet	Rutland Barrington	*BBar*
Old Adam Goodheart, Robin's servant	Rudolph Lewis	*Bass*
Rose Maybud, a village maiden	Leonora Braham	*Sop*
Mad Margaret	Jessie Bond	*MS*
Dame Hannah, Rose's aunt	Rosina Brandram	*Con*
Zorah, professional bridesmaid	Josephine Findlay	*Sop*
Ruth, professional bridesmaid	Miss Lindsay	*Sop*

GHOSTS

Sir Rupert Murgatroyd, first baronet	Mr Price	
Sir Jaspar Murgatroyd, third baronet	Mr Charles	
Sir Lionel Murgatroyd, sixth baronet	Mr Trevor	
Sir Conrad Murgatroyd, twelfth baronet	Mr Burbank	
Sir Desmond Murgatroyd, sixteenth baronet	Mr Tuer	
Sir Gilbert Murgatroyd, eighteenth baronet	Mr Wilbraham	
Sir Mervyn Murgatroyd, twentieth baronet	Mr Cox	
Sir Roderic Murgatroyd, twenty-first baronet	Richard Temple	*BBar*

Chorus of Officers, Ancestors, Professional Bridesmaids, Villagers

Songs and choruses

Act 1   Fair is Rose as the bright May-day (Bridesmaids)
           Sir Rupert Murgatroyd (Hannah, Bridesmaids)
           If somebody there chanced to be (Rose)
           I know a youth who loves a little maid (Robin, Rose)
           I shipped, d'ye see, in a Revenue sloop (Richard, Chorus)
           My boy, you may take it from me (Robin)
           The battle's roar is over (Richard, Rose)
           In sailing o'er life's ocean wide (Richard, Robin, Rose)

Jessie Bond as Mad Margaret in *Ruddigore* and Rutland Barrington as Sir Despard Murgatroyd in *Ruddigore*.

Cheerily carols the lark (Margaret)
To a garden full of posies (Margaret)
Welcome, gentry (Chorus)
Oh why am I moody and sad? (Sir Despard, Chorus)
You understand? (Sir Despard, Richard)
Hail the bride of seventeen summers (Chorus)
When the buds are blossoming (Rose, Hannah, Chorus)
Within this breast there beats a heart (Richard, Chorus)
Farewell! Thou hadst my heart (Rose)
Oh happy the lily (Rose, Richard, Despard, Margaret, Hannah,
    Adam, Zorah, Robin, Chorus)

Act 2   I once was as meek as a new-born lamb (Robin, Adam)

Happily coupled are we (Richard, Rose, Chorus)
In bygone days I had thy love (Rose, Chorus)
Painted emblems of a race (Ghosts)
When the night wind howls in the chimney cowls, (Roderic, Ghosts)
He yields! He answers to our call! (Ghosts)
Away, Remorse! (Robin)
I once was a very abandoned person (Despard, Margaret)
My eyes are fully open to my awful situation (Robin, Despard, Margaret)
There grew a little flower (Hannah, Roderic)
Having been a wicked baronet a week (Robin, Rose, Chorus)
Oh happy the lily (All)

Synopsis

Act 1

The village of Rederring in Cornwall possesses a chorus of professional bridesmaids but their services are not in demand due to the reluctance of pretty Rose Maybud to marry. The elderly Dame Hannah is asked to get married simply to employ the bridesmaids; but she relates how a witch roasted on the village green had cursed the baronets of Ruddigore – of whom Hannah's former suitor had been one – and of the need for each baronet to commit a daily crime or perish. Robin Oakapple, a young farmer in the village, loves Rose Maybud but, despite her own feelings of affection, she refuses to declare her love due to a fetish about correct behaviour. Unknown to the villagers, Robin is really Sir Ruthven Murgatroyd, the true Baronet of Ruddigore. He refuses to take his title because of the curse attached to it. The only person who knows of this, apart from Robin's servant, is Robin's half-brother, Richard Dauntless, a sailor who has just returned from a spell at sea. Having recounted his adventures, Richard agrees to approach Rose on Robin's behalf. However, he falls in love with Rose himself and when Robin and the bridesmaids appear they find the two together. But when Rose discovers that Robin loves her, she rejects Richard and accepts Robin. Mad Margaret is also a resident of Rederring. Her madness is caused by her love for Robin's younger brother – Sir Despard Murgatroyd – who has become Baronet of Ruddigore believing his older brother to be dead. Sir Despard rides into the village where he is approached by Richard who informs him of Robin's true identity. The wedding of Rose and Robin is about to begin when Sir Despard interrupts and claims Robin as his elder brother and therefore the true heir to Ruddigore and its problematic curse. Robin, now exposed, rushes off leaving Richard to approach Rose and Sir Despard to be reunited with Margaret.

Act 2

Robin and his servant – Adam Goodheart – have taken up residence at Ruddigore Castle, but neither relishes the prospect. Richard and Rose call at the castle asking for permission to marry but Robin refuses. In

211

despair at his plight, Robin appeals to his ancestors whose ghostly forms step from the picture frames in the gallery. Sir Roderic, one of these, demands an account of Robin's daily crimes but is not impressed by the trivial list. The ancestors insist that he should kidnap a woman or perish and Robin has no choice but to comply. He sends Adam to carry out the deed and then receives visitors, Sir Despard and Margaret, who have begun a reformed life together. They advise Robin to desist from his life of crime and he decides to defy his ancestors and suffer the consequences. But he has forgotten about Adam's mission and is mortified to find that Adam has carried off Dame Hannah who proves to be a handful for the two of them. Robin calls to Sir Roderic for aid, only to be further chastised when his ancestor recognizes Dame Hannah as his former lover! The situation is rectified when Robin realises that a Baronet of Ruddigore can only die by refusing to commit a daily crime and such a refusal is the same as suicide which is itself a crime – so the baronets had no need to die at all! The curse has now been lifted. Rose returns to Robin, Roderic claims Dame Hannah, Richard approaches a chief bridesmaid, Zorah, and so three weddings are planned – to the delight of the many bridesmaids!

The Yeomen of the Guard

Sub-title
The Merryman and his Maid

Descriptive billing
A new and original Opera in 2 Acts

Date and theatre of first performance
3 October 1888, Savoy Theatre, London

Length of original run
423 performances

Overture
Written by Sullivan

Setting
Act 1   Tower Green
Act 2   The same by moonlight

Time
The sixteenth century

Cast list, performers in first London season and voices
Sir Richard Cholmondeley, Lieutenant at
    the Tower   Wallace Brownlow   *Bar*

Colonel Fairfax, under sentence of death	Courtice Pounds	*Tenor*
Sergeant Meryll	Richard Temple	*BBar*
Leonard Meryll, his son	W. R. Shirley	*Tenor*
Jack Point, strolling player	George Grossmith	*Bar*
Wilfred Shadbolt, head jailor	W. H. Denny	*Bass*
Headsman	H. Richards	*Silent*
First Yeoman	J. Wilbraham	*Tenor*
Second Yeoman	A. Medcalf	*Bar*
Elsie Maynard, strolling singer	Geraldine Ulmar	*Sop*
Phoebe Meryll, the Sergeant's daughter	Jessie Bond	*MS*
Dame Carruthers, housekeeper	Rosina Brandram	*Con*
Kate, her niece	Rose Hervey	*Sop*
Chorus of Yeomen, Gentlemen and Citizens		

Courtice Pounds played
Colonel Fairfax in *The Yeomen
of the Guard*.

Songs and choruses

Act 1   When maiden loves, she sits and sighs (Phoebe)

Tower Warders, under orders! (Chorus of Yeomen and Crowd)

This the autumn of our life (Second Yeoman)

When our gallant Norman foes (Carruthers, Yeomen)

Alas! I waver to and fro! (Phoebe, Leonard, Sergeant)

Is life a boon? (Fairfax)

I have a song to sing, O (Point, Elsie)

How say you, maiden, will you wed (Elsie, Point, Lieutenant)

I've jibe and joke (Point)

'Tis done! I am a bride! (Elsie)

Were I thy bride (Phoebe)

Oh, Sergeant Meryll, is it true (Yeomen)

Didst thou not, oh, Leonard Meryll (First and Second Yeomen)

To thy fraternal care (Wilfred, Fairfax, Phoebe)

An escort for the prisoner (Fairfax and Yeomen)

Oh, woe is *you*? (Point)

All frenzied with despair I rave (Lieutenant, Chorus)

Act 2   Night has spread her pall once more (Chorus)

Warders are ye? (Carruthers)

Oh! a private buffoon is a light-hearted loon (Point)

Hereupon we're both agreed (Point, Wilfred)

Free from his fetters grim (Fairfax)

Strange adventure! Maiden wedded (Fairfax, Sergeant, Carruthers, Kate)

Like a ghost his vigil keeping (Wilfred, Point, Chorus)

A man who would woo a fair maid (Elsie, Phoebe, Fairfax)

When a wooer goes a-wooing (Elsie, Phoebe, Fairfax, Point)

Rapture, rapture! when love's votary (Carruthers, Sergeant)

Comes the pretty young bride (Female Chorus)

'Tis said that joy in full perfection (Phoebe, Elsie, Carruthers)

Oh, day of terror! Day of tears! (All)

Oh, thoughtless crew! (Point, Elsie, All)

Synopsis

Act 1

Phoebe Meryll sits alone on Tower Green tormented by the impending execution of the handsome Colonel Fairfax who has been accused of dealings with the devil. Sergeant Meryll, Phoebe's father, informs his daughter that her brother Leonard, having distinguished himself in battle, is now to become a warder at the Tower. Both father and daughter hope that when he arrives he will carry a reprieve for Fairfax. But Leonard brings no reprieve and so Sergeant Meryll contrives a plan whereby Fairfax is to be freed and will take the place of Leonard whom no-one has yet seen. In the meantime, Fairfax has been moved to the death cell. He has been falsely accused of sorcery by a relative who plans to inherit his estates after his demise. The condemned man asks the Lieutenant of the Tower, Sir Richard Cholmondeley, to find him a wife for the remaining hour he has left to live, and thus thwart his relative's evil ploy. Two travelling entertainers – Jack Point, a jester, and his partner Elsie Maynard – visit the Tower to perform, but the crowd proves boisterous and only the timely intervention of the lieutenant saves the entertainers from harm. The lieutenant sees Elsie as a suitable wife for Fairfax and broaches the subject to the two players. Elsie consents and is led away blindfolded to Fairfax's cell and returns shortly as a married woman. The Merylls now carry out their plan to free Fairfax. To obtain the key from the head jailor, Wilfred Shadbolt, without his knowledge, Phoebe plays on his love for her and then manages to distract the jailor's attention long enough to free Fairfax and return the key. Fairfax, now shaven and wearing a warder's uniform, is produced as Sergeant Meryll's son. Plans for the execution begin and three warders including the disguised Fairfax are sent to escort the prisoner, only to find that his cell is bare. Shadbolt is immediately arrested whilst Jack Point and Elsie are horrified at the situation that has resulted – realizing that Elsie's husband is still alive and now free.

Act 2

Two days have passed and there is no trace of the escaped prisoner. Both Shadbolt and Point are desperate and so they decide to lie by claiming to have shot the prisoner as he attempted to escape and then say that they watched him sink in the moat. Fairfax is concerned since he has no idea of the identity of his wife but to his pleasure he learns that it is Elsie whom he married. She feels affection for him but refuses to respond to his advances because she is already married to an unknown husband. Point attempts to woo Elsie, only to have his effort ridiculed by Fairfax who shows him how it should be done and, in the demonstration, proceeds to win Elsie for himself. Both Point and Phoebe are heartbroken at this development. Shadbolt is perplexed at Phoebe's jealousy of Elsie and realizes the true identity of the man masquerading as Leonard. Phoebe, distraught lest the secret gets out, agrees to become engaged to the jailor. The real Leonard arrives bearing a reprieve for Fairfax but the conversation between Meryll and his son is overheard by Dame Carruthers, the Tower housekeeper, who thereby discovers the plot, and Sergeant Meryll is forced to propose to her in order to ensure her silence. As news of Fairfax's survival and reprieve is announced, Elsie is resigned to accepting her unknown husband but is overjoyed on discovering that her husband is Fairfax, the man with whom she fell in love. Only Jack Point remains alone and falls senseless with grief at Elsie's feet.

The Gondoliers

Sub-title
The King of Barataria

Descriptive billing
An entirely original Comic Opera in 2 Acts

Date and theatre of first performance
7 December 1889, Savoy Theatre, London

Length of original run
554 performances

Overture
Written by Sullivan. His overture ended with the gavotte but Sir Malcolm Sargent added a new ending with the rousing cachucha.

Setting
Act 1   The Piazetta in Venice
Act 2   A Pavilion in the Palace of Barataria, three months later

Time
1750

Cast list, performers in first London season and voices

The Duke of Plaza-Toro, a grandee of Spain	Frank Wyatt	*Bar*
Luiz, his attendant	Wallace Brownlow	*Tenor*
Don Alhambra del Bolero, Grand Inquisitor	W. H. Denny	*Bass*
Marco Palmieri, a gondolier	Courtice Pounds	*Tenor*
Giuseppi Palmieri, a gondolier	Rutland Barrington	*Bar*
Antonio, a gondolier	A. Medcalf	*Bar*
Francesco, a gondolier	Charles Rose	*Tenor*
Giorgio, a gondolier	George de Pledge	*Bass*
Annibale, a gondolier	J. Wilbraham	*Spoken*
The Duchess of Plaza-Toro	Rosina Brandram	*Con*
Casilda, her daughter	Decima Moore	*Sop*
Gianetta	Geraldine Ulmar	*Sop*
Tessa	Jessie Bond	*MS*
Fiametta	Nellie Lawrence	*Sop*
Vittoria	Annie Cole	*MS*
Giulia	Norah Phyllis	*Sop*
Inez	Annie Bernard	*Con*

Chorus of Gondoliers, Ladies, Men-at-Arms, Heralds, Pages

Songs and choruses

Act 1 List and learn, ye dainty roses (Female Chorus)
   For the merriest fellows are we (Antonio, Chorus)
   Buon' giorno, signorine! (Marco, Giuseppi, Girls)
   We're called *gondolieri*! (Marco, Giuseppi)
   Thank you, gallant *gondolieri* (Gianetta, Tessa, Chorus)
   From the sunny Spanish shore (Duke, Duchess, Casilda, Luiz)
   In enterprise of martial kind (Duke)
   O rapture, when alone together (Casilda, Luiz)
   There was a time (Casilda, Luiz)
   I stole the Prince, and I brought him here (Don Alhambra, All)
   Try we life-long, we can never (Duke, Duchess, Casilda, Luiz, Don Alhambra)
   When a merry maiden marries (Tessa, Chorus)
   Kind sir, you cannot have the heart (Gianetta)
   Then one of us will be a Queen (Marco, Giuseppe, Gianetta, Tessa)
   For every one who feels inclined (Marco, Giuseppe, Chorus)
   Now, Marco dear (Gianetta, Tessa)
   Then away we go to an island fair (Chorus)

Act 2 Of happiness the very pith (Marco, Giuseppe, Male Chorus)
   Rising early in the morning (Giuseppe, Chorus)
   Take a pair of sparkling eyes (Marco)
   Here we are at the risk of our lives (Chorus of Girls)
   Dance a cachucha (Chorus)
   There lived a King, as I've been told (Don Alhambra, Marco, Giuseppi)
   In a contemplative fashion (Marco, Giuseppi, Gianetta, Tessa)
   With ducal pomp and ducal pride (Duke, Duchess, Chorus of Men)
   On the day when I was wedded (Duchess)
   Small titles and orders (Duke, Duchess)
   I am a courtier grave and serious (Duke, Duchess, Casilda, Marco, Giuseppi)
   Here is a case unprecedented! (Marco, Giuseppi, Casilda, Gianetta, Tessa)
   Now let the loyal lieges gather round (Don Alhambra, Chorus)
   The Royal Prince was by the King entrusted (Inez)
   This statement we receive (Marco, Giuseppi, Gianetta, Tessa)
   Once more *gondolieri* (All)

Synopsis

Act 1
Venetian girls are making bridal bouquets and singing of their love for two gondoliers – Marco and Giuseppe Palmieri, much to the irritation of

all the other gondoliers. The two brothers are expected to choose brides and they proceed to do so by means of a game of blind man's buff, and when they have won Gianetta and Tessa, everyone accompanies them to the church for the wedding. The Duke and Duchess of Plaza-Toro, arriving in Venice from Spain accompanied by their daughter Casilda, and their drummer-attendant Luiz, explain the reason for their journey to Casilda. She was married when an infant to a young prince who is now the King of Barataria, and the Plaza-Toros have come to Venice to enquire of the king's whereabouts from the Grand Inquisitor, Don Alhambra del Bolero. This news is disastrous for Casilda who has fallen secretly in love with Luiz. Don Alhambra arrives and reveals that, years before, he had had the young prince stolen and taken to Venice where he had hidden him with the Palmieris, a family of gondoliers. Unfortunately, due to 'a terrible taste for tippling' this highly-respectable gondolier could never tell the difference between his own son and the prince and inevitably had mixed them up. The only person who can tell the difference is the prince's foster-mother, Inez – who happens to be Luiz's mother. She had been entrusted with the care of the baby prince by the King, and has now been summoned. The wedding has taken place and the newly-weds are celebrating when Don Alhambra interrupts the proceedings to explain that either Marco or Giuseppe is King of Barataria. This pleases the two gondoliers and delights their wives. Until the king's identity is made known, Don Alhambra has arranged for them to rule jointly, and the gondoliers leave for Barataria with fond farewells from the girls whom they have just married but must now leave behind in Venice.

Act 2
Three months have elapsed and both gondoliers are together reigning over the island of Barataria. They have given all the other gondoliers positions at court which is run on the principle of universal equality. The girls have still not been allowed entry and the men miss their wives but to their surprise the girls suddenly arrive and a dance is arranged to celebrate the reunion. Don Alhambra appears and announces that the rightful king (whichever he is) was married to Casilda in infancy, and so this makes either Marco or Giuseppe a bigamist. The Duke and Duchess of Plaza-Toro also arrive with Casilda amid much splendour. The duke is now the Duke of Plaza-Toro Limited; and both he and the duchess have a busy time attending functions and advertising products that they would certainly never dream of using in order to raise cash. The problem is sorted out by the entrance of the elderly nurse, Inez, who tells that, to ensure the prince's safety, she had swapped him in infancy with her own son when traitors came to steal the baby prince, and then brought up the baby as her son. So Luiz ascends the throne as king with Casilda as his queen, whilst the gondoliers bid their farewells and thankfully enough return with their wives to Venice.

Utopia Limited

Sub-title
The Flowers of Progress

Descriptive billing
An original Comic Opera in 2 Acts

Date and theatre of first performance
7 October 1893, Savoy Theatre, London

Length of original run
245 performances

Overture
A short overture performed during the original run has been lost. Its authorship remains unknown

Setting
Act 1   A Utopian Palm Grove
Act 2   Throne Room in King Paramount's Palace

Time
1893

Cast list, performers in first London season and voices

Paramount the First, King of Utopia	Rutland Barrington	*BBar*
Scaphio, judge	W. H. Denny	*Bar*
Phantis, judge	John le Hay	*BBar*
Tarara, Public Exploder	Walter Passmore	*Tenor*
Calynx, Vice-Chamberlain	Bowden Haswell	*Bar*
Princess Zara	Nancy McIntosh	*Sop*
Princess Nekaya	Emmie Owen	*Sop*
Princess Kalyba	Florence Perry	*MS*
Lady Sophy, governess	Rosina Brandram	*Con*
FLOWERS OF PROGRESS:		
Lord Dramaleigh, a British Lord Chamberlain	Scott Russell	*Bar*
Captain Fitzbattleaxe, First Life Guards	Charles Kenningham	*Tenor*
Captain Sir Edward Corcoran, Royal Navy	Lawrence Gridley	*Bass*
Sir Bailey Barre, QC, MP	Enes Blackmore	*Bar*
Mr Blushington, county council	Herbert Ralland	*Bar*
Mr Goldbury, company promoter	Scott Fishe	*Bar*
Chorus of Maidens, Guards, Citizens of Utopia		

Songs and choruses
Act 1   In lazy languor – motionless (Female Chorus)
         O make way for the Wise Men (Chorus)

In every mental lore (Scaphio, Phantis)
Let all your doubts take wing (Scaphio, Phantis)
Quaff the nectar – cull the roses (Chorus)
My subjects all, it is your wish emphatic (Paramount)
Although of native maids the cream (Nekaya, Kalyba)
Bold-faced ranger (Lady Sophy)
First you're born – and I'll be bound you (Paramount, Chorus)
Subjected to your heavenly gaze (Paramount, Sophy)
Oh, maiden, rich (Female Chorus)
Five years have flown since I took wing (Zara, Fitzbattleaxe, Troopers)
Ah, gallant soldier, brave and true (Zara, Fitzbattleaxe, Chorus)
It's understood, I think, all round (Zara, Fitzbattleaxe, Scaphio, Phantis)
Oh, admirable art! (Zara, Fitzbattleaxe)
Although your Royal summons to appear (Chorus, Paramount, Zara)
When Britain sounds the trump of war (Zara)
Some seven men form an Association (Goldbury, Chorus)
Henceforward, of a verity (Paramount, Chorus)
Let's seal this mercantile pact (Chorus)

Act 2 A tenor, all singers above (Fitzbattleaxe)
Words of love too loudly spoken (Zara, Fitzbattleaxe)
Society has quite forsaken all her wicked courses (Paramount, Flowers of Progress)
Eagle high in cloudland soaring (Chorus)
With Fury deep we burn (Scaphio, Phantis)
If you think that when banded in unity (Scaphio, Phantis, Paramount)
With wily brain upon the spot (Scaphio, Phantis, Tarara)
A wonderful joy our eyes to bless (Goldbury)
Then I may sing and play? (Nekaya, Dramaleigh, Kalyba, Goldbury)
When but a maid of fifteen year (Sophy)
Oh, the rapture unrestrained (Sophy, Paramount)
Upon our sea-girt land (Chorus)
There's a little group of isles beyond the wave (Zara, Paramount, All)

Synopsis

Act 1

The women of the tropical island of Utopia are relaxing in the royal gardens. Calynx, the Vice-Chamberlain, announces that King Paramount's eldest daughter, Zara, is returning home to anglicise Utopia after five years of studying in England. Tarara, the Public Exploder, has read of the king's supposed immorality in a banned journal called 'The

Palace Peeper' and he is angered that he has not been ordered to dispose of the king. Two counsellors, Scaphio and Phantis, are the true power behind the throne. Phantis confesses to loving Princess Zara and Scaphio agrees to help him. King Paramount arrives and discusses 'The Palace Peeper' with Scaphio and Phantis. The king is being forced to write the articles himself by the two counsellors. Paramount is worried in case the magazine falls into the hands of Princess Zara or Lady Sophy (an English governess he has engaged to instruct his two younger daughters in correct behaviour) and whom he admires. His fears are well-founded for Lady Sophy appears holding a copy of the magazine but because of the King's apparent unwillingness to discover the writer of the article, she refuses to accept the love he has offered. Princess Zara returns home, escorted by troops of the Life Guards, and accompanied by Captain Fitzbattleaxe. Scaphio also falls in love with Zara and the two counsellors tell her of their feelings. Fitzbattleaxe, who is himself attracted to Zara, suggests the solution that Scaphio and Phantis should fight a duel but that in the meantime they should entrust the princess to his safekeeping. Zara reads a copy of the magazine and confronts her father with it. He breaks down and explains that he is being manipulated but Zara informs him that she has brought six 'Flowers of Progress' who can remodel Utopia along English lines and thereby remove the influence of Scaphio and Phantis. Paramount summons his court to explain the improvements that are to take place. The court approves the plan except for the two counsellors who are dismayed when Paramount proclaims Utopia to be a 'limited monarchy'.

Act 2

Captain Fitzbattleaxe and Zara are waiting to attend the first British-style cabinet meeting. The captain attempts to woo the princess but she is more interested in the successful progress of her imported experts. Scaphio and Phantis, dismayed at their loss of prestige, threaten the king, but he is not prepared to listen to them and so they discuss treason with Tarara. Two of the British experts, Mr Goldbury and Lord Dramaleigh, are perturbed by the cool response of the younger princesses and they explain to the princesses that English girls are by no means as retiring as Lady Sophy has led them to believe. Lady Sophy has pledged not to marry anyone but a perfect monarch and she had believed that Paramount was such a king until she read the damaging articles about his debauched lifestyle. Paramount, overhearing her remarks, rushes to her and confesses the true situation and Lady Sophy, overcome with relief, embraces him. The embrace is seen by the younger princesses, Goldbury and Dramaleigh as well as Zara and Fitzbattleaxe who all join in the celebrations. But Scaphio and Phantis have incited the populace to rebellion because Utopia has come to a standstill due to its new perfection. Zara realises that she has forgotten to introduce government by party whereby one party undoes all that another has built up. Paramount proclaims its adoption amid jubilation whilst Scaphio and Phantis are led away under arrest.

The Grand Duke

Sub-title
The Statutory Duel

Descriptive billing
An original Comic Opera in 2 Acts

Date and theatre of first performance
7 March 1896, Savoy Theatre, London

Length of original run
123 performances

Overture
Written by Sullivan

Setting
Act 1   Public Square of Speisesaal
Act 2   Hall in the Grand Ducal Palace

Time
1750

Cast list, performers in first London season and voices

Rudolph, Grand Duke	Walter Passmore	*Bar*
Ernest Dummkopf, theatrical manager	Charles Kenningham	*Tenor*
Ludwig, comedian	Rutland Barrington	*Bar*
Dr Tannhäuser, a notary	Scott Russell	*Tenor*
Prince of Monte Carlo	Scott Fishe	*Bar*
Viscount Mentone	E. Carleton	*Spoken*
Ben Hashbaz, a costumier	C. H. Workman	*Bar*
Herald	Jones Hewson	*Bar*
Princess of Monte Carlo	Emmie Owen	*Sop*
Baroness von Krakenfeldt	Rosina Brandram	*Con*
Julia Jellicoe	Ilka von Palmay	*Sop*
Lisa	Florence Perry	*Sop*

Chorus of Chamberlains, Nobles, Actors, Actresses

Songs and choruses
Act 1   Won't it be a pretty wedding? (Chorus of Actors and Actresses)
By the mystic regulation (Ludwig, Chorus)
Were I a king in very truth (Ernest, Chorus)
How would I play this part (Julia)
My goodness me! What shall we do? (Chorus)
Ten minutes since I met a chap (Ludwig, Chorus)
About a century since (Notary, Chorus)
Strange the views some people hold! (Ludwig, Lisa, Notary, Ernest, Julia)

Ilka von Palmay played Julia
Jellicoe in *The Grand Duke*.

222

The good Grand Duke of Pfennig Halbpfennig (Chamberlains)
A pattern to professors of monarchical autonomy (Rudolph)
As o'er our penny roll we sing (Baroness, Rudolph)
When you find you're a broken-down critter (Rudolph)
Come, hither, all you people (Rudolph, Ludwig, Chorus)
Big bombs, small bombs, great guns and little ones! (Rudolph, Ludwig)
Oh, a Monarch who boasts intellectual graces (Ludwig, Chorus)
Ah, pity me, my comrades true (Julia)
Oh, listen to me, dear (Lisa, Julia)
The die is cast (Lisa, Chorus)

Act 2   As before you we defile (Chorus)
At the outset I may mention it's my sovereign intention (Ludwig, Chorus)
Take care of him – he's much too good to live (Lisa, Ludwig)
Now, Julia, come (Ludwig, Julia)
Your Highness, there's a party at the door (Chorus)
With fury indescribable I burn (Baroness, Ludwig, Chorus)
Now away to the wedding we go (Baroness, Chorus)
All is darksome – all is dreary (Julia)
If the light of love's lingering ember (Ernest, Julia)
Now bridegroom and bride let us toast (Chorus)
I once gave an evening party (Baroness, Chorus)
The Prince of Monte Carlo (Herald)
We're rigged out in magnificent array (Prince, Princess, Costumier, Nobles)
Hurrah, Hurrah, Hurrah, Now away to the wedding we'll go (Chorus)
Happy couples, lightly treading (Chorus)

Synopsis

Act 1

In the Grand Duchy of Pfennig-Halbpfennig a theatrical company, managed by Ernest Dummkopf, is celebrating the forthcoming marriage of two of its members – Ludwig and Lisa. The company is involved in a conspiracy to overthrow the Grand Duke and replace him with Ernest as ruler of the kingdom. When he assumes the title Ernest intends to recruit the members of his court from his theatrical troupe according to their professional status. This is a sly way of compelling the leading lady, Julia Jellicoe, into marrying him. But the plot is revealed to the Grand Duke's personal detective by Ludwig, who mistakes him for a fellow conspirator. The Notary, Dr Tannhäuser, suggests the idea of a Statutory Duel, which involves the duellists in cutting a pack of cards. The higher card wins and the winner assumes the loser's responsibilities whilst the loser is regarded as dead. It is decided that Ludwig and Ernest should duel. The winner is to present himself before the Grand Duke and explain that, having discovered a conspiracy, a duel has been fought and the leader killed. Therefore, the theatrical company cannot be held guilty of any crime. As the effect of the duel expires on the following day, the loser then reappears when a pardon has been granted. The two 'fight' and Ludwig, having won by drawing an ace, goes off to find the Grand Duke. The Grand Duke himself meanwhile is having problems. He explains to his fiancée, the Baroness von Krakenfeldt, that his betrothal to the Princess of Monte Carlo in infancy would become invalid the following morning because her father is too poor to make the journey to Pfennig-Halbpfennig. The Grand Duke is now disturbed concerning the news of the conspiracy related by his detective. It is in this state that Ludwig finds him. Ludwig decides to change his plan and craftily suggests a further Statutory Duel which the Grand Duke Rudolph is to lose and then give up his title. Once the conspirators have succeeded in deposing Ludwig, Rudolph can return and claim his title. Rudolph agrees and Ludwig wins the dukedom by drawing another ace. When the troupe discovers that this has happened, Julia – as leading lady – immediately claims the role of Ludwig's duchess and this leaves Lisa heartbroken at losing Ludwig.

Act 2
The new duke is in power. The Baroness hears that Ludwig has decided to renew the Statutory Duel for a further one hundred years and she becomes the third to claim Ludwig as her husband-to-be – since she had been one of Rudolph's responsibilities. Julia is now left deserted as Ludwig and the Baroness plan to marry. The situation is further complicated by the sudden arrival of the Prince of Monte Carlo who has reversed his depleted fortunes by inventing the roulette wheel. He appears with his daughter, the Princess of Monte Carlo, who is just in time to claim the Grand Duke as her betrothed. The chaos is unravelled by the Notary who explains a minor error. He points out that in a Statutory Duel an ace is regarded as the lowest card in the deck, and as Ludwig had won on both occasions with an ace he had actually lost the duels. The period in which the duels had an effect has by now run out anyway and so Rudolph, Ludwig and Ernest revert to their former positions and to the Princess of Monte Carlo, Lisa and Julia respectively; and the Notary makes amends by officiating at a multiple wedding.

Gilbert: Chronological Listing of Major Works

Gilbert was a prolific writer of verse, short stories, playlets, plays, operas and extravaganzas. The listing which follows is principally of his stage works and is selective.

1856   'Laughing Song' translated from Auber's 'Manon Lescaut'

1861   Ballads and articles first published in *Fun*

1866   *Dulcamara*. Extravaganza. St James's Theatre

1867   *Harlequin Cock-Robin*. Pantomime. Lyceum Theatre

1868   *Robert the Devil*. Operatic extravaganza. Gaiety Theatre

1869   *An Old Score*. Play. Gaiety Theatre.
        Ages Ago. Opera. (Fred Clay) Royal Gallery of Illustration
        Bab Ballads. Book of ballads

1870   *Our Island Home*. Opera. (Thomas German Reed) Gallery of Illustration
        The Palace of Truth. Play. Haymarket Theatre

1871   *Great Expectations*. Play, after Dickens. Court Theatre
        Pygmalion and Galatea. Play. Haymarket Theatre
        Thespis. Opera. (A. S. Sullivan) Gaiety Theatre

1873   *More Bab Ballads*. Book of further ballads
        The Wicked World. Play. Haymarket Theatre
        The Happy Land. Play. Court Theatre

1874   *Ought We To Visit Her?* Play. Royalty Theatre
        Charity. Play. Haymarket Theatre
        Sweethearts. Play. Prince of Wales's Theatre

1875   *Broken Hearts*. Play. Court Theatre
        Trial by Jury. Opera. (A. S. Sullivan) Royalty Theatre

1876   *Dan'l Druce*. Play. Haymarket Theatre

1877	*Engaged*. Play. Haymarket Theatre
	The Sorcerer. Opera. (A. S. Sullivan) Opéra Comique
1878	*The Ne'er Do Weel*. Play. Olympic Theatre
	H.M.S. Pinafore. Opera (A. S. Sullivan) Opéra Comique
1879	*The Pirates of Penzance*. Opera. (A. S. Sullivan) Paignton
	Gretchen. Play. Olympic Theatre
1880	*The Martyr of Antioch*. Cantata. Leeds Festival
1881	*Patience*. Opera. (A. S. Sullivan) Opéra Comique
	Foggerty's Fairy. Play. Criterion Theatre
1882	*Iolanthe*. Opera. (A. S. Sullivan) Savoy Theatre
1884	*Comedy and Tragedy*. Play. Lyceum Theatre
	Princess Ida. Opera. (A. S. Sullivan) Savoy Theatre
1885	*The Mikado*. Opera. (A. S. Sullivan) Savoy Theatre
1887	*Ruddigore*. Opera. (A. S. Sullivan) Savoy Theatre
1888	*The Yeomen of the Guard*. Opera. (A. S. Sullivan) Savoy Theatre
	Brantighame Hall. Play. St James's Theatre
1889	*The Gondoliers*. Opera. (A. S. Sullivan) Savoy Theatre
1891	*Rosencrantz and Guildenstern*. Play. Vaudeville Theatre
1892	*Haste to the Wedding*. Operetta. (Grossmith) Criterion Theatre
	The Mountebanks. Opera. (Alfred Cellier) Lyric Theatre
1893	*Utopia Limited*. Opera. (A. S. Sullivan) Savoy Theatre
1894	*His Excellency*. Opera. (Osmond Carr) Lyric Theatre
1896	*The Grand Duke*. Opera. (A. S. Sullivan) Savoy Theatre
1897	*The Fortune Hunter*. Play. Theatre Royal, Birmingham
1898	*Songs of a Savoyard*. Book of songs and ballads
1904	*The Fairy's Dilemma*. Play. Garrick Theatre
1909	*The Fallen Fairies*. Opera. Gilbert's last opera. (Edward German) Savoy Theatre
1911	*The Hooligan*. Play. Gilbert's last play. Coliseum

Sullivan: Chronological Listing of Major Works

In addition to orchestral music, cantatas, oratorios and comic operas, Sullivan wrote various pieces for piano and cello, services and anthems, numerous hymns, various part-songs and carols and a considerable number of solo songs, vocal duets and trios. His regular publishers over extended periods included Novello, Cramer, Chappell, Metzler and Boosey. *Thespis* was not published and is lost; Metzler published *The Sorcerer* and *H.M.S. Pinafore*; and Chappell had the distinction of publishing the other eleven Gilbert and Sullivan operas. The general listing which follows is selective.

1850   'By the Waters of Babylon'. Anthem (unpublished)
1855   'O Israel'. Song. The first that Sullivan had published
1861   *The Tempest*. Incidental music. (text Shakespeare) Leipzig
1864   *L'Ile Enchantée*. Ballet. (choreography H. Desplaces) Covent Garden
        Kenilworth. Masque. (text H. F. Chorley) Birmingham Festival
        The Sapphire Necklace. Opera. (text H. F. Chorley) Not produced
1866   *In Memoriam*. Overture. Norwich Festival
        Symphony in E (the 'Irish') Crystal Palace
        Concerto for Cello and Orchestra in D. Crystal Palace
1867   *Marmion*. Overture. St James's Hall
        Cox and Box. Opera. (F. C. Burnand) Adelphi Theatre
        The Contrabandista. Opera. (F. C. Burnand) St George's Hall
1868   'O Fair Dove'. Song. (Jean Ingelow)
1869   *The Prodigal Son*. Oratorio. (text chosen from Bible by Sullivan) Worcester Cathedral

1870   *Overture di ballo.* Birmingham Festival
1871   'Onward Christian Soldiers'. Hymn. (Sabine Baring-Gould)
       Tune: St Gertrude
      'It came upon the midnight clear'. Carol.
      The Merchant of Venice. Incidental music. (Shakespeare)
       Prince's Theatre, Manchester
      'The Window'. Song cycle. (Tennyson)
      Thespis. Opera. (W. S. Gilbert) Gaiety Theatre
1872   *Te Deum laudamus.* For recovery of Prince of Wales.
      (liturgical text) Crystal Palace
1873   *The Light of the World.* Oratorio. (text chosen from Bible
      by Sullivan) Birmingham Festival
1874   *The Merry Wives of Windsor.* Incidental music (Shakespeare)
      Gaiety Theatre
1875   *Trial by Jury.* Opera. (W. S. Gilbert) Royalty Theatre
      The Zoo. Opera. (B. Rowe) St James's Theatre
1877   *The Sorcerer.* Opera. (W. S. Gilbert) Opéra Comique
      'The Lost Chord'. Song. (Adelaide A. Procter)
      Henry VIII. Incidental music. (Shakespeare) Theatre
      Royal, Manchester
1878   *H.M.S. Pinafore.* Opera. (W. S. Gilbert) Opéra Comique
1879   *The Pirates of Penzance.* Opera. (W. S. Gilbert) Paignton
1880   *The Martyr of Antioch.* Cantata. (H. H. Milman, adapted
      by W. S. Gilbert) Leeds Festival
1881   *Patience.* Opera. (W. S. Gilbert) Opéra Comique
1882   *Iolanthe.* Opera. (W. S. Gilbert) Savoy Theatre
1884   *Princess Ida.* Opera. (W. S. Gilbert) Savoy Theatre
1885   *The Mikado.* Opera. (W. S. Gilbert) Savoy Theatre
1886   *The Golden Legend.* Oratorio. (Longfellow, adapted by
      Joseph Bennett) Leeds Festival
1887   *Ruddigore.* Opera. (W. S. Gilbert) Savoy Theatre
1888   *Macbeth.* Incidental music. (Shakespeare) Lyceum Theatre
      The Yeomen of the Guard. Opera. (W. S. Gilbert) Savoy
      Theatre
1889   *The Gondoliers.* Opera. (W. S. Gilbert) Savoy Theatre
1891   *Ivanhoe.* Grand Opera. (Julian Sturgis, after Scott)
      Royal English Opera House
1892   *Haddon Hall.* Opera. (Sydney Grundy) Savoy Theatre
      The Foresters. Incidental music. (Tennyson) Daly's Theatre,
      New York
1893   *Utopia Limited.* Opera. (W. S. Gilbert) Savoy Theatre
      Imperial March. Imperial Institute
1894   *The Chieftain.* Opera. (F. C. Burnand) Savoy Theatre
1895   *King Arthur.* Incidental music. (J. Comyns Carr) Lyceum
      Theatre

1896   *The Grand Duke*. Opera. (W. S. Gilbert) Savoy Theatre
1897   *Victoria and Merrie England*. Ballet. (choreography C. Coppi) Alhambra Theatre
1898   *The Beauty Stone*. Opera. (A. W. Pinero and J. Comyns Carr) Savoy Theatre
1899   *The Rose of Persia*. Opera. (Basil Hood) Savoy Theatre
1901   *The Emerald Isle*. Opera. (Basil Hood) Music completed by Edward German. Savoy Theatre
1902   *Te Deum laudamus*. Thanksgiving for victory. (liturgical text) St Paul's Cathedral

Bibliography

Allen, Reginald: *The First Night Gilbert and Sullivan* (Heritage, New York 1958)

Ayre, Leslie: *The Gilbert and Sullivan Companion* (Allen, London 1972)

Baily, Leslie: *The Gilbert and Sullivan Book* (Cassell, London 1952; revised Spring Books 1966)

Baily, Leslie: *Gilbert and Sullivan and their World* (Thames & Hudson, London 1973)

Bettany, Clemence: *D'Oyly Carte Centenary: 1875-1975* (D'Oyly Carte Opera Trust, London 1975)

Bond, Jessie: *The Life and Reminiscences of Jessie Bond* (Bodley Head, London 1930)

Bradley, Ian: *The Annotated Gilbert and Sullivan* 2 vols. (Penguin Books, Harmondsworth 1982 & 1984)

Brahms, Caryl: *Gilbert and Sullivan: Chords and Discords* (Weidenfeld & Nicolson, London 1975)

Cellier, François and Bridgeman, Cunningham: *Gilbert, Sullivan and D'Oyly Carte* (London 1914)

Cox-Ife, William: *W. S. Gilbert: Stage Director* (Dennis Dobson, London 1977)

Dark, Sidney and Grey, Rowland: *W. S. Gilbert: His Life and Letters* (Methuen, London 1923)

Darlington, W. A: *The World of Gilbert and Sullivan* (New York, 1950)

Eden, David: *Gilbert and Sullivan: The Creative Conflict* (Associated University Presses, London 1986)

Ellis, James (ed): *The Bab Ballads by W. S. Gilbert* (Belknap Press, Cambridge, Massachusetts 1970)

Fitz-Gerald, S. J. Adair: *The Story of the Savoy Opera* (Stanley Paul, London 1924)

Gilbert, W. S: *The Savoy Operas* 2 vols. (Oxford University Press, Oxford 1962 & 1963)

Goodman, Andrew: *Gilbert and Sullivan at Law* (Associated University Presses, London 1983)

Goodman, Andrew: *Gilbert and Sullivan's London* (Spellmount Ltd, Tunbridge Wells 1988)

Grossmith, George: *A Society Clown* (Bristol 1888)

Haining, Peter (ed): *The Lost Stories of W. S. Gilbert* (Robson Books, London 1982)

Helyar, James (ed): *Gilbert and Sullivan: papers presented at the International Conference, Kansas in May 1970* (University of Kansas Libraries, Kansas 1971)

Hughes, Gervase: *The Music of Arthur Sullivan* (Macmillan, London 1960)

Hyman, Alan: *Sullivan and his Satellites: a survey of English operettas 1860-1914* (Chappell, London 1978)

Jacobs, Arthur: *Arthur Sullivan: A Victorian Musician* (Oxford University Press, Oxford 1984)

Jefferson, Alan: *The Complete Gilbert and Sullivan Opera Guide* (Webb and Bower, Exeter 1984)

Lytton, Henry A: *The Secrets of a Savoyard* (Jarrolds, London 1922)

Lytton, Henry A: *A Wandering Minstrel* (Jarrolds, London 1933)

Mander, Raymond and Mitchenson, Joe: *A Picture History of Gilbert and Sullivan* (Vista Books, London 1962)

Moore, Frank Ledlie: *The Handbook of Gilbert and Sullivan* (Arthur Barker, London 1962)

Pearson, Hesketh: *Gilbert and Sullivan* (Hamish Hamilton, London 1935: reprinted Penguin Books 1985)

Pearson, Hesketh: *Gilbert: His Life and Strife* (Methuen, London 1957)

Rollins, Cyril and Witts, R. John: *The D'Oyly Carte Opera Company in Gilbert and Sullivan Operas: A record of productions, 1875-1961* (Michael Joseph, London 1962)

Saxe Wyndham, Henry: *Arthur Seymour Sullivan* (Kegan Paul, London 1926)

Smith, Geoffrey: *The Savoy Operas* (Robert Hale, London 1983)

Stedman, Jane, W. (ed): *Gilbert before Sullivan* (Chicago 1967)

Sullivan, Herbert and Flower, Newman: *Sir Arthur Sullivan: His Life, Letters and Diaries* (Cassell, London 1927; revised 1950)

Walbrook, H. M: *Gilbert and Sullivan Opera* (White, London 1922)

Williamson, Audrey: *Gilbert and Sullivan Opera* (Rockcliff Publishing, London 1953; revised Marion Boyars 1982)

Wilson, Robin and Lloyd, Frederic: *Gilbert and Sullivan: The D'Oyly Carte Years* (Weidenfeld and Nicolson, London 1984)

Wolfson, John: *Final Curtain: The Last Gilbert and Sullivan Operas* (Chappell, London 1976)

Wolfson, John: *Sullivan and the Scott Russells: A Victorian love affair* (Packard, Chichester 1984)

Wood, Roger: *A D'Oyly Carte Album* (Black, London 1953)

Acknowledgements

I would like to thank Peter Joslin for the use of pictures from his personal collection, and Andrew Codd for his opera synopses.

Recordings

There have been numerous recordings of the Gilbert and Sullivan operas and also of a number of Sullivan's operas written with other librettists as well as recordings of Sullivan's diverse musical interests. The most important of these recordings are listed below. L.P.'s that have not been re-issued can sometimes be obtained second-hand on order from a specialist supplier such as Harold Moores Records, 2 Marlborough Street, London W1V 1DE (off Regent Street), tel. 01-437-1576.

In the list which follows LP denotes a long-playing disc, TC denotes a tape cassette, CD denotes a compact disc and VR denotes a video recording.

The abbreviations used are: AOC Ambrosian Opera Chorus, CBSO City of Birmingham Symphony Orchestra, DCOC D'Oyly Carte Opera Company, DCOCh D'Oyly Carte Opera Chorus, GFC Glyndebourne Festival Chorus, LSO London Symphony Orchestra, NSO New Symphony Orchestra, NSWOC New Sadler's Wells Opera Chorus, NSWOO New Sadler's Wells Opera Orchestra, OROH Orchestra of the Royal Opera House, PAO Pro Arte Orchestra, RLPO Royal Liverpool Philharmonic Orchestra, RPO Royal Philharmonic Orchestra, SO Symphony Orchestra.

Thespis
Spencer, Fulham Light Op Soc, Light Op Orch SRRE 132-3 (music from Sullivan's little-known operas fitted to Gilbert's lyrics by Max Miradin)

Trial by Jury
Sargent, GFC, PAO LP EX749696-1, TC EX749696-4, CDS 747779-8
Godfrey, DCOCh, OROH LP 417 358 1DY2, TC 417 358 4DY2
Norris, DCOCh, DCOC CDZ8052-2
Faris, AOC, LSO VR Savoy Video VHS S1010

The Sorcerer
Godfrey, DCOC, RPO LP 414 344 1DY2, TC 414 344 4DY2
Godfrey, DCOCh, SO (rec.1933) CD Z 8068-2
Faris, AOC, LSO VR Savoy Video VHS S1004

HMS Pinafore
Sargent, GFC, PAO LP EX749594-1, TC EX749594-4, CDS7 47779-8
Phipps, NSWOC, NSWOO LP TER 2 1150, TC ZCTED 1150, CD TER 2 1150
Godfrey, DCOC, NSO LP 414 283 1DY2, TC 414 283 4DY2
Sargent, DCOCh, Orch CD Z 8052-2
Nash, DCOC VR VHS VITC 2021
Faris, AOC, LSO, VR Savoy Video VHS S1002

The Pirates of Penzance
Sargent, GFC, PAO LP EX749693-1, TC EX749693-4, CDS7 47758-8
Godfrey, DCOC, RPO LP 414 186 1DY2, TC 414 186 4DY2, CD 414 286 2DY2

Elliott, New York Shakespeare Fest LP K62035
Faris, AOC, LSO VR Savoy Video VHS S1001
Elliott, New York Shakespeare Fest, Joseph Papp production VR VHS
VHA 1080

Patience
Sargent, GFC, PAO LP EX7 49597-1, TC EX7 49597-4, CDS7 47758-8
Godfrey, DCOC, NSO LP 414 429 1DY2, TC 414 429 4DY2, CD 414
286 2DY2
Groves, GFC, RLPO, CDC 747783-8
Faris, AOC, LSO VR Savoy Video VHS S1003

Iolanthe
Sargent, GFC, PAO LP EX7 49597-1, TC EX7 49597-4, CDS7 47831-8
Godfrey, DCOC, Grenadier Guards Band, NSO LP 414 145 1DY2,
TC 414 145 4DY2
Faris, AOC, LSO VR Savoy Video VHS S1000

Princess Ida
Sargent, DCOC, RPO LP 414 426 1DY2, TC 414 426 4DY2
Norris/Byng DCOCh, Orch LP GEMM 129-30
Faris, AOC, LSO VR Savoy Video VHS S1006

The Mikado
Sargent, GFC, PAO LP EX7 49696-1, TC EX7 49696-4, CDS7 47773-8
Godfrey, DCOC, NSO LP 414 341 1DY2, TC 414 341 4DY2
Godfrey, DCOCh, SO (rec.1936) CD Z 8051-2
Nash, DCOCh, RPO LP SKL 5158, TC K22 K22, CD 417 296 2DY2
Faris, NSWOC, NSWOO LP ESDW 1077183
Robinson, English National Opera and Chorus LP TER 1121, TC Z
CTER 11121, CD TER 1121
Faris, AOC, LSO VR Savoy Video VHS S1009
Godfrey, DCOCh, CBSO VR BHE Production

Ruddigore
Sargent, GFC, PAO LP EX7 49693-1, TC EX7 49693-4, CDS7 47787-8
Godfrey, DCOCh OROH LP 417 355 1DY2, TC 417 355 4DY2
Phipps, NSWOC, NSWOO LP TER 2 1128, TC ZCTED 1128,
CDTER2 1128
Faris, AOC, LSO VR Savoy Video VHS S1008

The Gondoliers
Sargent, GFC, PAO LP EX7 49696-1, TC EX7 49696-4, CDS7 47775-8
Godfrey, DCOC, NSO LP 417 254 1DY2, TC 417 254 4DY2, CD 417
254 2DY2
Norris, DCOCh, Orch LP GEMM 141-2
Nash, DCOCh, RPO LP SKL 5277-8
Faris, AOC, LSO VR Savoy Video VHS S1005

The Yeomen of the Guard
Sargent, GFC, PAO, LP EX7 49594-1, TC EX7 49594-4, CDS7 47718-8
Sargent, DCOCh, RPO LP 417 358 1DY2, TC 417 358 4DY2
Faris, AOC, LSO VR Savoy Video VHS S1007
Lloyd-Jones, New World Phil Orch VR VHS VITC 2022

Utopia Limited
Nash, DCOCh, RPO LP 414 359 1DY2, TC 414 359 4DY2
Landis, Lyric Theatre Co and Orch LP SHEZ 505-7

The Grand Duke
Nash, DCOCh, RPO LP 417 342 1DY2, TC 417 342 4DY2
Harding, Cheam Op Soc Choir, Southern Fest Orch LP SHE 516-7

C.H. Workman's Gilbert and Sullivan
LP GEMM 135

John Reed: I have a song to sing o
DCOC LP SKL 5254

Valerie Masterson and Robert Tear Sing Gilbert and Sullivan
Alwyn, Bournemouth Sinfonietta LP ASD 4392

Here's a how-de-do: A Gilbert and Sullivan Gala
Hickox, Northern Sinfonia LP EL 2701701

D'Oyly Carte The Last Night
27 February 1982 – Faris/Goulding DCOC LP DCLN 1-3

A Gilbert and Sullivan Gala
Alwyn, Bournemouth Sin/Hickox, N. Sinfonia (Masterson, Armstrong, Tear, Luxon) CDC7 47763-2

Sullivan
(includes three 'lost' songs from **Yeomen**) Murray, Gilbert and Sullivan Festival Orch LP SHE 509

The Art of the Savoyard 1900-1922
LP GEM 118-120

The Art of the Savoyard Vol 2
(includes voice of Sullivan) LP GEMM 282-3

Gilbert and Sullivan, The Early Records
1898-1912 LP ED 29 0422 1

The Hey-Day of Gilbert and Sullivan
1926-1936 LP EX 29 0480 3

Gilbert and Sullivan with Band and Voice
Taylor, Band of the Welsh Guards LP BND 1024

Cox and Box
Sargent, PAO CDS7 47758-8
Nash, DCOC, RPO, LP TXS 128
Godfrey, DCOC, NSO LP 417 355 1DY2, TC 417 355 4DY2
Faris, AOC, LSO, VR Savoy Video VHS S1010

The Zoo
Nash, DCOC, RPO LP 414 342-1, TC 414 342-4

Ivanhoe
Murray, Gilbert and Sullivan Fest (selection) LP SHE 509

Sullivan without Gilbert
(selection) LP OPAL 831

Haddon Hall
Harding, Southern Fest Orch, Cheam Op Soc LP SHE 566-7

The Chieftain
Adams, Sawston Light Opera Group LP SRRE 181-2

The Beauty Stone
Lyle, Consort Orch, Chorus of Gilbert and Sullivan Soc of Edinburgh
LP SHE 579-80

The Rose of Persia
Walters, Orphean Singers and Orch LP SRRE 152-153
Lyle, Edinburgh, Gilbert and Sullivan Soc Chorus, Prince Consort Orch
LP SHE 588-9

The Emerald Isle
Lyle, Chorus of the Gilbert and Sullivan Society of Edinburgh, Consort
Orch LP SHE 574-5

Pineapple Poll
Mackerras RPO LP ESD 7028, TC ESD 7028, CD Z 8016

Concerto for Cello and Orch in D
J. Lloyd Webber, LSO (recons. Mackerras) LP EL 270430-1, TC EL
270430-4, CDC 7 47622-2

In Memoriam-Overture in C
Dunn, CBSO CDS 7 47758-8

Imperial March
Nash, RPO LP SKL 5225, TC K2C17, CD 414 359-4

Marmion – overture
Nash, RPO LP SKL 5277-8

Overture di Ballo
Groves, RLPO LP ESD 1077541, TC ESD 1077544, CDS 7 47831-8
Faris, Scottish Chamber Orch CD NI5066
Incidental music to **Henry VIII** Nash, RPO LP TXS 113
Incidental music to **The Merchant of Venice** Dunn, CBSO
CDS 7 47787-8
Incidental music to **The Tempest** Dunn, CBSO CDS 7 47787-8
Symphony in E (Irish) Groves, RLPO CDC 7 47783-8

Selections of Sullivan's vocal and choral works appear on LP OPAL 831
including songs from **The Golden Legend** and **The Prodigal Son**.

The songs 'Let me dream again' and 'Sweethearts' (the latter with words
by Gilbert) are included on LP CFC 156, TC MCFC 156, CDCFC 156.

The song 'The long day closes' is included on LP CFC 145, TC MCFC
145, CDCF 145

The song 'The Lost Chord' is included on LP TRX 101, TC TRXC 101,
CDTRXCD 101
Selections of Sullivan's chamber and instrumental music appear on LP
SHE 512 and LP SHE 533

Index

Bold entries indicate illustrations